D1565841

The Responsive Self

THE ANCHOR YALE BIBLE REFERENCE LIBRARY
is a project of international and interfaith scope in which
Protestant, Catholic, and Jewish scholars from many countries
contribute individual volumes. The project is not sponsored by
any ecclesiastical organization and is not intended to reflect
any particular theological doctrine.

The series is committed to producing volumes in the tradition
established half a century ago by the founders of the Anchor
Bible, William Foxwell Albright and David Noel Freedman.
It aims to present the best contemporary scholarship in a way
that is accessible not only to scholars but also to the educated
nonspecialist. It is committed to work of sound philological and historical scholarship, supplemented by insight from
modern methods, such as sociological and literary criticism.

John J. Collins
General Editor

THE ANCHOR YALE BIBLE REFERENCE LIBRARY

The Responsive Self

Personal Religion in Biblical Literature of the Neo-Babylonian and Persian Periods

SUSAN NIDITCH

 Yale
UNIVERSITY
PRESS

NEW HAVEN
AND
LONDON

Published with assistance from the foundation established in memory of James Wesley Cooper of the Class of 1865, Yale College.

Yale University Press books may be purchased in quantity for educational, business, or promotional use. For information, please e-mail sales.press@yale .edu (U.S. office) or sales@yaleup.co.uk (U.K. office).

Set in Adobe Caslon and Bauer Bodoni types by Newgen North America.

Library of Congress Control Number: 2015930848
ISBN 978-0-300-16636-1 (cloth : alk. paper)

A catalogue record for this book is available from the British Library.

This paper meets the requirements of ANSI/NISO Z39.48-1992 (Permanence of Paper).

Contents

Acknowledgments

The completion of this book was greatly aided by two sabbatical leaves supported by Amherst College. I thank the Trustees of Amherst College for their ongoing support. The work developed as I taught groups of talented students, especially in the course "Personal Religion in the Bible," offered two times during my involvement with this project. My students' questions and comments, as always, allowed me to sharpen ideas and clarify concepts, and urged me to think about familiar passages in new ways. I have presented portions of the book at public lectures and at the summer seminar I attend each August, the Colloquium for Biblical Research. I thank participants at these events for their excellent ideas and questions. Without the prodding of John J. Collins, the editor of this series, I probably would not have written the book. I thank him as always for his friendship, encouragement, and creative ideas. Other colleagues with whom I have shared my work and ideas in written or oral form and who have influenced the final product include James Ackerman, Susan Ackerman, Elizabeth Bloch-Smith, Marc Zvi Brettler, Cynthia Chapman, William Brown, Alan Cooper, Avraham Faust, Edward L. Greenstein, Paul D. Hanson, Theodore J. Lewis, Peter Machinist, Dean S. McBride, P. Kyle McCarter, Patrick D. Miller, Saul M. Olyan, David Schloen, Mark S. Smith, Sidnie Crawford White, and David S. Vanderhooft. Robert Doran, my husband of forty years and the kindest man in the world, is a constant source of support and encouragement. I dedicate this book to him and to our daughters, Rebecca Doran and Elizabeth Doran, who not only make us proud but also have helped to shape who we are.

The Responsive Self

The Responsive Self

Introduction

Upheaval and instability are wellsprings of personal and cultural creativity. In the history of early Judaism, the period from the conquest of Judea by Babylonia through the subsequent takeover and rule of Judea and Samaria by the imperial Persians provides settings for the composition of a rich and varied corpus of works preserved in the Hebrew Bible. These writings evidence a strong interest in the religious responses of individuals and an intimate engagement with the nature of personal experience in a world controlled by a powerful and enigmatic deity. This book deals with matters of self-representation and the presentation of selves. How does late-biblical literature portray individuals' emotions, disappointments, desires, and doubts within particular cultural and religious frameworks? The goal is to explore ways in which followers of Yahweh, participating in long-standing traditions and specific sociohistorical settings of late-biblical times, are shown to privatize and personalize religion.

I am interested in a variety of phenomena, including the use of first-person speech in literary creations, the assumption of seemingly autobiographical forms and orientations, the emphasis on individual responsibility for sin and punishment, the creative and daring challenge to conventional ideas about the way the world operates, the interest in the emotional dimensions of biblical characters, the portrayal of everyday small things that relate to essential aspects of worldview, and descriptions of self-imposed ritual. This set of interests lends itself to exciting approaches in the contemporary study of religion, rooted largely in the sociology of religion. The concept of "lived religion," developed by Robert Orsi, Meredith McGuire, and others, and related ideas about material religion, explored, for example, by Colleen McDannell, involve understanding and describing what people do and believe in cultures of religion. I argue that religion as lived is as relevant a concept to ancient Israelite tradition as it is to contemporary religions, allowing us to think about its variety, syncretisms, and synergies and to appreciate the interplay between individuals and communities, tradition and innovation, official and unofficial religion. Within the context of lived religion, writers of the period under study expressed and experienced their religious identities in a variety of ways that emphasize the individual. Personal religion in this sense is not confined to late writings, but I make the case that it finds a good deal of overt expression in the preserved literature of this period and that there are reasons of setting and worldview that make it so.

Preexilic Israelite religion as described by Judean writers who put their stamp on the Hebrew Bible was rooted in a national communal identity related to key shared institutions: the homeland, the monarchy, the temple. Land, king, and temple continue to have deeply symbolic and mythological significance even in modern Judaism, but the Babylonian exile brought significant challenges to the social structure and accompanying adjustments in worldview. The monarchy was no more, and Solomon's temple was destroyed, to be replaced by a more modest building funded by Persian conquerors. The holy land was a holding of imperialist and colonialist outsiders. Perhaps in response to these perceived tears in the social fabric and related adjustments in worldview, early Jewish literature written and preserved by an array of writers increasingly included an emphasis on the individual's relationship to God, his or her psychology, and view of his or her place in the world.

Israelite religion, among Judeans of the South and Israelites of the North, had always included prayer, a means of individual connection with the deity.[1] There had always been incantations, a means by which human beings could attempt to overcome adversity or encourage hope. There are ancient graffiti from the First Temple period, such as those at Kuntillet 'Ajrud, that provide a window on individual, spontaneous, immediate religious sensibilities, a kind of fast-food religion. People believed that divine beings could appear to individuals in powerful theophanies, accepted the revelatory significance of dreams and visions, and relied upon the efficacy of divinatory techniques. Material culture of the First Temple period included the presence of female figurines found buried beneath households. These figurines surely had some connection to matters of fertility and the

personal address to higher powers believed to bestow such blessings. Carol
Meyers, Joseph Blenkinsopp, Rainer Albertz, and others point to evidence
in literature and material culture of additional aspects of "household religion," such as family altars.[2] Death customs and burial sites reveal loci for
individual religious expression in the face of personal crisis throughout the
history of Israel.

The literature of the exile and early Second Temple period, however, is
especially rich in expressions and media of personal religion. Authors have
preserved in writing concerns and content that emphasize and represent
the individual, personalizing in various ways the religion of ancient Israel
even while drawing upon traditional forms and threads in pan-Israelite
culture, itself a diverse and complex phenomenon. This literature reveals
the special concerns and orientations to life that emerged from particular
theological, political, and cultural challenges in the wake of the Babylonian
conquest.[3] Ways of thinking about "religion as lived," and related concepts
of "material religion" and "personal religion," are thus relevant to the study
of ancient Israel in general and to an understanding of the late-biblical
period in particular.

Lived Religion

The sociologist of religion Meredith B. McGuire begins her book *Lived
Religion* with a reflection on her own changing realizations about the nature of religious identity. Early in her career, she "thought it would be easy
to find out what each interviewee's religion was," and she "assumed that
individuals' religious worlds would be linked (sometimes firmly, sometimes
loosely) with the beliefs, moral norms, and religious practices promoted by
the particular religious organizations of which they were members."[4] She
describes having come to realize that her interviewees' religions were much
more complicated than she had originally thought. Focusing on individuals, diversities within groups and practices, the interplay between "official"
and "unofficial" belief, and the cultural threads that influence and intertwine in surprising ways within religious identities, McGuire concludes
that religion at the individual level is "an ever-changing, multifaceted, often messy—even contradictory—amalgam of beliefs and practices that are
not necessarily those religious institutions consider important."[5] She writes
of "personal religion" and "lived religion," examining the experiences that
people "consider most important" and "the concrete practices that make

up their personal religious experience and expression."[6] She grapples with "how to comprehend individuals' religion as practiced, in all their complexity and dynamism."[7]

Most interesting for our study of personal religion in the Neo-Babylonian and Persian periods, McGuire asks whether these questions and approaches to the study of contemporary religion apply as well to religious identity in premodern cultures. McGuire answers in the affirmative and presents a case study from medieval Christianity that reveals the relevance of her approach for the study of cultures in which informants are not live, observable subjects. I intend to follow McGuire's lead and explore religion as lived in the period following the Babylonian exile. Key terms serve as headings to important concepts. Already mentioned are "concrete practice," "diversity," "official and unofficial," "dynamism," and "individual." Related terminology includes "material religion," "embodied practice," "syncretism," and "the self." Let us unpack the ideas suggested by these key terms with help from an array of scholars in sociology, anthropology, and religion and begin to explore how they may be relevant to the religion of ancient Israel in general and to the Neo-Babylonian and Persian periods in particular. The biblical book of Ruth provides an excellent example.

Set in the period of the judges, the tale purports to tell the story of David's ancestor heroine, a young Moabite widow of an Israelite man who embraces Yahweh and, with her mother-in-law, Naomi, travels to the older woman's home in Bethel. There, in the romantic and fecund time of the harvest, Ruth meets and marries Naomi's wealthy kinsman Boaz and bears him a son in her deceased husband's name in a rough approximation or evocation of the levirate law of Deuteronomy 25:5. A postexilic dating seems probable for this anthological narrative that is based on Genesis 38 and includes direct allusions to it. The movement of action in the Genesis tale, with its terse dialogue and minimalist description, contrasts with the beautiful monologue of Ruth 1:16–17, the more expansive interactions between characters in the story, and the way in which the author builds up to the scene at the threshing floor. The book of Ruth is a short story or romance rather than a folktale, as indicated by stylistic issues explored in more detail in chapter seven. I argue that Ruth is from the Persian period and that it richly exudes qualities of personal religion and religion as lived.

The sociologist of religion Robert Orsi urges us, when we study people's religion, to think of "the circle of friends and kin among whom they lived, memories they held (their own or those borrowed or inherited from others), their sense of place in their immediate world . . . the stories they were told by relatives they loved, bonds of commitment and loyalty to particular friends and kin."[8] The biblical tale of Ruth, with its emphasis on family and return to the land of one's origins, its sensitivity to the movement of the seasons with their related patterns in the agricultural cycle, and its frequent mention of God's blessings and induced trials evoke these concerns of lived religion, as do the "intimate contexts" in which religion is expressed and contoured:[9] invocations of the deity between a mother-in-law and daughter-in law, between potential lovers at a threshing floor, between elders at the city gate. Orsi reminds us that religion is always "religion-in-action," "religion in relationships between people"[10]—for example, the kindness offered one's kinsfolk at the harvest time. Orsi is interested in "what people do with religious idioms, how they use them, what they make of themselves and their worlds . . . and how they are fundamentally shaped by the worlds they are making as they make these worlds." He explores religion as "situated amid the ordinary concerns of life, at the junctures of self and culture, family and the social world"[11]—such scenes dominate the book of Ruth.

Orsi seeks to undermine the boundary often maintained by scholars of religion between private and public, noting that "lived religion cannot be separated from practices of everyday life" or from the ordinary, mundane spaces where life unfolds:[12] in the case of Ruth, the field, the town, the household. McGuire similarly points to the artificiality of boundaries drawn between sacred and profane.[13] Scholars of lived religion pay special attention to the physical, material aspects of religious identity, expression, and engagement, including an emphasis on the personal body itself, loci where culture and the individual, society and self, sacred and profane, and ordinary and transcendent can come into intimate contact. Colleen Mc-Dannell notes that "people build religion into the landscape, they make and buy pious images for their homes, and they wear special reminders of their faith next to their bodies.[14] She adds, "Experiencing the physical dimension of religion helps bring about religious values, norms, behaviors, and attitudes."[15] The body, our own physicality, is critical to the material dimension of religion, for as McDannell writes, "Human beings cannot appropriate religious truths or be 'grasped by an ultimate concern' without involving their bodies."[16] McGuire describes a contemporary religious setting in which the hands are a veritable channel to the divine, "conduits of God's power," filled with healing power. She describes objects, cloths, boxes, and pendants that take on religious meaning and that are integral to religious identity and experience.[17] Material religion in these manifestations is also critical to understanding Yahwism as lived.

In contrast to McDannell, Orsi, and McGuire, we cannot talk to interviewees or observe what they do, what objects they hold dear, or how they employ their bodies, but we do have access to ritual and narrative accounts that, however literary or stylized, richly reveal their composers' views of religion as lived and the impressions they preserve. We have blessings and curses etched into walls or painted on pieces of clay pots or sherds. Graffiti may provide great insight into religion as lived and into the personal needs, experiences, worries, and desires of the writer and may provide quintessential examples of personal religion. And thanks to the work of archaeologists, we can visually reconstruct the contours of domestic spaces—the setting, for example, of home altars.[18] Indeed, our work with archaeological evidence is not so different from McDannell's use of a photograph to speculate on a subject's religious orientation or identity. The subjects are no longer alive, the interpretation is hers, the objects are static and were possibly arranged by the photographer, and yet information can be gleaned from them, even though, as McDannell notes, the scholar needs to stay aware of her own orientations, prejudices, and sociocultural settings.[19]

Archaeologists have discovered a variety of religiously relevant objects, paraphernalia, statuary, and painted images, tactile media that exemplify what Patricia Cox Miller, a scholar of late antiquity, has called "a touch of the real."[20] Joseph Blenkinsopp has coined the phrase "religion in ordinary time."[21] For the Persian period, we might point to Melody Knowles's discussion of incense altars, suggesting tactile religious practice that stimulates the senses.[22] Miller invokes this language of the real to describe a particular aesthetic of self-identity that is critical to any study of personal religion. She inquires further whether certain periods and settings are more conducive to manifestations of the religious real than ones that tend to locate the self in more transcendent ways, for example, by reference to cosmic imagery. Similarly, McGuire asks whether particular settings tend to manifest personal and private religion, popular and unofficial dimensions, rather than the official, realizing there is always a feedback loop between the two sides of this dichotomy.

To be sure, people always pray independently in unofficial settings, and family-home-based customs are common in any cultural group, as noted above. The question is, however, when are manifestations of unofficial religion preserved in official sources and manifested in official settings? An illustration is provided by my own experience as an American Jew during childhood and adulthood. In the 1950s in the suburbs of Boston, where I grew up, there were no public, noticeable manifestations of "unofficial religion." The service in the Conservative synagogue attended by my family was always the same in order and in content, led by an ordained Jewish Theological Seminary–trained rabbi who followed the traditional liturgy, as practiced in any American Conservative synagogue of the period. There were no folksongs or modern poems, no healing circles, no meditation classes, nor any impromptu discussions with the congregation concerning the day's Torah reading—all of which did appear in synagogue services of the 1980s. The same could be said of the Catholic and Protestant churches in my hometown—no rock groups, no special affects, no talking in tongues (in non-Pentecostal churches).

I would argue that such patterns are reflected in ancient Israelite religion as well and that the early exilic and Persian periods are those in which preserved sources reveal increased emphasis on the real or material, the individual or personal, and the unofficial or popular aspects of religion. There is also evidence of the interplay between unofficial and official, personal and public dimensions of religious experience and expression. With a nuanced approach, Knowles urges us to think of aspects of religious life in the Persian period "such as private prayer and unrecorded communal gatherings, as well as practices that have left only textual evidence, such as the development of penitential prayer."[23] We might also mention in this context the exilic-period graffiti accompanied by line drawings in the burial cave near Khirbet Beit Lei. In Frank Cross's reading, the writing on the wall includes a request for deliverance: "Deliver [us] O Lord"; a request for absolution: "Absolve [us] O merciful God! Absolve [us] O Yahweh"; and "a prophetic oracle in which Yahweh speaks in the first person, and in poetic form."[24] Cross suggests that these prayers and the oracle were left behind by a prophet and his followers fleeing the troubles in Jerusalem. They are personal requests to God in a time of emergency, formulaic in form and thus part of a shared communal cultural identity, and made material and permanent by having been written on a physical surface, where they remain to this day.

These particular writings are in a cave, unofficial and immediate. However, we also know much about what we are calling "personal religion" from the nature and content of the datable works preserved in the public, official tradition of the Hebrew Bible that were being collected at this time. Knowles, for example, views Psalms 120–134 as possible evidence of pilgrimage customs in the Persian period. In her view, these psalms at least "reflect the concerns that pilgrims manifest."[25] And once again, as Orsi notes, "the study of lived religion directs attention to institutions *and* persons, texts *and* rituals, practice *and* theology, things *and* ideas."[26] The pilgrimage is a personal, moving experience for the individual, undertaken at his or her own physical and financial cost, but it is also a communal and ritualized event, and a public display of religious identity enjoined in written texts preserved and approved by the official, institutional representatives of ancient Judaism.[27] We will examine manifestations of these complex, interactive patterns in culture in due course, but we first need to attend to the theme of religion and the self, the meaning of "selfhood," and a related issue concerning the typological nature of traditional literature and the voice of the individual.

The Self, Convention, and Individuation

Suggesting that the "self was a religious concept" in antiquity, David Brakke, Michael Satlow, and Steven Weitzman ask, "What can be recovered of ancient selves, or of ancient perceptions of the self from the surviving textual sources?"[28] Influenced by Judith Butler, they ask further, "Does a text that purports to describe an author's inner life give access to a real self, or is that self a fiction—not what generates the text, but what the text generates?"[29] When we read Jeremiah's confessions or Nehemiah's memoir, are we learning about these men, or are we reading "persistent tropes"? Are these works "shaped by shared perceptions about what selves are supposed to be like?"[30] As Brakke and colleagues note, the text is "a product of a cultural process in which linguistic conventions, social institutions, and individual agency, as well as individual experience, collude in creating and re-creating selves."[31] Saul Olyan suggests that we can find individual voices in special and creative uses of topoi. When authors innovate upon traditional forms, we can begin to identify the self.[32] The Tibetologist and scholar of comparative religion Janet Gyatso too has explored portrayals of the self in traditional cultures. Gyatso examines the interplay between the individual and the typological, portrayals of the self and the demands of cultural convention, in the autobiography of a Tibetan lama of the eighteenth century who, to complicate matters further, is believed in his tradition to be a reincarnation of a previous lama. She notes that cultural historians have long suggested that "a sense of personal individuality [is] a unique marker of modern Western identity."[33] Gyatso, however, shows that the genre of this Tibetan work is indeed autobiography and that traditional authors, like modern ones, engage in "discourse in which the question 'who am I?' is answered by a narrative that tells 'how I became who I am.'"[34] Yes, there are conventions and tropes, but there is also "room for personal variation."[35] Like Olyan, she asks how one distinguishes trope from detail, the traditional and culturally shared from the individual, and seeks to understand the historical settings conducive to the production of autobiography or lack thereof.[36]

Stephen T. Katz's comments on the new and yet derivative aspects of mystical experiences and reports provide a relevant parallel. On the one hand, the mystical experience can be viewed as radical, powerfully personal, and a challenge to religion as usual. On the other hand, tradition rather conservatively influences the contents and form of the mystical experience and the language in which it is described.[37] Indeed, many mystics study canonical literature, whose form and content then make their way into mystical experience. In a largely oral culture in which texts as texts are not studied, the oral tradition has an equally strong or even stronger influence upon the content of a vision or the way the underworld looks. John Miles Foley has pointed to the "immanently referential" quality of language and experience in traditional societies in which the deity looks a certain way, certain phrases evoke certain emotional responses, and the larger tradition brings itself to bear on any piece of it that is employed or re-created.[38] Thus, as we trace some of the recurring literary forms in which personal religion is preserved and presented, we will point to specific individual and sometimes innovative scenes and messages that are nevertheless clothed in the imagery, meaning-world, and linguistic expectations of the tradition. Katz's work, like that of Brakke, Gyatso, Orsi, and McDannell, points to the way in which official and unofficial religion, the cultural and the individual, the self and tradition, interact and interface. Exploring these overlapping categories so central to an understanding of personal religion as presented in late-biblical material offers special challenges.

Challenges

A recurring subtheme of this study involves the difficulty of dealing with Yahwist cultures and literatures of the Neo-Babylonian and Persian periods, as underscored by the lively debates among scholars. The distinguished Israeli biblicist Shemaryahu Talmon frequently observed that the entire Hebrew Bible is to some degree a Second Temple–period document.[39] What Talmon meant is that while Hebrew Scriptures contain writings and traditions datable to earlier periods, the Hebrew Bible, a complex anthology or library of works, was given its essential compositional form during the intensely creative period of scribal activity following the conquest of the southern kingdom by the Babylonians in 586 BCE, the destruction of the great Solomonic temple in Jerusalem, and the exile of the Judean elite. Babylonia itself was defeated by Persia later in the sixth century BCE, and a replacement temple was built under the auspices of the Persian government, which allowed for the return of willing Judeans to the homeland. In the context of Persian rule and perhaps, in part, under the influence of Persian culture, the collecting, composing, and preserving of older and newer traditions took place. I agree with Talmon that an understanding of the Babylonian–Persian–early Second Temple period is crucial for an appreciation of the literature and culture of ancient Israel.

In the last few decades there has been an explosion of interest in Jewish cultures of the period following the Babylonian conquest. Certain themes emphasized in scholarly conversations have a direct bearing on ways in which we approach matters of religious identity and expression among Jews in the period following the conquest.

A first critical area comes under the heading of physical environment. Scholars including Oded Lipschits, Avraham Faust, Kenneth Hoglund, Charles E. Carter, Jeffrey R. Zorn, and Menachem Stern have mined archaeological evidence in an attempt to draw a picture of the contours and contents of the physical environment that reflected and helped shape daily life and religious practice.[40] Observations about the physical and material worlds where people lived lead to disparate expectations and ideas about their religious responses and expressions. The physical and material environment integrally relates to a range of cultural and psychosocial maps, affecting identity and modes of self-expression. A second related area of concern involves questions about continuity and discontinuity in material culture as it relates to social realities.

Many articles on material culture in the Persian period begin with their authors' declaration—an apology of sorts—that the available archaeological evidence is extremely difficult to interpret and that new evidence may well alter present conclusions. Lively debates question whether the material culture of Judah, or Yehud, during particular periods and places is characterized by essential continuity or evidence of disruption and transformation. Those arguing for essential continuity in material culture in Yehud in the wake of the conquest point to evidence of vitality in Gibeon, Mizpah, and Bethel, claiming that only Jerusalem suffered the affects of the conquest;[41] others point to significant diminishment and disruption.[42] Hans Barstad, for example, writes of the "myth of the empty land," emphasizing resilience and continuity, whereas Hoglund writes of "ruralization," which occurred as survivors fled urban centers and established new agricultural rural homesteads, and Faust describes Yehud as "a post-collapse society."[43]

Scholars who take the "discontinuity" position would not suggest that Yehud was ever utterly emptied out by the Babylonians. It has long been recognized that the biblical view of the extent of the exile reflects the ancient writers' worldview rather than social reality. Nevertheless, where one stands on this range of views is relevant to thinking about lived religion and personal religion. Did the presence of social, economic, and cultural continuity in Yehud lead to religious conservatism among Jews? Life did not change that much. On the other hand, if people were not as insecure as some have suggested, was there a greater likelihood of theological and literary innovation? Does significant disruption in communal ways of life lead to more emphasis on personal modes of religious expression, and to what ends?

Paradoxically, religious expression in bottom-up, personal religion may be either conservative or innovative. How people bury their dead or how they pray need not change. These activities are rooted in custom, oral tradition, the way it has always been. Does the absence of normative enforcers, however, allow for experimentation or for being more overtly influenced by neighbors' forms of religious expression? Alternatively, in the absence of former Judean official structures and in protest against foreign influence over important aspects of life, did Yahwists seek to maintain old traditions quite conservatively, holding on tightly to perceptions of the way things were? These are the sorts of questions we need to consider as we assess religious attitudes in late-biblical literature and representations of individual voices. There may be a spectrum of responses from the sources, and whether one agrees with Barstad or Faust, the implications of continuity or discontinuity are not easy to ascertain.

That the conquest brought significant disruptions seems indisputable. There was obvious physical destruction in Jerusalem, and psychic disruption among all Jews, even among those who found homes in parts of Yehud that did not suffer the devastation of Jerusalem and its environs. An American in the early part of the twenty-first century did not have to live near Ground Zero to feel the effects of the destructive attacks of 9/11. Those events, which were less invasive than the conquest of Yehud and the destruction of its mythic and political center, have nevertheless had an enormous influence on U.S. worldviews. Thus, Ephraim Stern reads the lack of female figurines throughout Yehud (during the monarchy, these buried figures were ubiquitous) as suggesting that subsequent to the Babylonian conquest, a kind of conservative reformation took place.[44] Whether or not we agree with Stern's interpretation of the silence of evidence, he is to be commended for trying to take account of the material situation on the ground as an indication of religious identity and expression. In a different vein, William Schniedewind regards the Persian period as a time of retrenchment in which a paucity of resources and the decline of classical Hebrew made for an unlikely environment for the flowering of literature written in Hebrew.[45] Charles Carter and Raymond Person argue, however, that despite the diminishment in resources, the Persian period could well have given rise to rich literary production.[46] I agree with Carter and Person, but appreciate the way in which all three scholars think in terms of the interrelationship between the physical realities of daily life and the literature that preserves and shapes worldviews.

A third important area to consider is "non-Judean Jews." Various settings and influences beyond Yehud relate to religious identities and voices represented in the Hebrew Bible: Samarian versus Judean, the diaspora versus the homeland, exiled status versus those left behind in the land—and later, those who returned to the land versus those who stayed in exile. Scholars have explored each of these dichotomies from a variety of perspectives. I mention a few studies to give some sense of the richness of contemporary scholarship and to underscore issues we need to consider in approaching questions about personal religion. For example, would we expect works written in the diaspora to reflect a wider array of possibilities for religion as lived, the bricolage resulting from direct contact with a non-Jewish culture, or might we expect Jews abroad to work harder to define "us" over against "them"?

Jill Middlemas examines anew religious identity and practice and the social, political, and economic status of those left in the land during the exile of the elites.[47] Joseph Blenkinsopp describes an ideology of "theocratic polity in the province of Judah" stemming from conservative threads in the tradition, which was "taken over by [an] ultradevout Judeo-Babylonian group," whereas Jeremiah W. Cataldo questions whether ancient Yehud actually can be defined as a theocracy.[48] Jon L. Berquist has explored with insight Persian-period Jewish literature in the light of postcolonial studies.[49] Daniel L. Smith approaches the experience of exile and deportation from comparative sociological and psychoanalytical perspectives, asking how genres of religious expression reflect responses to such social trauma.[50] Gary Knoppers explores Samarian-Judean relations,[51] and David Vanderhooft examines the differences between Neo-Babylonian and Persian rule as they relate to economic revitalization, administrative organization, and possible roles for ethnic minorities in postexilic settings.[52] He and others also explore linguistic shifts and the language of the exile.[53] All these works point to what Morton Smith called "the parties and politics" of the era, variations and tensions that that relate to worldviews and ways of living religion.[54]

A fourth area of concern is the role of the Persian Empire and Persian culture, and their relationship to Yehud. One excellent example of work in this vein is a set of readings edited by James Watts dealing with questions related to the formation of the Pentateuch in a Persian-period setting.[55] How much political, ideological, legal, and compositional autonomy did the authors have? How centralized was Persian control over Yehud, and did it extend to influencing the collection, preservation, and form of the Pentateuch itself? What ultimately was the role and place of the Persian Empire in the formation of Jewish identity? Work continues as well concerning priestly groups that seem to have had strong ties with Persia, their self-perception and self-presentation in the Hebrew Bible, their political, sociohistorical identities, and tensions between the groups.[56] Some Persian-period writers were pro-Persian, others were not; some looked for a new ruler descended from David, some did not. Some hoped for an overturning of reality, some upheld the status quo, and others hoped to survive by what David Daube calls "collaboration with tyranny."[57] Some were "liberal" on socioeconomic issues but "conservative" on intermarriage. Some appeared to be the opposite—they intermarried but seemed oblivious of the plight of the poor, or became rich by oppressing the poor—or at least they were accused of doing so. Finally, Brent Strawn explores the fascinating intersection of the symbols of Persian art and Second Temple–period literature, reminding us once again of the importance of material religion, of the critical ways in which unspoken and visual dimensions reflect and shape people's religion as lived.[58]

A fifth area of concern is chronology. In exploring late-biblical literature and its settings as they relate to personal religion, we need to consider diachronic and synchronic dynamics. Difficulties abound in ascertaining the sociocultural settings behind the compositions in Trito-Isaiah, Zechariah 9–14, and other prophetic works, such as Joel and Malachi. Morton Smith's views of Yahweh-alone and syncretist parties, and Hanson's theory concerning competition between those who held to different religious worldviews, one visionary and the other pragmatic, still provide useful categories and point to some of the tensions in late-biblical Israel,[59] a tension reflected in the literature. The picture, however, is surely even more complex than either allowed. In a thoughtful introduction to a work dealing with the role that Jerusalem played in religious life and imagination in the Persian period, Knowles points to many of these continuing debates.[60]

Scholars also disagree about which biblical compositions count as windows on Persian-period worldviews—Ruth, Job, Ecclesiastes? Some do not date these works to the Persian period at all. As scholarly conversations indicate, there is considerable continuing debate about the redaction history of biblical priestly literature.[61] How do we talk about the Priestly Source (P) and the Persian period? What about the frameworks for apocalyptic works? Some preserved sources indicate the worldview of those who urge action in order to precipitate the eschatological battle, while others urge patient waiting for the Lord, a variation in orientation found among contemporary apocalyptists as well. Indeed, commenting on these many debates and difficulties, Yigal Levin begins a recent work on the period suggesting that a goal of his project is to "present the reader with a lifeboat, or at least to extend a paddle."[62] Methodological approaches and theoretical considerations drawn from the study of contemporary religion and described above inform our work and help us deal with these complex issues.

Case Studies

Each of the case studies that follow grapples with manifestations of and innovations upon personal religion within the sociohistorical challenges offered by the Babylonian and Persian periods of Judaism. A first study deals with treatments of sin and responsibility and explores the emphasis on individual responsibility for sin found in sixth-century-BCE biblical texts. Of special interest is a saying found in Jeremiah and Ezekiel, "The parents eat [have eaten] sour grapes, and the teeth of the children twinge" (Ezekiel 18:2–3; Jeremiah 31:29; see also Lamentations 5:7) and the fascinating rhetorical tour de force that follows in Ezekiel 18.[63] In content and form, these texts provide an important challenge to conventional wisdom and exemplify individualized interpretations of traditional literary forms.

A second, related study explores God's justice as it affects individuals' situations in life, particularly as seen in Job and Ecclesiastes. Like Edward L. Greenstein concerning Job[64] and C.-L. Seow concerning Ecclesiastes,[65] I date both works to the Persian Period. As in chapter one, I show how these works challenge conventional wisdom or turn it on its head by adapting or recontextualizing traditional forms and debating inherited, community-shared theological truths. The use of first-person language and images of embodiment help to frame vital concerns in personal terms.

A discussion of the self leads to a trajectory of tradition that links incantations, the personal lament of Lamentations 3 and a number of Psalms, the confessions of Jeremiah, and the memoir of Nehemiah. The self found in these works, explored in chapter three, is an increasingly insistent and autobiographical self, even while the literary forms are traditional, typological, and formulaic in language and content.

The making of a vow frequently concludes the lament as the speaker promises to give or do certain things if the deity intercedes on his behalf. The vow is an important means by which individuals establish ties with the deity and with members of the community. Vows are also expressions, assertions, and reflections of self-definition. A fourth case study provides a close examination of Numbers 6, a description of the Nazirite vow; Numbers 30, a text dealing with women's vows; and other references to vows, often in narrative contexts. These examples reveal an important thread in the social, theological, economic, and personal dimensions of Judaism in the Persian Period. Vows relating to war (Jephthah, Saul, and the ban) provide interesting contrasts with late-biblical examples from Numbers 6 and 30.

Chapter five explores the relationships between literary texts and objects, spaces, and pictorial representations as they relate to the study of personal religion in the Neo-Babylonian and Persian periods. This chapter focuses fully on material religion as manifested in a burial site, in prophetic visionary experiences, and in the form of performance art exemplified by the sign act.

Chapter six focuses further on the self within the prophetic visionary tradition. The portrayal of seers in late-biblical material puts increasing
emphasis on individual experience, even though conventions in language
and content remain fully visible. This chapter explores the development of
biblical vision texts in order to emphasize the way in which these literary
forms come to reflect an interest in the individual seer and his immersion
in the experiential dimension of religion. A comparison between preexilic
and postexilic texts presents an important trajectory.

The final case study, which relates well to observations concerning
late-biblical seers, deals with characterization in Persian-period literature.
Characterization in Ruth and Jonah is subtly developed through exquisite
attention to detail, to dialogue, mood, setting, and motivation. Comparisons between Ruth and Tamar (Genesis 38) and between Jonah and other
prophetic works are especially useful. Ruth and Jonah may well be based
on portrayals of Tamar and other prophets, such as Elijah; juxtaposing the
earlier and later works reveals differences that highlight late-biblical characterization as it relates to personal religion and the interest in individuals.

As we approach this fascinating corpus and explore manifestations of
and attitudes to personal religion among Yahwists of the Neo-Babylonian
and Persian periods, we do well to think in wider humanistic terms about
the significance of our findings. The following studies have relevance not
only for appreciating worldviews of the particular ancient community that
is the subject of this study but also for understanding ways in which all
human beings seek to deal with the realities and adversities of life within
particular social, cultural, and historical contexts. This set of studies examines the complicated negotiations that construct identity, pointing to the
relationships between the personal and the communal, the material and
the metaphysical. Throughout, attention is paid to shared conventions and
specific variations in the ongoing interplay between the individual and the
cultural that draws upon and re-creates tradition.

1 Sour Grapes, Suffering, and Coping with Chaos

Outlook on the Individual

Parents eat [have eaten] sour grapes,
and the teeth of the children twinge.
Ezekiel 18:2; Jeremiah 31:29

The saying, quoted by Ezekiel and Jeremiah, provides a first case study in exploring engagement with the individual in the context of lived religion of the sixth century BCE. As with all traditional forms, the meanings and messages of this deceptively simple saying are variable, complex, multiple, context driven, and difficult to ascertain. Our study pays special attention to the ethnic genre *māšāl* and related matters of content, structure, and meaning, examining the proverb in hypothesized performance contexts. A critical review of more typical scholarly approaches to the proverb in its biblical settings and an overview of approaches to questions of sin and punishment preserved in the Hebrew Bible lead to alternate suggestions for possible meanings of the proverb, ones influenced less by theological considerations than by work in religion as lived and the field of folklore studies. An analysis of the proverb in Ezekiel and Jeremiah asks what the intended audience may have had in mind about the saying and how this interpretation might contrast with each prophet's ideas. Finally, we return to questions about the proverb's place in personal religion to explore whether Jeremiah and Ezekiel are concerned with individual human beings in a retail, life-experiencing sense. Some details of translation need to be addressed first.

Translation

The root translated above as "sour grapes" could also connote "unripe fruit," but the same message would be conveyed whether the hearer imagines one image or the other: fruit with a certain piquancy has an effect on the consumer's (offspring's) teeth. The verb *qhh*, employed with certainty at only one other biblical location, Ecclesiastes 10:10, is a more difficult problem. It has frequently been translated "to make blunt" or "to set on edge." The passage that includes Ecclesiastes 10:10 is difficult. The *māšāl* follows one of the author's ironic collections of overliteralized sayings that emphasize his theme of life's seeming absurdity. The message of the set, taken as a whole, seems to be that the outcome of particular actions is not as expected.

> He who digs a pit will fall into it.
> He who breaks through a wall, a snake will bite him.
> He who quarries rocks will be hurt by them.
> He who splits logs will be endangered by them.
> *Ecclesiastes 10:8–9*

Turning to Ecclesiastes 10:10, we note that scholars usually translate *qhh* as "blunt," drawing an oppositional parallel with *qlql* in 10:10b, which they translate as "sharpen." The verb *qlql* actually means "to move back and forth," as in the motion involved in whetting a knife or ax. It may be that the iron referred to in verse 10 is not what one sharpens, but the steel upon which one sharpens an instrument or weapon. I would translate thus:

> If the iron is in bad condition [*qhh*],
> and it does not whet edges,
> warriors it will make mighty
> and skill will be the advantage.[1]

Rabbinic texts expand the meaning of the root *qhh* to include "tough," "hard," "unyielding," "difficult," "unsolvable." The iron in Ecclesiastes 10:10 does not work well.

The author seems to suggest again that the results of an action are not as one would expect. Warriors become mighty when the sharpener fails. A sharpened weapon is not necessarily an instrument of victory. Relying on wisdom or skill is what leads to success. The *qhh* root, thus understood, should have negative nuances regarding condition or effectiveness. While "blunt" or "set on edge" would work, I prefer a phrase that emphasizes the immediate negative reaction of the teeth, their condition, the way they feel. Carole R. Fontaine suggests "pucker,"[2] but I translate the term as "twinge."

Form, Context, and Meaning

Having provided a translation, we can move on to questions about the *māšāl*, its texture, structure, and context.[3] In the biblical tradition, the term *māšāl* is applied to a variety of communicative forms that we might call parable, proverb, oracle, or icon. A form of "oblique and artful communication, drawn from personal memory and experience and built upon the traditions claimed by a folk group to be its collective memory,"[4] the *māšāl* is rooted in the notion of analogy and comparing, which is the literal meaning of the verb *mšl*. The person performing a proverb, a type of *māšāl*, draws a comparison between the real-life setting of the listeners and the content of the saying. The proverb may serve as critique, approbation, or neutral observation.

Influenced by the folklorist Alan Dundes and others, Fontaine nicely describes the structure of the proverb and its texture. Dundes suggests that proverbs are composed of one or more topics and one or more comments on the topics, which linguistically often relate to subject and predicate. Fontaine views the topics in this proverb as "fathers/children" and the comments as "eat sour grapes/twinge."[5] One might also see the topic as the first half of the proverb—what the parents do—and the comment as the result—the children's suffering the twinging of their teeth. The theme is clearly generational, not unlike the proverb "like mother, like daughter," also employed by Ezekiel, which, apart from Ezekiel's context, could be used in a positive or negative way, depending upon performance context and tone. Similarly, in U.S. culture, one might say "he's a chip off the old block" to point out that a son is successful like his father or a rogue like his father. The sour grapes proverb causally links an action or event and a subsequent negative experience, not unlike the proverb pattern, "When X sneezes in Y, Z catches a cold in W." Presumably, an action or event could have a positive outcome across time or place, as in the Chinese proverb "One generation plants the trees and another gets the shade," or "Each generation will reap what the former generation has sown." In the latter example, negative and positive possibilities of meaning are available, depending upon the specific situation implied by the saying and the context in which it is performed or quoted.

Were we situated in ancient Israelite culture, we could observe the ways in which the sour grapes saying is employed or ask people to imagine such a setting and describe it. We could listen to the inflection of the speaker and assess the relative status of the speaker of the proverb and those to whom it is addressed. Folklorists including Barbara Kirshenblatt-Gimblett and Alan Dundes engage in this sort of ethnographic work.[6] They find that proverbs have differing connotations even within the same folk group. The meaning conveyed depends upon the specific context and situation that gives rise to proverb performance, the relationship between the speaker and those who are addressed, the tone of the speaker, the version of the proverb to which the addressees had been previously exposed, and other factors. Kirshenblatt-Gimblett, for example, points to a survey indicating that a certain percentage of hearers of the proverb beginning with the topic "a friend in need" understand the comment and conclusion to be "is a friend indeed," whereas others hear the completion of the proverb to be "is a friend in deed." Moreover, in each case the proverb can be applied differently. She shows further how the message of the proverb "money talks" depends upon the economic situation of the speaker and the receiver, the situation upon which the speaker comments, whether the tone is sarcastic or bitter (implying perhaps that a person's money has not led to his advancement), or guilty (implying, for example, that the speaker himself has succeeded through his father's wealthy connections whereas his friend who hears him quote the proverb has not), or sympathetic (for example, directed at a person who has missed out on some benefit because of a lack of money).

Options for performance settings and interpretations of the proverb about eating the sour grapes are many. The saying may serve as a criticism of the way that people reared their children. For example, if parents show no devotion to their children, do not discipline them, or provide bad role models, the children lack self-confidence, ambition, or happiness. Perhaps they run wild or become sociopathic, and suffer the consequences. This use of the proverb might imply a modern view that child miscreants are shaped within family environments and therefore they are not responsible for their crimes. Theologically oriented views explored below suggest that the prophets reject this notion, whereas the people cling to it in an ancient version (or parody) of conservative and liberal approaches to crime. The proverb could be applied to a specific person and his parents. One might use the proverb to comment on the way a neighbor child experiences life (the bad seed, the withdrawn child, the child with an eating disorder). One might say the proverb about him to his parents or to a third party. The proverb might be deployed to generalize about the joblessness of young workers whose parents did not prepare them for work or who ruined the economy.

Other interpretations of the proverb that inform performance settings might explain children's conditions or actions without judging their parents negatively. The "eating" and the subsequent "twinging" do not point to a process of delayed punishment for previous acts of wrongdoing. Rather, the parents have been exposed to suffering, so their children suffer. For example, poverty in one generation can prevent parents from providing their children with proper resources, leading to poverty in the next generation. The bitterness of the fruit they eat leads to the children's discomfort. Alternatively, the ancestors might have unwittingly done something that leads to future generations' problems, for example, smoking in the days before people recognized the health hazards of secondhand smoke.

The proverb can be relevant in all the cases described above whether one knows who the ancestors are or what they did and experienced. That is, it can be applied to specific parents and children or to the links between generations of people. The cause of contemporary suffering is assigned to the unseen, the actions or experiences of those who are perhaps already dead. Deeds long past somehow pile up problems for later. Wrongdoing, whether intentional or unintentional, may lead to the downfall of the perpetrators, but may not. Either way, curse-like, it may float on through generations to lead future people to suffer its consequences. Religious worldviews work out the implications of the floating curse in their own ways.

Why is this proverb cited in these exilic-period texts, and can we tell from the written contexts what it may have meant to the audiences of Ezekiel and Jeremiah and to the prophets themselves? What is the conventional wisdom that each prophet quotes? And what do the saying and its quotation have to do with questions about the representation of individuals and the interest in personal religion? First, some comments on the function of proverbs.

Dundes writes, "Folklore provides a socially sanctioned framework for the expression of critical anxiety-producing problems as well as a cherished artistic vehicle for communicating ethos and worldview."[7] Dundes suggests that forms of communication such as the proverb, which have culturally recognizable structures and flexible, wide-ranging application, help people grapple with challenges, the twinging that human beings, set in culture, experience during their lifetimes and that becomes especially acute in periods of crisis, communal or individual. Fontaine notes that proverbs function as problem-solving media, pointing to tensions faced by people and the need to address these tensions: "The greater the conflict with which a person is confronted, the more apt he or she becomes to fall back on internalized systems of categorization and problem-solving . . . The traditional saying deals with these kinds of content."[8] Surely, the period of Babylonian conquest, like any situation of war, with its deaths, deprivation, and forced migrations, induced inner turmoil and conflict. Scholarly approaches to this particular proverb are generally less attuned to the sort of attention paid to context and function by folklorists than to matters of theology.

In 1987, the biblical scholar Robert A. Oden published *The Bible without Theology*.[9] Oden was interested in the place and evolution of biblical studies within the context of, and often in tension with, the field of religious studies as informed, in particular, by anthropology. The book deals with trajectories in intellectual history and with scholarly subjectivity. Oden explores what scholars' approaches to the Hebrew Bible say about their own sense of self, identity, and place in the world. As I review contemporary colleagues' treatments of this proverb, I find myself thinking about Oden's title and his project, noting that interpretations of the allusions to the proverb in Jeremiah and Ezekiel are consistently and almost exclusively framed in theological terms of disobedience to God and consequent punishment. Scholars point to the tension between people's self-image of innocence and the reality of their sinfulness, and frequently raise questions about responsibility for sin and whether this responsibility is collective or individual, having to do with the self or the community, and how these two sides of a seeming dichotomy relate or intertwine.[10]

Another area of interest among scholars concerns the nature of wrongdoing. Is it a matter of criminal lawbreaking, dealt with in the human realm, or a matter of sin, falling within the divine purview?[11] A third important and central area explored by scholars concerns the transgenerational implications for punishment projected by the proverb and its challenge to God's justice. Some of these studies compare Jeremiah and Ezekiel's incorporation of the proverb, seeking to understand the views of theodicy expressed by each prophet and by those presumed to have employed the proverb.[12] Finally, some raise broader issues about the nature of the moral self and the moral community.[13]

A set of quotations about the proverb cited in Ezekiel 18 sets the interpretive interests of scholars in relief and helps frame the set of questions that I wish to explore.

> The people are expressing their worldview—that their fate is determined by the actions of their fathers; their own moral choices are irrelevant. In the rest of the chapter Ezekiel sets out to refute this notion, and to reassert the relevance of virtuous moral selfhood as the only accurate way of understanding their situation.[14]

> The people hide behind the old conception of an extended retribution . . . in order to avoid their own responsibility for their plight.[15]

> Thus, implies the prophet, those in exile are there for their own sins and not those of their parents, and since their relationship with God is not an intractable or inherited fate they can take responsibility for it and return to YAHWEH.[16]

> The prophet addresses an audience who are blaming previous generations for the disaster of exile . . . He rejects this saying and with it his audience's denial of responsibility for their fate.[17]

These approaches, one way or another, express interest in the way the proverb relates to assignments of blame for the Babylonian conquest and the exile of elites, whose voices are so strongly represented in the written texts of the Hebrew Bible; the proverb is quoted and then rejected in order to insist that the blame for the unfortunate course of events that characterizes the Babylonian conquest lies with the people, not with evil enemies or ancestors or poor leadership or chance. The people themselves are responsible for the disaster; their moral choices count. The Judeans are portrayed as trying to deny responsibility, to refuse to admit to their own sins, to be unwilling to accept that they themselves are the source of their troubles.

Behind the interpretations and interests represented by this selection of scholarly views, there can be no genuine attention to the individual, whatever the distinctions some scholars draw between individual and corporate responsibility; the proverb and its rejection are said to be about the people's sin, the nation's wrongdoing, however that is phrased in individual terms. And yet it seems unlikely that during the Babylonian crisis, the deployment of this proverb in ordinary situations might not have had to do with individual experience. What about the three-year-old child who died as a result of the invasion? Was he or she guilty of sin? Was every priest corrupt? Was the poor, honest workman necessarily guilty of sin? Were the prophets or their countrymen who are said to quote the proverb not concerned with basic questions about why bad things happen to good people? Such questions do not generally inform scholarly dialogue about the proverb, its function, and its range of meanings.

Scholarly interpretations represented by the above quotations, moreover, pay inadequate attention to the structure, content, and contexts of the proverb, and to its possible meanings in various performance settings. As we have noted, proverbs, like other forms of folklore, are flexible, adaptable media that can take on different meanings in different contexts, depending upon tone, speaker, situation, the relationship between speaker and listener, and so on. The folklorist Wolfgang Mieder writes, "Only a specific context will reveal what a proverb really wants to say."[18] There has not been sufficient attention paid to the range of conventional wisdom that may be implied by the proverb, to the multiple and sometimes contrasting explanations people offer for the uncontrollable difficulties they face in life, or to variations among biblical treatments of matters of blame and causation regarding life's difficulties.

A number of contemporary scholars do point out that no pattern from preexilic to exilic times traces a simple evolution from corporate identity to individualism.[19] Rather, as we discussed in relation to personal religion, an awareness of community and shared cultural identity is present in all religious cultures. At the same time, such cultures are also characterized by forms of private religious expression and experience that are integrally related to individual identity. And in some periods and situations, an increased emphasis on and concern with the personal and the individual come to the fore. Many biblical examples of the so-called blessings-and-curses theology, whereby blessings accrue to those who follow covenant and curses to those who do not, can be read as comments on and evaluations of society: the ways in which it treats widows and orphans, the ways in which violence is prevalent or controlled, honesty expected or infrequent, leadership tolerant and fair or tyrannical. Those societies characterized by violence, dishonesty, oppression, neglect, and indifference to suffering will be swept away. And yet in some contexts, the authors appear to chastise actions by and attitudes of individuals. The classic biblical statement of blessings and curses found in Deuteronomy 27–28 points to a tension between questions about the tone and tenor of society versus the actions of individuals, and between the consequences of actions for the group as a whole versus the individual. Thus Deuteronomy 27:15–26 specifically curses anyone who acts in a particular way, for example, by taking a bribe or by lying with an animal, whereas Deuteronomy 28:12 refers to the whole people Israel's blessed capacity to "lend to many nations" and to their shared suffering destruction, disaster, and panic, in the case of the communal curse of Deuteronomy 28:20. Moreover, there is no simple dichotomy between criminal actions, which are adjudicated by human beings and punished in accordance with social norms, and sins, acts of wrongdoing that are the express purview of God. To be sure, Israelites believed that God is aware of certain acts of criminal or civil wrongdoing that escape human legal responses, and there are acts, for example, within the realm of liturgical behavior or embodied religion, that especially affect a person's relationship to God, for example, being unclean during the performance of ritual sacrifice. But the distinctions are frequently blurred: to murder is to break covenant and insult the deity, and being knowingly unclean in a setting requiring ritual purity is legally wrong. There are no neat divisions between humanly proscribed wrongdoing and divinely punished sins.

There is a shared belief reflected in the Hebrew Scriptures that communities try to punish those responsible for breaking their laws, all of which are believed to be divinely sent or approved, and this punishment is to be applied not to the parents of those who break covenant, but to the wrongdoers themselves (Deuteronomy 24:16). At the same time, there is a thread in the Scriptures that regards certain kinds of wrongdoing, for example, breaking the ban and stealing God's war spoil, as in the case of Achan (Joshua 7), as attaching a contagious and cancerous otherness to those around the miscreant, who must also be rooted out.[20]

Suffering and death itself are the result of sin, and everyone sins, even though sins differ in seriousness; it is the nature of being human. Thus, death or suffering can always be explained by sin (Deuteronomy 27–28). It is, moreover, entirely possible to believe that some suffering is the result of one's own sins and some an inheritance from ancestors, that some punishment for sin is immediate and other punishments are delayed (see Deuteronomy 27–28; Exodus 20:5, 34:6–7; Numbers 14:18). The way in which writers blame misfortunes following the death of the good king Josiah on the misdeeds of his grandfather, Manasseh, is an excellent historiographic example of the delayed wages of sin. Similarly, Lamentations 5:7 can be read to suggest that subsequent generations bear the sins of their deceased ancestors: "Our ancestors sinned; they are no more / We their sins bear."

Alternatively, the saying in Lamentations 5:7 might be read as a comment on the human condition: we all sin and we all suffer. Ezekiel 33:10, another saying attributed to the people, seems to suggest precisely this view of sin and suffering. We suffer under the burden of sin, and so, as they ask, "How can we live?" All these possibilities are reflected in the Hebrew Bible and all relate to the desire to explain and acknowledge suffering in a world that somehow makes sense.

The proverb, in both forms included by the prophets, addresses central and troubling ambiguities that define the human condition. Death, illness, economic devastation, and physical suffering are some of the many faces of chaos, the uncontrollable and inexplicable aspects of our existence. This proverb is one way to cope with anomie, the senselessness of suffering, the sources of disruption and dislocation. As the social anthropologist Clifford Geertz has written, "The effort is not to deny the undeniable—that there are unexplained events, that life hurts, or that rain falls on the just—but to deny that there are inexplicable events, that life is unendurable, and that justice is a mirage."[21] Defining chaos as "a tumult of events which lack not just interpretations but interpretability," he points out that chaos "threatens to break in upon man: at the limits of his analytical capacities, at the limits of his powers of endurance, and at the limits of his moral insight."[22] The Babylonian conquest presented each of these challenges, pointing to the "gap between things as they are and things as they ought to be if our conceptions of right and wrong make sense."[23] There must have been those who remembered Isaiah's promises about the inviolability of Jerusalem and divine protection for Yahweh's people (Isaiah 29:5–8, 31:4–9, 37:33–35). There must have been those whose innocent children had been injured or killed. There must have been people who believed themselves to be living in decency and faithfulness and yet whose lives were utterly disrupted. If they could say that previous acts by those over whom they had no control had caused current suffering, they somehow might explain the trauma and accept it. That is just the way life is. An alternate explanation is that we ourselves are the cause, for we all sin, in ways large and small, and this view was also common among ancient Israelites. And indeed, all these possibilities exist at once.

The proverb quoted by Ezekiel and Jeremiah thus offers a piece of conventional wisdom that comforts—not, as many scholars suggest, because it deflects the people's own responsibility for sin, but because it offers some reason for anomie, suffering, dislocation, and death. It is one of many such explanations that make suffering interpretable. And here we return to questions about the function and form of the *māšāl*, its context and performance, and the ways in which the prophets grapple with the saying as an indication of their worldviews in a time of crisis, worldviews concerned with the individual.

Fontaine suggests that there is a difference between what the "people believe to be the situation and what Yahweh knows to be the case," and that the prophets attribute "hypocrisy" to the people's "popular piety."[24] I suggest rather that the prophets and the people approach the proverb from different directions or worldviews. The prophets are concerned with God's fairness. The one God ideally should be consistent in his treatment of individuals. Ezekiel and Jeremiah describe an ideal world where innocents do not suffer and each person suffers for his own wrongdoing. Undeserved suffering is simply not fair. The people however, see the proverb as a way to make unfairness comprehensible. The world may be unfair, but it is not, to reprise Geertz's formulation, utterly mad. Indeed, we might think again about Geertz's description of the three ways in which chaos threatens: a challenge to understanding, to endurance, and to moral insight. One might suggest that the events of the sixth century BCE challenged Judeans' endurance on various levels; the prophets see the events as a challenge to moral insight, whereas nonprophetic speakers of proverbs might well perceive their situation as a challenge to understanding. Attribution of suffering to events and generations of the past helps one cope, even if the suffering does not seem fair. Suffering is at least explicable. As Geertz notes, "The problem of suffering is, paradoxically, not how to avoid suffering, but how to suffer, how to make of physical pain, personal loss, worldly defeat, or helpless contemplation of others' agony something bearable, supportable—something as we say, sufferable."[25] Suffering is what human beings share, the human condition. One has sympathy for those who suffer, but without laying upon them blame, recrimination, or guilt in the absence of evidence that somehow they deserve their distress. Like a healing ritual explored by Geertz, the proverb about sour grapes has "the ability to give the stricken person a vocabulary in terms of which to grasp the nature of his distress and relate it to the wider world."[26] The prophets, however, wrestling with questions of theodicy, are disturbed to think that the one God may be punishing innocent victims, an idea that is anathema to them. For the people, suffering is an unexplained problem, whereas for the prophets it is a moral dilemma. How can God punish those who have not sinned?

A close look at the proverb in its literary contexts points to each prophet's orientation toward this piece of folk wisdom. Jeremiah begins his contextualization with formulaic language of the oracle, "Behold, days are coming . . ." His message from God sets up a contrast between the present situation and what the future holds—in this case, a hopeful contrast between a time of desolation and a time of hope and rebuilding. Yahweh is going to sow the house of Israel with humans and animals (Jeremiah 31:27). This image of fertility is followed by a promise that is then illustrated by the proverb.

> And it will be: as I was watching over them
> to pull up and to pull down,
> and to tear down and to destroy,
> and to do harm,
> thus I will watch over them
> to build and to plant, utterance of the Yahweh.
> In those days they will say no longer,
> "The parents have eaten sour grapes
> and the teeth of the children twinge."
> Rather, a man for his own sin will die.
> Every human being who eats sour grapes,
> twinge will his teeth.
> Behold days are coming, utterance of Yahweh,
> and I will cut with the house of Israel and the house of Judah a new
>   covenant.
> *Jeremiah 31:27–31*

Former realities involved God's pulling up and tearing down, his doing harm, but in this utopian, hoped-for future he will build and plant. The punch line about then versus now is provided by the proverb. Thus contextualized, the use of the proverb suggests that Jeremiah, like those he addresses, considers accurate the perception that undeserved suffering results from what the ancestors have done. He, however, is not satisfied with simply explaining the people's suffering. Rather, he feels that the whole proposition leads to moral questions. Why should the people suffer because of a floating curse? Rather, "in those days" to come, there will be a new system: each person will be punished for his own sin. This promise will be a feature of the new covenant, the new deal that God is making with the people. This new deal, of course, still poses a moral dilemma that the proverb itself seeks to address, namely, the suffering of the good. Jeremiah insists that suffering is the result of sin, but if the good suffer, it must mean that even they sin. Thus Jeremiah 31:33 adds to his utopian description the view that a time will arise when no one will sin. The law will be placed in each person, a new heart, so that moral choices, large and small, will always be good ones, and no one will need to be punished.

The new covenant is characterized by an internalization of the law within each person: the law is written on their hearts (31:33). They absorb knowledge of the Lord in an instantaneous, immediate way; having been forgiven for previous sins, they are able to make a fresh start under the new covenant. In this way, Jeremiah imagines a reality in which sin leads to punishment no more, whether ancestors' sins or one's own, because people are, in a sense, one with the law. Questions concerning divine justice are no longer necessary. There is no undeserved suffering because there is no longer suffering at all. The model here is radical, a leap of imagination, and utterly utopian. It discards the conventional wisdom of the proverb, which seeks to make suffering explicable, and it accepts the premises of the prophet's theology and his concept of theodicy while insisting that its terms will no longer be necessary because no one will sin. Moral insight is no longer in self-contradiction. Things will be as they ought to be.

Ezekiel's approach in Ezekiel 18, which appears to stop short of this utopian vision, is oriented to the significance of performing the proverb in the present rather than the applicability of the proverb in the future, but Ezekiel can ultimately be seen to reach much the same point as Jeremiah, once one considers the fuller corpus of his oracles. Ezekiel is insistent that the blessings-and-curses theology is valid for each person. That being the case, and since God is in control of all "living souls" and what happens to them, the notion of inherited sin is invalid, as is indeed the notion that ancestors' righteousness inoculates subsequent generations against punishment or mitigates the punishment. Even if Noah, Daniel, and Job, paragons of righteousness, were present, there would be no reprieve for sons and daughters. These three would be saved, but not those who sin after them (Ezekiel 14:13–20). To reprise Geertz, the proverb creates for Ezekiel a contradiction between how things are supposed to be and how things are, if one's concept of right and wrong is correct. Thus, a lengthy monologue in 18:5–24 develops this train of thought, providing examples and elaborating on the implications of this fair deal for the disposition of individual actors.

Several points need to be made about Ezekiel's monologue as it relates to representations and views of self and the prophet's interpretation of the proverb. Throughout, Ezekiel explores the implications and consequences of an individual's actions: if a man is righteous (18:5); if he bears a son who is violent (18:10); if a wicked man repents (18:21). A formulaically framed list of quintessential markers of behavior, good and bad, is reiterated: stances regarding idol worship, adultery, the oppressing of people, holding pledges, robbery, feeding the poor, and so on. These behaviors are attributed to fathers and sons, individuals. Possibilities for repentance are offered, as is the recognition that one might slide into sin after a good and moral life. One need not act like one's father, whether he was righteous or wicked. A father's deeds, good or evil, will not accrue to the son. Ezekiel insists that the people are wrong to claim that God is unfair by saying, "not right is the way of the Lord" (18:25). Rather, he declares, within a strongly theological model, that they are not taking responsibility for their own sin. They should not use the proverb (as he understands it) to make sense of their situation. They have brought trouble upon themselves. The sin is not their ancestors' but their own.

While 18:5–24 deals with individuals, 18:25–32 relates to the community, the tone and tenor of society. Are the ways of the community righteous or not? Do they turn away from evil or not? This juxtaposition of individual and community is evident in Deuteronomy 27–28, as noted above. In Ezekiel 18:25–32, the house of Israel is addressed in wholesale fashion, and yet the actions of each individual dominate the first half of the passage, and thus it seems reasonable to suggest that Ezekiel is also deeply concerned with individuals. It is interesting that 18:32 returns to the individual: "I take no delight in the death of anyone who has died." The same theme dominates the response in Ezekiel 33 to the people's insistence that they cannot escape sin and its consequences (33:10). Again we find the words of God, an echo of 18:32, this time in an oath formula, "As I live, says Yahweh God [literally and implicitly, "let me not live"], if I delight in the death of the wicked." As in chapter 18, the good person can fall into sin and die (33:12–13, 18), and the evildoer can repent, act differently, and live (33:14–16, 19). Indeed, Ezekiel 33:1–10 deals with the prophet's personal responsibility as a sentinel whose responsibility it is to warn Israel, in this case taken as a communal whole. If he does his job and people fail to heed him, he is free from guilt, but if he shies away from this responsibility and does not warn them, their blood is on his hands. It is as if he himself is a murderer (see also Ezekiel 3:17–21). Sin and responsibility are thus seen in both communal and individual terms, and the link between sin and death is made explicit.

Ezekiel, like other postexilic writers, understands the events of the sixth century BCE to be explained by the people's sinfulness. There is nothing new here. But he puts an intense emphasis on individual behavior. Calamity occurs not merely because society en masse is evil or because of the leadership of an idolatrous king. It is each person's choices that bring him down. A society can be composed of those who sin and those who do not, and their treatment by God will differ accordingly. Ezekiel tells the people that each is in control of his or her life. They need a new orientation, a new heart and a new spirit, and then they will live (18:31). Ezekiel 18:32, like chapter 33, also seems to emphasize that death itself is the result of sin, whether an entire people's demise or that of individuals: "He dies for his own iniquity" (18:18); "He shall surely live" (18:19); "The person who sins, that one shall die" (18:20). This view of the cause of death is a very old notion in many cultures, including ancient Israel. We all die because one way or another we all sin. The author of Job of course contests this point of view, this other aspect of conventional wisdom that reflects the effort to make sense of our lot in life. Nevertheless, in chapters 18 and 33, Ezekiel insists it is possible not to sin.

One must assume, however, that Ezekiel himself could not ignore the fact that people cannot simply avoid sin and choose the good. He must still grapple with the death of those who are too young to make choices. Do their deaths serve as punishment for their sinful parents? Why then do some children die and others live? And thus Ezekiel, like Jeremiah, comes to a more utopian view, a hope for the future that human beings will be so transformed that they will no longer sin.[27]

Ezekiel 36:25–38 imagines a cleansing rite of passage whereby, in priestly fashion, water sprinkled upon the people takes away their uncleanness and a "new heart and a new spirit" replaces their "heart of stone." The presence of the Lord's spirit within people allows them to follow God's commandments and sin no more. Only then can they be assured of the bounty of God's blessings, at peace in the land, a new Eden. This passage treats the community as a whole, as if it has one heart, but the transformation has implications for questions about individual sin raised in Ezekiel 18, just as the tale about the garden of Eden in Genesis 2–3 is understood to have implications for each human being's life cycle and experience. Only the sort of transformation predicted in Ezekiel 36 can allow Ezekiel's view of the way the world works to stand. In this way, his vision is as radically utopian as that of Jeremiah.

2 Personal Religion in Ecclesiastes and Job

Conventional Wisdom, Responses in the First-Person Voice, and the Problem of Suffering

Questions raised by the *māšāl* of sour grapes concerning individual responsibility, divine justice, and ways of coping with life's trials lead to the biblical books of Qohelet (Ecclesiastes) and Job. Each complex work has been variously dated, and different suggestions have been offered concerning the redaction history of the works and the origin of the seemingly disparate pieces joined to constitute each book. First we explore tensions in these compositions, briefly outlining major trends in scholarship and the ways in which readers might make sense of competing themes and forms in each. Then we turn to specific passages that relate integrally to themes of this study: personal religion, self-representation, and characterizations of the individual. What do the books of Qohelet and Job reveal about the privatization and personalization of religious identity, and how is the appreciation of these works enhanced by paying attention to religion as lived in a late-biblical context?

Tensions in Qohelet and Job

Qohelet moves readers in different directions. One thread appears to offer or at least to preserve typical, conventional wisdom about accepting one's lot, working hard, doing the best one can within the confines of an often difficult reality (for example, 3:13, 5:12, 5:18–20). Such messages, which are compatible with the collection of sayings in the book of Proverbs, are conveyed not only by proverbial sayings in Qohelet but also by an insistence on God's power and the implicit need, as a modern evangelical might say, to put oneself in the hands of the Lord (3:14). Another thread in Qohelet appears to declare life incomprehensibly absurd, decidedly unfair (for example, 1:1–11, 2:17, 2:26, 3:19, 4:7, 4:16, etc.). The choice seems to lie between either being consumed by bitterness and depression or eating, drinking, and being merry while one can.

One might approach the book as a philosophically radical work that has been framed and softened theologically by a pious redactor who has the last word at 12:13–14. Despite the efforts of this redactor, the work is dominated by a kind of ancient existentialism, captured by the recurring and difficult-to-translate phrase "all is vanity" (or "emptiness" or "vapor" or "futility" or "absurdity").[1] Conventional wisdom of the kind offered without irony or sarcasm in Proverbs thus appears to be quoted in order to be rejected as untrue or condemned as unfair.[2] Alternatively, one might regard Qohelet as philosophically more mainstream, at least from an ancient Israelite perspective: it acknowledges the challenges of human life on earth but insists on the relevance of the powerful deity who understands how it all makes sense, even if this knowledge is hidden from mere mortals.

Michael V. Fox's approach to Qohelet contributes to this second view of the book's overall message. Fox sees a kind of wholeness in the very contradictions in worldview that characterize the work. He writes, "As I see it, Qohelet's contradictions state problems rather than resolving them, and the interpreter likewise must leave many of the observations in tension." God remains God despite "the uneasy tensions . . . characterizing Qohelet's attitudes and world view." The author himself is neither "consistently pious or consistently skeptical and pessimistic."[3] C.-L. Seow points to a number of specific contradictions in the work concerning attitudes to wisdom, to pleasure, to life, and to the degree of divine involvement in human affairs.[4] He suggests the possible work of an editor in 12:13b–14, but agrees that the book exudes consistency of perspective despite the purposeful contradictions.[5]

Like Qohelet, the book of Job confronts the reader with incongruity and ambiguity. Carole Fontaine has pointed to some of the incongruities in Job, for example, the unexpected portrayal of Yahweh as involved in a "wager" and the fact that God's "answer to Job seems to be so little to the point." She finds the behavior of Job and his supposed comforters to be "puzzling."[6] Other tensions emerge in the style, content, and structure of the work. David Penchansky explores varieties of dissonance in Job, concentrating on the complicated nature of the frame narrative and its internal tensions, tensions between that frame and the "center," and the result of this juxtaposition of parts.[7]

The framing story, with its simplicity, its traditional-style repetitive language and content, its trickster troublemaker (a member of the divine council), its good hero (a favorite of the deity), and its plot of loss and restoration, seems ill-suited to the complex, poetically baroque dialogue rooted in traditional forms of lament and lawsuit. The speeches of Elihu seem to reprise what has already been said. Are they essentially a summary, do they provide emphasis for certain key messages, or do they provide nuance for what precedes them in the work? Are the speeches from the whirlwind, with their strong component of mantic wisdom, in tension with the work as a whole or integral to it? As in the case of Qohelet, one might well question whether Job works as a whole, thematically and literarily. Do the seams of originally separate layers and contributions shine through with such force that one is struck by the composite nature of the work? Scholars have taken various positions about these matters of continuity and discontinuity, but a consensus has emerged that the book as it stands works as an integrated whole.[8]

On Conventional Wisdom in Qohelet and Job

Following upon the close contextual reading of the proverb concerning sour grapes, I am interested in exploring what the authors of Job and Qohelet suggest about the nature of conventional wisdom in regard to the ways of the world, the individual's fate in life, responsibility for that fate, and questions of fairness. How do these authors approach what they perceive to be conventional wisdom and how, in the process, do they reveal a personalized and privatized religion? The components of this conventional wisdom in Qohelet emerge as the author first describes how one might think the world works or want the world to work, and then rejects the validity of this view or explains how wrong the notion is. Alternatively, he mentions conventional wisdom in a framework that rejects it as an inaccurate picture of the realities experienced by people.

Thus conventional wisdom holds that work is worth the effort, that it provides gain (Ecclesiastes 3:13, 5:12). So states, for example, Proverbs 6:6–11. The reality, however, is otherwise (Ecclesiastes 1:3, 3:9, 2:21, 6:7). Another component of the conventional view is that one can be wise and act according to the tenets of wisdom and that wisdom will benefit the practitioner (Ecclesiastes 1:16–17, 2:14, 7:19, 9:16, 10:12). So says Wisdom, personified in Proverbs 1–8, and yet in Qohelet "this is a chasing after wind" (Ecclesiastes

1:17, 6:9, 7:23, 9:16). Similarly, a conventional view would suggest that enjoyment and pleasure are to be savored in life, but this notion too is vanity (Ecclesiastes 2:1). Wealth should provide security, but wealth can disappear in an instant because of economic twists and turns over which one has no control (Ecclesiastes 5:13–17). Finally, and most closely related to questions explored in chapter one, the just should be blessed and thrive (Ecclesiastes 3:16–17), but in fact bad things happen to good people, evildoers appear to prosper, and the same death awaits all (Ecclesiastes 8:14, 9:1–2). These concerns, of course, are at the heart of Job, the quintessential tale about the suffering of the just, a debate about theodicy.

In contrast to Qohelet, the book of Job places aspects of the conventional wisdom in the mouths of different characters.[9] As Edward L. Greenstein has noted, Job and his friends seem to accept a "principle of just retribution."[10] Job seems to believe that it is possible for a human being to be blameless, that he is an example of one such decent person (Job 9:20–24, 27:5–6, 31:1–40, although see the equivocation at 19:4), and that his suffering is unfair. He thus accepts the blessings and curses theology (Job 24:18–20, 27:13–23), but does not understand why the curse should be upon his head, especially given that so many obvious evildoers seem to thrive (21:7–18). Indeed, in line with the observations of the author of Qohelet, Job notes that the good sometimes die suddenly while "the earth is given into the hands of the wicked" (9:23–24). Job mentions the view, reflected in the traditional saying about the sour grapes and children's teeth, that the curse of the parents is saved for their children (21:19), but finds that assertion, even if true, not a satisfying way to explain the conventional view of the consequences of good and evil. The evildoer is gone, and what does he know or care about those descended from him (21:21)?

Job's "friends" point to aspects of conventional wisdom concerning the causes of suffering and the role of individual sin in death. They insist that no one who is innocent perishes (Eliphaz, in 4:7–16) or is rejected (Bildad, 8:20), that God is always just (Eliphaz, 4:17; Bildad, 8:3), and that all human beings commit some degree of sin, which perhaps explains why we all suffer the ultimate judgment and eventually die (Eliphaz, 4:17, 15:14–16). Suffering is good discipline (Eliphaz, 5:17), and if God reproves a person, he also redeems him (Eliphaz, 5:19–20). They suggest that if you are an innocent sufferer and seek him, you will be restored (Bildad, 8:5–7), and that only God knows the truth about a man's sin (Zophar, 11:4–6). Repentance is possible, and with it restoration (Zophar,

11:13–19); and evildoers are ultimately doomed (Zophar, 11:20). In short, if your suffering is unabated, you somehow deserve it (Eliphaz, 15:20–35, 22:1–11; Bildad, 18:5–21; Zophar, 20:12–29). Elihu's speech reviews these assumptions: God is utterly in charge, so one must not doubt him or argue with him (33:12–14, 34:13); the wicked will be punished, as is fair (36:6); the "impious" or "haughty of heart" die young (36:13–14); and suffering has a disciplining and saving function (36:15). What social and historical contexts might frame the grappling with, challenge to, and defense of conventional wisdom about good and evil, reward and punishment, as expressed in Qohelet and Job?

Chronology

A range of dates has been offered by contemporary scholars for Qohelet: the Persian period from the second half of the fifth century to the first half of the fourth century BCE;[11] the Hellenistic period from the fourth to the third centuries BCE;[12] and somewhat later in that period, to around the mid-third century.[13] Arguments for dating are based on linguistic and thematic criteria, orientations to life expressed in the work. Seow suggests, for example, that indications in language tally with an implied socioeconomic world of boom and bust that point to the Persian period.[14] Others are not convinced by Seow's reliance on the absence of Greek loan words to suggest an earlier period, and instead emphasize the author's possible affinities with or awareness of Greek philosophical orientations.[15] For our purposes, a date from the fifth to the third century places Qohelet in the late-biblical period in which communities find themselves in a colonialist setting, one in which First Temple–period institutions are gone or altered, a time of uncertainty and transition when, I would argue, authors express concerns with self and provide us access to their versions of personal religion.

Job has also been variously dated, although a consensus of scholars dates the final composition to earlier or later in the period following the Babylonian conquest. John Gray sees the work as "substantially composed between 450 and 350 BCE."[16] Robert Gordis places the work early in the Second Temple period.[17] Marvin Pope, whose excellent overview of features of Job suggests links in worldview and form with an array of ancient Near Eastern works, leaves the date "an open question," but suggests that the dialogue was composed in the seventh century BCE.[18] Avi Hurwitz, who bases his study on comparative linguistic criteria, has convinced a consensus of scholars that the narrative that frames the dialogue is a composition of the sixth century BCE.[19] As in the case of Qohelet, the problems posed by the work as a whole and its overall orientation suggest a context in the late-biblical period and themes central to our study of personal religion. Gordis, for example, emphasizes the interest in the individual, which, in his view, "becomes paramount in religious thought" during this period.[20] While noting that writers of the ancient world had long taken account of what Geertz calls the gap between the way things are and the way they ought to be, given our conceptions of right and wrong, Gray suggests that "the collapse of the state and the social order" in the wake of the Babylonian conquest profoundly affects perceptions of the "traditional ethic with its balance in favor of the principle of reward and retribution with God's order." Indeed, in his view, this ethic "could no longer be maintained on traditional evidence."[21] I agree with the observations by Gordis and Gray, and turn next to views of death, a most personal and central human concern with which all religious orientations must deal.

Death as Personal

Death is always personal, involving fears for one's own life and the loss of dear ones. The authors of Qohelet and Job compose their works at a critical time in Jewish thought—before the full flowering of belief in resurrection, but at a time when the older, conventional answers about why we die and how we cope with death seem particularly unsatisfying. Qohelet and Job both ask profound questions concerning death and fairness as they relate to individuals. Both works provide a window on what many in late-biblical times would like to believe is true, thereby revealing important aspects of shared and assumed worldviews—conventional views that the authors of Job and Qohelet reject.

Qohelet and Job both point explicitly or implicitly to the ways in which people try to make sense of death. As in prophetic responses to the saying about sour grapes, the authors of Qohelet and Job raise questions about the fate of the good versus the fate of the evil, implying that some (including Jeremiah, Ezekiel, and the voices behind passages such as Exodus 20:5–6 and Deuteronomy 27:15–26) would like to believe that fairness operates in regard to one's fate. Job and Qohelet are dominated by the notion that death is final and eternal, and most interesting for our purposes, they explore suffering in relation to actions of individuals and what they experience rather than having to do with the tone and tenor of societies and communal well-being.[22]

Thus, the author of Qohelet opines that the wicked sometimes prolong their lives and the righteous perish (7:15). The wise die, as do fools (2:16). He thus allows that there are wicked and righteous, wise and foolish, but the same fate, death, comes to all (9:2):

> to the righteous and to the evil,
> to the good and to the clean and to the unclean,
> to the one who offers sacrifice, and to the one who does not offer sacrifice,
> as for the good so for the sinner,
> one who swears an oath is the same as one who fears an oath . . .
> one fate is for all.
> *Ecclesiastes 9:2–3*

Voicing a protest, the author describes this situation as "an evil in all that happens under the sun." As noted above, his attitude to this reality can be variously interpreted and admits of tension and contradiction in light of the work as a whole (see, for example, 7:17–18). Nevertheless, however one approaches such tensions—the views of different writers or one author's acceptance of and effort to point to the contradictions ever present in human experience—Qohelet preserves both the typical messages and expectations of certain threads in conventional wisdom, for example, the good should prosper and the evil fail, and a critique of such wisdom. And whereas passages such as Deuteronomy 27–28 and Ezekiel 18 veer back and forth between describing the actions of individuals and those of communities, and the outcomes faced by one or all, Qohelet focuses solely on individuals, their actions, their fate, their inevitable death. Going beyond questions of a nation's fate or the fate of a particular community, the author focuses on the human condition, what each person faces in life. As part of that focus on humanity, Qohelet deals with the distinction between animals and humans, suggesting that some believe animals and human beings experience death differently, that human beings go to a better or other place when they die.

Ecclesiastes 3:19–21 explores an essential question about human identity relevant to the life cycle of every person. On the one hand, it is clear that people are mortal, in contrast to the divinity and his heavenly cohort. As the later rabbinic tradition notes, we are unlike the heavenly beings in our mortality and like the beasts of the earth in that we die (for example, Genesis Rabbah 8:11). Of course, the Rabbis believe that the righteous will live again in the world to come, but the author of Qohelet has no such hope. Whereas Psalm 49:13–15, another example of late-biblical thought, might be read to suggest that the "soul" of some people is somehow "redeemed from the hand of Sheol," the underworld where the dead are consigned, Ecclesiastes 3:19–21 insists that our fate in regard to death is like that of the animals.[23] We all die. We all become dust and go to the same place in the end. Ecclesiastes 3:19 seems to suggest, however, that some believe that the human "spirit" ascends after death, whereas the animal "spirit" descends, but Qohelet does not buy it. There is no consciousness after death, there is nothing:

> For the living know they will die,
> but the dead know nothing.
> No more is their reward,
> for forgotten is the memory of them.
> Even their love, their hate, their passion—
> already lost.
> They have no portion any longer, eternally,
> in anything that is done under the sun.
> *Ecclesiastes 9:5–6*

The passages from Psalm 49 and Ecclesiastes 3 raise interpretative difficulties. Is the psalmist being metaphoric, as in so many laments in which the sufferer is loosed from the cords of death at the end and rescued by God? What do terms for "wind"/"spirit" and "soul"/"life force" connote conceptually in each passage? The least we can say is that the author of Ecclesiastes 3:19–21 is grappling with complex questions about the nature of being a human, questions that rise in bold relief as each of us faces the prospect of death. These are questions of personal religion relating to the very nature of personhood. The author concludes that each of us has is a limited life span of unpredictable length. Whether animal or human, foolish or wise, righteous or wicked, we all die and there is no promised endtime in which we return, a time when matters of fairness can be sorted out and judged. For the author of Qohelet, this is just the way life is. Life is not fair. Geertz might say that the author, like people who quote the proverb about sour grapes, is responding to the challenge of comprehending our condition, to the way in which "chaos threatens at the limits of our analytical capacity."[24] The author does not, however, presume to solve the moral dilemma posed by the fact that we all share the same fate at the end. He does not deal with the threat of chaos at the limits of "moral insight."[25] Job, by contrast, blames God for the unfairness he observes and experiences, accusing the deity of breaking a deal that promises blessings for righteousness and suffering for wickedness; see, for example, Job 12:6, 21:7–13. Death itself figures in his challenge to the deity, a challenge to conventional wisdom.

Like Qohelet, Job emphasizes that death is eternal. Those who descend into Sheol do not return (Job 7:7–10, 10:21, 16:22). He writes, "For the tree has hope." If it is cut down, it can be transformed or renewed. The author describes the way it can put forth new branches from the seemingly dead stump. The mere scent of water can cause it to sprout (14:7–9), "but a human being lies down in death and does not rise up / until the heavens are no more / they will not awake / they will not be roused from their sleep" (Job 14:12). He can imagine a situation in which death is not eternal, stating that if renewed life could follow a period of being dead, he "would wait all the days of his service" until his "transformation" would come (14:14), but, alas, this is only an imagining for Job. Like the author of Qohelet, the author of Job points out, moreover, that the good and the wicked come to the same end (21:23–26). Death, eternal and unremitting, is the fate of all. For Job, however, this bitter truth is an example of what Geertz would describe as the threat of chaos at the limits of our moral insight. Job refuses to accept the unfairness of this reality, and his protest takes the form of direct argumentation with the deity and with those who insist upon God's justice despite the seeming unfairness of Job's suffering and that of other decent human beings. Both authors employ first-person speech to claim and present their points of view in an intensely personal and self-referential way.

First Person and Self

Several recent studies have focused on the use and significance of first-person speech in Qohelet. Drawing a distinction between his work and that of previous studies, Kyle R. Greenwood does not treat the use of person as a possible indicator of layers of authorship and redaction history, but explores the use of person in Qohelet as a matter of voice.[26] The first-person voice, "taking on the persona of Solomon," expresses the attitude of "the skeptic, whose views will ultimately be defeated by" the voice in the third person, that of the "Preacher."[27] For Greenwood, voice and shifts in voice are essential to the dialectical and narrative structure of the work as a whole.[28]

The interests of Eric S. Christianson are closer to this study's focus on self-representation and representations of self. Christianson emphasizes the use of the pronoun *ănî*, "I," in Qohelet: "The cumulative effect of the sheer abundance of first-person reference, especially in chs. 1–2 is visually remarkable. The explicit self-referential quality of Qoheleth's language is visually depicted in a series of suffixed *yod*s which for its density is unprecedented in the Hebrew Bible."[29] In his view, the use of the first person serves "to intensify the presence and significance of Qoheleth's experience."[30]

Christianson writes that this interest in "I" in Qohelet suggests "a literary strategy that . . . does raise questions about the self as subject."[31] He points to the difficulties of identifying or defining a self in literary contexts, a particular challenge when dealing with the purposeful anonymity and formulaic quality of traditional literatures, as discussed in the introduction.[32] Christianson also explores the range of relevant meanings conveyed by key terms such as *lēb* (literally, "heart," but meaning "mind" also), *nepeš* (a term applied variously to the soul or life force or personhood), and *rûaḥ* ("wind" or "spirit"). The many passages that employ first-person speech in Qohelet might be explored from three directions: evidence of self-reflection, the mention of accomplishments that evoke autobiography, and a more general assertion of the self conveyed.

As Christianson notes, the reference to the heart can relate in Qohelet to "searching and/or testing," to "reasoning" or "inner dialogue," to a range of emotions, or to knowledge.[33] What interests me are references to "my heart" that connote self-searching, self-reflection, talking to oneself, and gaining self-knowledge, for example, 1:16, literally, "I spoke did I with my heart." This self-consultation overlaps with the speaker's admissions about his attempts at self-reinforcement as he thinks of his accomplishments: his knowledge surpasses that of others, and his experience (literally, "his heart's seeing") has given him much wisdom and knowledge. He concludes, of course, that all this is but a chasing after wind (1:17). The realization is a climax to deep and critical self-evaluation.

Similarly, at 2:1 the author tries to convince himself that he can achieve a path to happiness, saying, "I said did I with my heart, 'Come now, I will test myself by joy, and [say] look at the good!'" The author's self-dialogue appears in various contexts, and is followed by different conclusions and realizations, many of which point to the speaker's dissatisfaction with or surprise at the end of his conversation with himself (see, for example, 2:15, 3:17, 3:18). Other phrases employing "the heart" suggest searching within oneself for a proper course of action, an act of self-consultation (2:3), or taking something to heart (9:1). Psychoanalytical dimensions, questions of mood and emotion, the desire for enlightenment, and the search for self-realization inform these passages in which the speaker employs "my heart." In a similar vein, some passages that do not employ "my heart" use a verb in the first person to invoke an act of self-refection: "I knew/perceived" (2:14) and "I considered" (literally, "turned to look," perhaps turning something over in one's mind [2:11, 2:12]).

As in Qohelet, the use of first-person speech dominates the book of Job. Job himself, his "friends," and the deity all self-refer via the first person as actors in a series of monologues and dialogues. In this respect, Job's speeches share much formally with the lament discussed in the next chapter.

Job refers to "the day I was born" (3:3) and asks, "Why did I not die from birth?" (literally, "from the womb" [3:11]). He declares, "I loathe my life" (10:1), "my eye has seen" (13:1), and alludes to "my request" (6:8). He pictures himself before God: "I would" (23:3–5). God says, "Look at Behemoth that I made" (40:15). Eliphaz, the most self-referential of the friends, says, "But I myself would" (5:8) and "I have seen fools" (5:3) and "I will show you" (15:17). Zophar declares, "The discipline of my ignominy I hear" (20:3). The use of first-person speech in Job does not reveal changing self-realization, an evolution of ideas, or implicit self-criticism concerning previously accepted personal views, as in the case of Qohelet. All the characters in Job are self-referential, self-absorbed, and self-justifying, almost narcissistically. They focus on their rights (in Job's case) or their knowledge (in the case of the "comforters") or their power (in the case of God).

Eliphaz, moreover, describes a personal, experiential event, a visionary episode in which he viscerally felt a spiritual force:

> To me a word was brought in stealth
> and my ear received an inkling from it.
> In disquieting thoughts from visions of the night
> when the god-sent deep sleep falls upon humans
> dread summoned me and trembling.
> It filled my bones with dread.
> A spirit swept by my face
> and the hair of my flesh bristled.
> Something stood but I could not recognize its appearance.
> A form was in front of my eyes.
> There was silence, and I heard a voice.
> *Job 4:12–16*

First-person speech and finely wrought description draws the reader into the embodied experience of the speaker. We are made to empathize with his vision report as our own hair bristles at his words. Indeed, attention to the body is one of the major features of Job that marks the work as an exemplar of personal religion.

Three terms that are important in Qohelet, especially when employed in Job with the first-person possessive pronoun, deeply convey an introspective, emotional dimension and qualities of personal religion: *lĕbābî* ("my heart, mind"); *napšî* ("my soul, being, life"); *rûḥî* ("my spirit"). In Job 17:11, the protagonist says, "My days have passed by / my plans have been torn apart / the possessions [or desires] of my innermost heart." The language used is unusual (for example, the way in which the word that usually connotes "wicked designs" simply seems to mean "plans"; also, the odd term for "desires"), as indeed it is throughout Job, underlining a unique voice. The tricolon suggests self-review, interiority, intense self-reflection. The language in 27:6 also focuses on the inner self: "To my righteousness I will keep hold / and I will not let go / my inner heart does not reproach me for my life" (literally, "my days"). "Heart" here might be translated as "conscience."

Self-contemplation is also conveyed by the phrase "my *nepeš*," which I would translate as "myself" or "my self": I do not know myself (9:21); I feel loathing for myself (literally, "My *nepeš* feels loathing for my life" [10:1]); I made myself bitter (27:2). The phrase "my spirit" conveys a similar self-reference and a concern with one's inner being, as in the poisoning of 6:4,[34] the distress of 7:11, and the ruining or breaking of 17:1.

Job also reflects, in Martin Buber's terms, the relationship between "I and thou" as it relates to God but also to his friends. Dialogue is the dominant form of the work, and an interaction between "I" and "you" structures the central portion of the work as Job makes his case and the human speakers respond. Job's comments directed at the deity (as "you") and the deity's eventual first-person response to Job (as "you") provide some of the most powerful interactions of the work, which is, after all, a narrative in which the protagonist, Job, reveals his innermost thoughts in the first-person voice while responding or reacting to a series of antagonists, the most powerful of whom is the deity, who speaks climactically near the end of the work.

Job addresses the deity directly, saying, "If I sin what do I do to you, watcher of mankind?" (7:20–21). The bitterness and emotional dimension of Job's speech is in part shaped by the insistent references to "I" and "you." An interpersonal relationship is at stake between the human and the deity, underscoring qualities of personal religion. Chapter 10 offers particularly good examples of Job's approach to God in real time and in his imagination. He says, "I will say to God, do not condemn me as wicked" (10:2). Saying, "Your hands shaped me and made me" (10:8), Job describes the intimacy of the relationship going back to Job's very creation. Notice the wordplay between the word for "shape" and the root meaning "pain" ('ṣb). Similarly, bemoaning his fate, Job asks God, "Why from the womb did you bring me forth?" (10:18). After many more comments and questions posed to God, the deity finally answers: "Can you draw out Leviathan with a fish-hook? And with a cord can you press down its tongue?" (40:25 in the Hebrew text; 41:1 in English). The series of questions that follow are clearly meant to put Job in his place, but the deity does so by addressing the hero in the second person. The list of questions, which emphasizes the deity's great accomplishments, is thus another aspect of the personalization of each speaker as a character who self-refers.

Conveying Personal Accomplishments: Qohelet and Job

A number of first-person comments early in Qohelet point to the author's accomplishments, his awareness of what he has done and observed in life, what he as an individual has learned. As Christianson notes, Qohelet's work has an autobiographical dimension.[35] The book is punctuated by narrative interludes; the speaker is endowed with personality as he speaks about himself in the first person.

The introductory verse at Ecclesiastes 1:12, leading to the sort of first-person reflections discussed above, projects an autobiographical orientation. Again, 'ănî is employed by the speaker, who names himself Qohelet and tells us that he was king over Israel in Jerusalem. Assuming the identity of a royal figure responsible for a literary work presented as part of the preserved tradition is not unique to Qohelet, as we know from the opening attribution of the book of Proverbs to Solomon or the attribution of particular psalms to David. Here, however, information about his supposed royal identity is offered by the fictional author himself, a part of his self-story. Material in Ecclesiastes 2:4–10 provides another important autobiographical component, a list of his activities and accomplishments.

In the first person, the author declares that he built houses and planted vineyards (2:4), that he made "for himself" gardens and parks and planted in them all sorts of fruit-bearing trees (2:5). He mentions the irrigation system he constructed (2:6) and the male and female slaves he acquired (2:7), his many possessions in animal wealth, gold, and silver (2:7–8). He had male and female singers and access to all sorts of pleasure.

The author thus paints an archetypal picture of the successful potentate who sits on top of the material world, a master of all he surveys, the possessor of a hefty and seemingly admirable résumé. And yet, as he tells us, he comes to realize that all his wealth, power, and pleasure are somehow meaningless (2:11). In fact, the author's self-representation partakes of a recurring pattern in the life stories of a host of heroes. The hero is apparently successful or content in his wealth and environment and then comes to realize that he has been deluded, that all ends in death, or that his material well-being was a mere illusion. This pattern applies to the Mesopotamian Gilgamesh, to Shakyamuni Buddha, and to a host of early Christian heroes such as "the man of God."[36] Qohelet's particular version of this pattern of realization is, however, presented as autobiography. The author comments upon his own experience, reflects upon the significance of what he has done. This work, however fictionalized the character who speaks about his life, offers a personalized framing of a conventional set of themes about material experience and accomplishment and thus provides an excellent example of the ways in which late-biblical writers express interest in the individual, albeit within the contours of a traditional narrative pattern.

Job's self-proclaimed accomplishment is righteousness, his doing of good deeds and his avoidance of the bad. Two speeches by Job, in particular, point to this matter of self-image: Job 29, in which the protagonist describes how he used to experience life, and chapter 31, in which Job details what he has never done, the varieties of evil in which he as a good person has never been involved. Both passages reveal Job's sense of who he is or was as a person and how he considers righteousness to be his greatest accomplishment, the quality that characterizes him as an individual, a source of pride and positive identity.

The list of accomplishments in chapter 29 includes having the deity's friendship (29:4–6); having the respect of other people, old and young, princely and noble (29:7–11), the poor and the widowed, because of his righteous deeds (29:13–17). Like Qohelet, Job describes himself as being on top of the world, living like a chief, dwelling like a king.

Job 31 lists all the bad activities he has avoided: falsehood (31:5), adultery (31:9–12), indifference to others' rights or suffering (31:13–23, 32), smugness about his wealth and status (31:24–25), foreign worship (31:26–28), joy at enemies' downfall (31:29–30), misuse of land and tenant farmers (31:38–40).

It turns out, of course, that Job's self-satisfaction is short-lived. Convictions concerning rewards for his righteousness and assumptions about a happy stability rooted in his own accomplishments are misguided and delusive, as were Qohelet's views of his material success. Success, material and social, is perceived as being rooted in the activities of the individual, his accomplishments, his righteousness, and his relationship with others, including the deity.

Ecclesiastes 12: Reflection on the End

Most interesting in this concern with the individual is the reflection on the end-time in Ecclesiastes 12, a passage that returns to that most personal of human experiences, death. C.-L. Seow notes that the language in Ecclesiastes 12:2 "sounds ominously eschatological": "Apparently the author has reused an old poem about the travails of old age and infused it with eschatological allusions. He depicts a scene of an end-time . . . It is humanity that is going to the grave (12:5b). It becomes clear, then, that it is not merely the end of the human life span of which the author speaks, but the end of human life in general. The text is not about the demise of an individual, but about the end of humanity."[37] I would suggest, to the contrary, that eschatological imagery and language has been taken from a more typical apocalyptic framework and applied to the individual's inevitable demise. The engagement with one's own end-time relates to material religion—the material of the body subject to death and decomposition.

> [1] And be mindful of your "well"/creator
> in the days of your youth
> before come the days of calamity
> and approach do years concerning which you will say,
> "There is no pleasure in them for me."
> [2] Before the sun becomes dark
> and the light and the moon and the stars,
> and return do the clouds after the rain.
> [3] On the day in which the guards of the house tremble
> and bent down are the mighty men,
> and ceased have the "grinders" because they are few,
> and grow dark do those who look through the windows.
> [4] And closed are doors in the market
> in the lowering of the sound of the one who grinds,
> and one arises to the sound of the bird

and bowed down are all the daughters of song.
⁵ Even from high up they are frightened
and terrors are on the way,
and distained is the watchful one.
And bear a heavy load does the grasshopper,
and frustrated is the caperberry.
For go does the human to his eternal home,
and process in the market do the mourners.
⁶ Before the silver cord is stretched,
and crushed is the golden bowl,
and broken is the jar in the spring,
and the wheel is crushed against the well.
⁷ And return will the dust upon the earth,
and the spirit will return to God who gave it.
Ecclesiastes 12:1–7

A first challenge is the translation of *bwr'yk,* which, as vocalized in the Masoretic Text (MT), means "creator." The author seems to ask each member of his audience to remember his maker while he is in youthful vigor. One might well ask why not remember the deity late in life? Some would emend the MT to read "your cistern," which could be translated as "spring," "well," or "grave" (in the sense of burial pit). Pointing to the burial-related possibility, Thomas Krüger suggests that the heard message is dual—take cognizance of your vulnerabilities and realize that a feature of your creation is the return to dust at the end of life.[38] The notion of a dually heard message is appealing, but I would suggest the second meaning is not "your grave" but "your well"—with sexual nuances, as in Proverbs 5:15. The wisdom offered in Proverbs 5 is to stay away from strange or foreign women and to "drink water from your own well, flowing water from your own font." Given that the final line of verse 1 refers to the loss of pleasure (in the sense of desire) and that the term for young man in 12:1b is associated with vigorous manly youth, the author is here telling the young male to pay attention while he can enjoy life, to fully appreciate the womanly "well" that allows for amorous pleasure. The interest in sexuality and fertility is evoked later in the speech as well.

Ecclesiastes 12:2 fully embraces apocalyptic imagery in which the natural world is turned upside down: the sun becomes dark, as do the other luminaries created by God to light the day and night. After the rain, the sun does not come out; instead, clouds return to create more stormy weather.

Similar imagery of darkening that appears to reverse the characteristics of the cosmos established in Genesis 1 is found, for example, in Isaiah 13:9–10, Ezekiel 32:7–8, and Joel 2:10. As Michael Fox notes, for the author of Qohelet, these eschatological nuances do not "depict the disaster to a nation or the world at large," as is the case for Jeremiah or Joel; rather, "for Qohelet they represent the demise of the individual . . . All values are solitary, measured by benefit or harm to the individual."[39]

Images of an upside-down world, applied to the inevitable life history of the mortal, continue in subsequent verses: guards, instead of being bulwarks and protectors, tremble with fear; mighty men or warriors are bent over (12:3a, b). The last two lines of 12:3 again invoke sexuality. The term "grind" is synonymous with sexual activity in several biblical passages, as noted by the Rabbis. In Job 31:10, the beleaguered hero states that if he has committed adultery, then he should suffer just deserts and his "wife should grind for another / and upon her may others kneel." Kneeling is the position of the lover, grinding the action in which the couple is engaged. Similarly, Deutero-Isaiah's visceral condemnation of a fallen Babylon, who is pictured as a wayward woman, powerfully presents the metaphor that equates grinding millstones with sex.

> Take millstones and grind flour,
> remove your veil,
> strip off [your] skirt,
> reveal the thigh,
> pass through rivers.
> Your nakedness will be revealed.
> Also will your shame be seen.
> *Isaiah 47:2*

The line in Ecclesiastes 12:3c that alludes to "grinders" is paralleled by imagery evocative of a kind of ancient red-light district.

In ancient Near Eastern literary tradition, those pictured gazing from windows are archetypally female figures.[40] Susan Ackerman has shown that the pose in the window often connotes an aristocratic woman. We might think of the Sisera's mother, gazing out the latticework window while awaiting her general son's return (Judges 5:28). In Ecclesiastes 12, the grinders and the gazing women are not aristocrats, but sex workers. Juxtaposed with the loaded language of grinding, these women are said to grow dark in an eerie fade-out. There is no sex to be had.

Images of desolation and alienation continue in 12:4. Commercial activity (perhaps including the purchase of pleasures of the flesh) has been suspended, since the doors to the open market have been closed. Pointing to parallels such as Deuteronomy 3:5, Joshua 6:26, 1 Samuel 23:7, Isaiah 45:1, Jeremiah 49:31, and Sirach 49:13, Seow notes that what are imagined are "the double-doors in the street bazaar," possibly city gates.[41] We recall that Rahab the harlot is said to live in the city-gate district in Joshua 2. The lowering of the sound of the grinder may, in fact, be a double entendre referring both to the preparation of grain and to sexual activity.

Relevant is Jeremiah 25:10, in which the doom and devastation predicted by the prophet are captured in the banishing of particular sounds and sights: the sound of mirth and the sound of joy, the sound (or voice) of the bridegroom and the sound of the bride, the sound of the millstones, and the light of the lamp. It may be that the last two images are meant to invoke the domestic realm of comfort that follows the wedding, with its food preparation and light. The millstone is, after all, used to grind grain, as the Israelites do in preparing manna for food at Numbers 11:8. In Jeremiah 25, however, as in Ecclesiastes 12:4b, the mention of the sound made by millstones may well partake of a double entendre involving food preparation and sexual activity, in this case, the lovemaking of the newlyweds.

The sound of the bird has been variously understood, translated, and emended, but I agree with Seow's suggestions about the association between the shrieking sound of the bird and death in ancient Near Eastern and international folklore. Noting that the term *ṣippôr* "may refer to birds of prey (Ezek 39:4)," he suggests that the cry of the bird in Ecclesiastes 12 refers either to "birds hooting ominously" or to "birds making a commotion when they sense death."[42] One thinks of the opening of Alfred Hitchcock's film *The Birds* for a modern invocation of this motif. The daughters of song are perhaps to be associated with women's mourning practices (see Amos 8:3).[43]

Another set of reversals appears in Ecclesiastes 12:5–6 concerning the expected workings of the world—indeed, concerning the very laws of nature. Such reversals, often associated with eschatological texts, here apply to the individual's life pattern. As Fox writes of the author, "He audaciously invokes images of general disaster to symbolize every death; more precisely—the death of you."[44] Thus, instead of being safe from the lookout position of a high place, people are filled with fear. Here I am reading not with the MT tradition, which vocalizes the root *r'h* (translating "they see"), but with other manuscript traditions that read the root *yr'* (translating "they fear").

Scholars often translate 12:5c as referring to the blossoming of the almond tree, the *šāqēd*.[45] It is not clear, however, in what way this fecund image, at home in the normal workings of nature, suits the context of reversals and chaos. The root *šqd*, when employed as a verb, also means "to watch," as in Jeremiah's wordplay in the symbolic vision at Jeremiah 1:11–12, in which an almond rod (*maqqēl šāqēd*) seen in the vision is interpreted to mean that the deity is "watching over" (*šōqēd*) his word to fulfill it. The verb is found in a number of late-biblical texts, including Jeremiah, Job, and Proverbs, in which the watcher is the vigilant or wakeful one, a term sometimes used in parallel with *šmr* (Psalm 127:1), in the sense of keeping guard. The verb, often translated as "to blossom," as if it were from *nṣṣ*, might be rooted in *n'ṣ*, "to spurn" or "to show contempt," in the *hophal*, which we are translating as "is distained." Thus, the person who should be respected for his watchfulness is regarded as contemptible. This image seems to be compatible with those of trembling guards and bent mighty men (12:3). The end-time is one of reversals. The next two lines of 12:5 point to reversals in nature. To understand the reference to the grasshopper's load, we need to look to ancient Mediterranean folk-wisdom traditions contrasting laziness and ambition, the sluggard and the hard worker.

Proverbs 6:6–11 is a praise song for the ant! The lazybones is told to go to the ant and observe its ways, how it gathers food in summer to prepare for the winter. The social and cooperative characteristics of this insect creature is noted, how it sets to its task without chief or officer or ruler. While the fable of the grasshopper and the ant is not found in Hebrew Scriptures, it is preserved most famously by Aesop (Thompson type 280A); it contrasts the image of the ant, preserved in Proverbs 6:6–8, with that of the fun-loving, lazy grasshopper, which never plans ahead and ends up starving like the lazybones mentioned in Proverbs 6:9–11. Thus, to suggest that the grasshopper bears a heavy burden is again to imagine the opposite of what is expected. His contrary-to-nature hard work is paralleled by the failure of the caperberry, an aphrodisiac. It is frustrated or made ineffectual. Again sexual nuances enter, and nothing operates as expected. Subsequent lines in Ecclesiastes 12 follow suit.

Following the phrase that literally means "until that not," usually understood to mean "before," as in 12:2, comes a series of reversals: the silver cord stretches (literally, "is extended"; see Isaiah 26:15, concerning the extension or enlarging of boundaries), an unlikely event because silver will break rather than elongate. The golden bowl breaks, another unlikely crossing of material expectations. The water jar is broken against the water spring, and the wheel is crushed against the well (taking the verb from *rṣṣ*, "to crush" rather than *rwṣ*, "to run"). We are in a land of opposites where water breaks a jar and the waterwheel is crushed rather than constructively spinning.

And finally, after this surreal imagery there reemerges in overt form the theme of each individual's death, the essence of the human condition foretold in the myth of Eden. Dust returns to the earth, and the life spirit bestowed by God returns to him. Every living human being is a representative of mankind and its earthly environment.

The death of each individual, including the author and every receiver of his writings, is identified with the end of the world; each individual is a microcosm. The Rabbis warn witnesses in capital cases about the need for scrupulous certainty and honesty, lest they cause the death of an innocent person; the witness, who may be complicit in ending a human being's life, is to think of the death of each individual as if it were the death of the whole world (Mishnah Sanhedrin 5:3). In Ecclesiastes 12, the reflection on the death of each person as eschatology joins with other contemplations on the self: the intensive use of first-person forms and verbs connoting self-reflection; the review of the writer's personal accomplishments; and views concerning the inevitability of death as a quintessential form of self-definition. Together, these threads provide insights into the writer's deep and dark personal religion.

Death is ultimately an issue of embodiment. Some, indeed, have suggested that several of the images in Ecclesiastes 12 are metaphors for the physical decline of the body, for example, the grinders are the teeth that no longer work, those who grow dark are the dimming eyes, and so on. In Job, the emphasis on the body is clear, another insistent aspect of the personal and the material as it relates to embodiment.

Body and Person in Job

Job's suffering is distinguished by particularly visceral imagery. His body, again described in the first-person possessive, is seen as flesh, worms, skin, pain. Personal religion thus intertwines with material religion in the very physicality of Job's condition, a situation of suffering that his friends blame upon supposed sin. To Job, however, his body's fate is inexplicable, given what he thinks he knows about the conduct of his life. In Geertz's terms, chaos confronts Job, at the limits of endurance.

Job describes his condition. "My flesh is clothed in worms / my skin coagulates and runs" (7:5). Job 16:7–17 is rich in embodied imagery: being seized or compressed (16:8), being torn (16:9) by an enemy, perhaps the deity himself. Again, language is framed in first-person terms: "*my* skin," "compressed *me*," "he has gnashed against *me* with his teeth" (16:9). God or an unnamed enemy's body, pictured as that of a wild beast, lacerates Job. In verse 10, the enemy, now referred to in the plural, strikes Job's ("my") cheeks, an image common in lament literature.[46] The reference to body parts is especially striking in Job's speeches: "To my skin and my flesh cling my bones" (19:20); "the night bores out my bones from me" (30:17); "my bowels are made to boil" (30:27). Embodiment, seen in the context of a challenge to his physical endurance, is thus integral to Job's perspective on his relationship to the deity; his frustration with a physical suffering that should be the wages of sin, but that is not; and his efforts to chart a personal religious identity that is at the same time somehow compatible with conventional wisdom and consonant with his view of his own righteous comportment.[47]

Job and Qohelet, two complex compositions from the late-biblical period, grapple with questions concerning God's justice, revealing a deep engagement with personal identity. The use of voices in the first person, key terms connoting self-reflection and interiority, the emphasis on individual accomplishments and reassessments of their meaning and ultimate value, reflections on death and disillusionment concerning the assignment of suffering, and the related themes of embodiment and personal, physical materiality point to a rich engagement with self-representation and individual experience. Many of these themes are found as well in a trajectory traced in the following chapter from the incantation to the lament, the confession, and the memoir.

3 From Incantation and Lament to Autobiography

The incantation is a form of verbal folklore, rooted in the desire to control the uncontrollable, to heal, to ease hardship, or to prevent it. Control is achieved by invoking the assistance of divine powers, whether a deity, a deceased holy person, a departed relative, or any intermediary figure believed to have the capacity to channel supernatural power and intervene on the petitioner's behalf to control the future or alter the present. The incantation shares a border with prayer, and in the ancient Near East it exhibits a formal pattern that includes some or all of the following motifs: a description of or allusion to the problem that needs to be addressed; the intervention by the speaker or writer, who requests protection or amelioration from a divine helper or casts a protective spell; the mention of helping agents; and the declaration that relief is at hand or assured. This essential pattern, in fact, characterizes a trajectory of related forms in the Hebrew Bible that point to late-biblical authors' interests in the individual and the creation of self in first-person narration, found in the laments of Lamentations, Psalms, and an array of other biblical works; the so-called confessions of Jeremiah; and the memoir of Nehemiah.[1] In this chapter, we explore examples of the pattern, building a kind of form-critical study that further delves into modes of self-representation in biblical literature of the Neo-Babylonian and Persian periods. We begin with incantations.

Incantations

The incantation is often prepared or performed by an adept who knows how to manipulate its formulaic language and the material upon which it is set down in written form, although, as in other varieties of personal religion, dichotomies between elite and nonelite, both regarding executors of the incantation and those whom they serve, should not be overdrawn.[2] Theodore Lewis has pointed to the wide array of terms employed in the Hebrew Bible to refer to the experts or professionals (often translated, for example, as "enchanter," "sorcerer," "exorcist") and has gathered together a list of the passages where they appear.[3] As a verbal art form, the incantation can be performed orally or written down on a document of skin, metal, wood, or clay. An incantation can be engraved into a wall or inked upon it or upon a piece of pottery. It can be carried on the person or buried in the ground, placed in a home or a burial tomb. It can involve interaction with other material objects and a kind of performance art.

Aramaic incantation bowls, originally buried under houses in the Aramaic-speaking worlds of late antiquity, have been studied by a number of scholars, including James Montgomery, Charles Isbell, Joseph Naveh, and Shaul Shaked.[4] They offer an entryway to the trajectory we trace. While these postbiblical materials are later in date than the works and worlds that are the focus of this book, the literary form of the incantation is an ancient one in the Levant, a point emphasized by some excellent Old Babylonian texts explored below. These nonbiblical examples of incantations, Jewish and non-Jewish, help us outline the essential form of the written material and some basic human, internationally evidenced assumptions about people's interaction with powers that seek to do them harm. These texts implicitly offer reasons for life's challenges and testify to the human need for such explanations.

The problems addressed by the bowls are generally framed rather generically[5] but sometimes seem to suggest specific circumstances: for example, dangers related to fertility and childbirth.[6] The incantations can be prophylactic—an effort to prevent future problems—or a way to deal with a present situation. Throughout, the assumption is that there are devils, demons, and other forces that mean harm to those who dwell in the house where the bowl is buried. The bowl does its preventive or healing work either by trapping the sources of evil or by serving as a kind of beacon of protection and healing that emanate from the words upon it.[7] Bowl 1 in the 1985 collection by Naveh and Shaked, for example, mentions demons, liliths, devils, spells, and other usual suspects (ll. 1–6), but also the pressing down of "his sickness," (l. 11), implying a specific need for cure. The verb "to press down" is common in these texts, suggesting not only the way to deal

with demonic forces but perhaps also the physical position of the bowl, pressed down like a cover (a term also frequently found) in the earth.[8] Such terminology, along with language of divorce, overturning, binding, and the banishing of enemy forces, juxtaposed to language of sealing, saving, and fortifying the person for whom the incantation is prepared, is a means of addressing the problem. The intervention includes the invocation of divine helpers such as Yahweh, angelic beings, and biblical characters, and the quotation of passages from the Hebrew Bible. The bowl mentioned above, in Naveh and Shaked's 1985 study, for example, contains language of sealing, guarding, and expelling but also invokes "your Father who is in heaven . . . who makes peace and wins the suit" (ll. 9–10). The language is juridical, since the incantation successfully pleads the case of one whose home and person are under attack from malevolent forces. The incantation ends with a note of assurance that the person named is guarded (l. 13). The incantation is thus composed of expected, essential motifs: problem (attack by forces, illness); intervention (the charm itself and the invocation of the deity, with juridical nuances); the declaration that help is at hand.

The same pattern provides a frame for a number of the early Mesopotamian incantations collected and translated by Jan Van Dijk, Albrecht Goetze, and Mary I. Hussey.[9] Text 6 seems to allude to problems in the region of the head: "on the skull / from the skull to the forehead, from the forehead to the ear, from the ear to the nostril" (ll. 2–8). The deity Ninkarrak is invoked (l. 9), and the adjuration is that the illness rise from the patient "in the way of locusts" (l. 10–11). Text 7 seems to address a cattle plague (problem); the goddess Ningirim is addressed for relief (intervention); and the speaker vows a gift to the great gods—"I will keep placing sundisks on the garments of the great gods with tender care" (ll. 14–16)—as a means of ensuring or encouraging their positive interest in the speaker's situation.

Laments

In the Hebrew Bible, Lamentations 3, a composition evocative of the biblical book of Job, which is in many ways a long-form lament,[10] provides a good case study for exploring the trajectory from incantation to autobiography. As in the Jewish and Old Babylonian incantations, the composer employs a motif pattern consisting of a complaint or problem, an intervention or request for relief, the mention of helping agents, and the assurance of alleviation. Looking closely at Lamentations 3 while keeping incantations and Job in mind allows us to see the way in which this pattern lends itself to expressions of personal religion in the wake of the Babylonian conquest.

As Lamentations 3 now stands, the portion in verses 40–51 moves the composition in communal directions by using the first-person plural and explicitly mentioning the people's sin, divine anger, and Israel's fate: to be cut off from the deity and scattered as "scrapings and refuse" (3:45) or "that which is scoured away" and "that which is rejected" among the peoples. The enemies are in control, and the speaker describes his grief in this situation of war and defeat. The majority of the chapter, however, is concerned with individual suffering. The lament in a received form that includes verses 40–51 presents this suffering in the context of a sociohistorical setting of war, invasion, and dislocation.

The opening situation requiring intervention, like that of Job, is framed by God's anger and animus. Steeped in personal religion, the speaker states that this anger is directed "especially against me" (3:1–3). The language is embodied, physically and psychoanalytically. Just as in Job, the author's expressed condition involves the wasting away of flesh and skin, the breaking of bones (3:4), being made to sit in dark, grave-like settings like the eternal dead (3:5), being weighed down by chains of bronze (3:7), being torn to pieces (3:11), and the grinding of one's teeth and cowering in ashes (3:16). As in Job and many of the laments in Psalms, others mock his condition and taunt him (3:14). In these biblical forms, evocative of the incantation, the source of trouble is otherworldly—the deity, in this case—but people also participate in his suffering. The speaker's hope rests with the deity, since he requests that the Lord have compassion and cease to reject him (3:31–32). As in the case of Job, the intervention must be made by the source of his problem. Finally comes the assurance of vindication, as in Job and as in the basic incantation: "I called / you heard" (3:55–56); "You have redeemed my life" (3:58). A part of the vindication motif particularly suggestive of the incantation is the speaker's urging the deity to pay back those who mocked him in his trouble, to curse them and make them suffer (3:64–66). Similarly, in Isbell, bowl 2:6, the incantation maker "brings down upon you (the enemies of his client, "the evil haters and the potent adversaries," 2:3) the ban, the prohibition, and the anathema which came down upon Mount Hermon and upon Leviathan the sea-monster and upon Sodom and upon Gomorrah."[11] In the Aramaic example, the curse against enemies is enhanced by reference to iconic saving events by the deity, preserved in the biblical tradition.

The most extensive biblical corpus of literature characterized by the pattern from complaint to intervention and amelioration is found in the Psalms. The so-called personal laments, generally agreed to have been composed in their current form during the period of and following the conquest by Babylonia, offer numerous examples of the motif pattern seen in the incantations and in Lamentations 3 and raise important issues pertaining to the tensions between individual expression and conventionalized speech, and between social contexts and personal expression. Compositions such as Psalms 5, 13, 17, 22, 25, 26, 27, 28, 31, 35, 38, 54, 59, 69, 70, 88, and 109, to which we will make reference, are characterized by traditional, formulaic language and imagery and by recurring themes and messages, all employed within the contours of the pattern of content observed in the incantations and Lamentations 3. As in Qohelet and Job, the use of the first person is marked, as is the language of embodiment; the emotions conveyed are strong, and the sense of pathos is compelling. However formulaic, the psalms give an impression of the voice of an individual who uses conventionalized language and content. The traditional language and content, nevertheless, are also the voice of shared history, community, and communication. The psalms are part of a postbiblical liturgical tradition, but liturgy also has to be considered an original life setting for many of these prayers.[12]

An analysis of two sets of these psalms, Psalms 17, 70, and 31 and Psalms 13, 26, and 54, including references to some of the others listed above, points to variations on the shared pattern of suffering and complaint, intervention, and expression of hope for assurance. Within the theological framework of a particular kind of Yahwism and within a sociohistorical setting in which suffering is understood to have particular causes in past sin, the key motifs may be expanded to include expressions of innocence by the speaker, reference to the special relationship with Israel's deity, insistence upon his power and desire to bring relief to the just, and a vow to repay the deity with sacrifice or praise. The psalms, like Lamentations 3, veer back and forth between addressing individual need and referring to the experience of the community of believers. These psalms underscore the flexibility and adaptability of literary forms and linguistic conventions within traditional cultures. The medium is available, recognizable, and easily reproduced, but it is contoured to fit a particular situation or context, personal, cultural, or literary.

Psalms 17, 31, and 70 begin with a request in the imperative form of the verb for assistance, even before the reader or listener knows what problem needs to be addressed: "listen / pay attention"(17:1), "turn your ear to me / save me quickly" (31:3), "hasten to my assistance" (70:2). The speaker in Psalm 17 pleads innocence, a Job-like righteous figure who insists he does not deserve what is happening to him and who therefore shares the conventional wisdom discussed in relation to the proverbs about sour grapes that wrongdoing brings punishment in the form of personal or national suffering (17:3–5). The psalms then continue with a request to turn back troubles or enemies, thereby specifying somewhat the difficulties faced by the speaker. Enemies seek his very being; the psalmist employs the terminology of *nepeš* that figures prominently in Job, as noted in chapter two (Psalms 70:3, 17:9, 31:10; see also Lamentations 3:58 and Psalms 35:4, 38:13, 54:5). Language is of affliction, *ʿŏnî* (Psalm 31:11, 70:6; Lamentations 3:1, 19; Job 30:16, 27; Psalms 25:18, 88:10). As in Lamentations 3 and Job, visceral imagery of the body, of corrupted and broken flesh and bones, is common in psalms of lament (Psalm 31:10–11, Lamentations 3:4, Job 30:17), as is that of being surrounded (Psalm 17:9–12), isolated, mocked, and disgraced (Psalms 17:10, 31:12–14, 70:3–4; Lamentations 3:61–63; Psalm 88:9). The formulaic patterning of language combines a verb for guarding from, rising up against, or shaming—some form of defeating the enemy—with language for the enemy to be conquered—evildoers, those who seek his life (Psalms 17:7–9, 17:13–14, 31:18b, 70:3; Lamentations 3:64–66, 54:7). The hope for vindication often combines with the intervention itself as the speaker prays for just deserts, that his enemy should suffer as he has (Psalms 17:13–14, 70:3–4; Lamentations 3:64). Thus, the lament frequently includes an imprecation or curse, suggesting the genre's ties to the basic incantation in form and function.[13] The power of the deity to intervene on the speaker's behalf is emphasized (Psalms 17:15, 31:20–25, 70:5–6).

Psalms 13, 26, and 54 provide versions of the motifs found in the set above as well as parallel uses of language, for example, the imperative request for intervention: "look! answer me" (Psalm 13:4); "execute judgment for me!" (26:1); "save me / plead my cause!" (54:3). Enemies or other sources of negativity attack the person, who prays, as indicated implicitly (26:1) or explicitly (13:3, 54:5). The deity is invoked for help; the prayer sometimes points to the speaker's innocence and worthiness (26:2, 4–7); and hope or assurance is expressed for amelioration and victory (13:6, 54:6–7). Imagery is visceral and emotional: life is in danger (54:5); sorrow afflicts (13:3).

These three laments, like many others, include an important feature in the hopeful-assurance element of the psalm: the speaker's vow to offer something to the deity in return for rescue. The speaker promises to sing to the Lord (Psalm 13:6), to bless the Lord in public assemblies (26:12), or to offer sacrifice (54:8). In his work on vows, Tony Cartledge points to the seeming incongruity of the speaker's sudden shift from sorrow and a state of utter alienation to a joyous and confident attitude and a vow to repay the deity for his rescue with some gift of song, praise, or physical offering. He takes issue with those who see these portions of the compositions as separate redactional pieces, and with suggestions that the work was composed or delivered not during the time of distress but after the poet found relief, so that the psalm functions less as a lament than as a song of thanksgiving. Cartledge suggests that the laments function as wholes and that fulfillment of the vow is contingent upon the deity's offering relief, as are other vows in biblical and wider ancient Near Eastern contexts.[14] Much more is said about vowing in the next chapter, but I agree with Cartledge that the promise at the end of the lament points to the relationship of reciprocity between the deity and the composer. Vowing is an interpersonal ritual in which fulfillment of the vow is contingent upon the actions of the vower's counterpart, the partner in his deal. The deity does need or desire praise; he does appreciate the savor of free-will offerings. He is a participant in this ritual from the lamenter's perspective. Indeed, the verbal insistence on the part of the composer that God will come to his aid also helps bring about this train of events. Words are powerful media. Just as the lamenter's curse upon his enemies is intended to have real consequences, so is the declaration that, eventually, all will be well. There is no doubt something very basic here in human psychology in the direction of wish fulfillment, reflected in profound beliefs about the way the world works or should work.

Language connoting the person, the physical body, and personal attack is thus drawn from a traditional corpus, as is the essential pattern of content, including complaint, intervention, and assurance of relief, framed by faith in the rescuing deity; often an insistence on the speaker's deservedness; a visceral desire for physical vengeance upon enemies; and a promise of praise or sacrifice that underscores the reciprocity between the deity and the lamenter. Can we, however, speak of individual lamenters, set in time and social context, people who produced these works or spoke them? Who might the speakers have been, and who were the enemies so exquisitely described? Can we even include such works as relevant to the study of representations of self? Is a self to be found in the so-called individual or personal laments of Psalms?

Patrick D. Miller, who beautifully explores recurring, stereotypical language in the laments, comes to some similar questions, concluding "The very nature of the psalms and the language with which such persons are described both obscure the immediate identification of the enemies and at the same time suggest that they may have many identities."[15] He adds that this openness allows for appropriations of language for any individual situation. Moshe Greenberg points to the "mixture of spontaneity and prescription" that characterizes prayers included in biblical narratives, seeing the combination as characteristic of "a traditional society."[16] Similarly, Esther Menn writes, "The suggestive vagueness of this stereotypical imagery appears to be a deliberate strategy that allows people facing any number of horrors to adopt the psalm for ritual use."[17] Writing about the psalms and prayer, Greenberg states, "It has long been noted that, despite the genuine fervor that pervades the psalms, for the most part, the circumstances they describe lack particularity; they speak in general terms of individual and communal distress and salvation. Whatever their origin, it seems that they functioned as stock compositions of trained liturgical poets, utilized by individuals and assemblies at temple celebrations."[18]

In a similar way, the incantations explored above are stereotypical in content and form, allowing the professional to complete a traditional template by specifying the problem at hand and the name of the sufferer or the one needing protection. Menn suggests that that the laments had origins "as a liturgical expression of an ordinary individual's suffering and restoration within the context of small group rites."[19] She has us imagine the "performance of rituals that centered on the well-being of seriously ill individuals" and points to various scholarly suggestions concerning contexts for the composition and recitation of these set pieces, including situations of mental, social, and physical suffering.[20] Menn and Miller thus point to possible contexts of lived religion in which such compositions would have taken on life, meaning, and efficacy. Similarly, Hermann Gunkel points to the superscription of Psalm 102:1, which introduces the lament with an indication that it is a "prayer of one afflicted, when he is faint and pours out his complaint before the Lord."[21] To fully appreciate such performances, of course, one would have to have observed them, spoken to the people reciting the psalms, inquired about the situation that gave rise to their lament, and asked about their training or how they had learned to lament. One would have taken account of the physical spaces where the psalms were recited and assessed whether they were extemporaneous oral compositions by those with access to the tradition. What we can say is that Israelites could imagine how such psalms might be used, and much is to be learned from them.

Greenberg's skillfully crafted lectures on biblical prose prayer explore the ways in which biblical authors describe characters who offer spontaneous prayers in situations in which they need to call upon the help of their God, but it is difficult to find laments used in such imagined contexts.[22] Greenberg is working with a common denominator, a basic pattern of prayer consisting of an address to the deity, a petition, and a motivating sentence, all of which may be found in expanded form in the lament under the headings we have called the problem and request for intervention. Greenberg notes that the basic elements can be added to or subtracted from. As we have seen, however, the lament described by Miller, myself, and others is characterized by a particular vocabulary, content, and framework, related, I argue, to incantations, on the one hand, and to extended works such as the confessions of Jeremiah, on the other, and this more specific and fully articulated form is not generally placed in the mouths of biblical characters in narrative contexts.[23] One interesting exception, however, is found in the book of Jonah. The Jonah narrative, about a prophet who flees on a ship to avoid God's command to go to Nineveh and warn its inhabitants to repent, is an ancient short story, the product, as Morton Smith might suggest, of literati in the period following the Babylonian conquest. Much more is said in a subsequent chapter about its composer's style, messages, and context as they relate to our study of personal religion and self-representation, but it is important to note that the author of Jonah placed in his protagonist's mouth a lament, uttered during an experience of utter alienation and dislocation, a time of lost hope, deep from within the belly of the huge fish that has swallowed him!

The pattern of the lament is clear: the request (Jonah 2:2) and the hope for release—"I call from my trouble to the Lord and he answers";[24] a description of the problem, namely, his drowning, literal and metaphorical, his isolation, and his confrontation with death (2:3–5); anticipation of rescue (2:7–8); and his vow to offer a sacrifice to the deity he petitions (2:10).

Jack Sasson has done substantial work on Jonah's prayer, exploring parallels between its language and the formulaic expressive conventions of other biblical compositions, in particular, for our purposes, the lament of Psalm 88.[25] Sasson points to shared language and imagery involving encompassing, deadly waters, and waves in Psalm 88:7 and Jonah 2:4. These phrases, very similar in vocabulary, reflect a more broadly used formula pattern: a verb connoting movement plus a phrase pointing toward an underworld direction: "my life at Sheol arrives" (Psalm 88:4b); "you put me in the pit of the underworld / in the dark regions of the deep" (Psalm 88:7); "you throw me to the depths, into the heart of the sea" (Jonah 2:4a); "your river surrounds me" (Jonah 2:4b); "all of your breakers and waves over me pass" (Jonah 2:4c); "surround me does water to my being" (Jonah 2:6a); "the Deep surrounds me" (Jonah 2:6b); "at the extremities of the mountains, I descend earthward" (Jonah 2:7). Sasson takes note also of the formulaic expression for the speaker's reaching for God in Psalm 88:3 and Jonah 2:8 (a form of *bw'*, literally, "to come" plus "to you / before you" plus "my prayer").

To be sure, the lament in Jonah is particularly rich in the imagery of water, although as Sasson notes, virtually every image in Jonah 2 is found in one or another biblical prayer, and being surrounded by water in fear of imminent death by drowning is a favorite image of biblical composers describing a character in difficult straits.[26] The problem motif of the lament in Jonah 2, however, is literalized and specified as an actual matter of drowning, as is appropriate for the tale. In considering questions about occasions for the recitation of laments, we should note that the author includes a lament as what a person might say in facing calamity. He is, to paraphrase Erving Goffman, following a script, a culturally framed and reinforced idea about individual action under particular circumstances.[27] The actions and words of an individual person are prepared for by a larger shared tradition, but it is individual experience that motivates the person to draw upon that tradition. In this case, an author chooses or constructs a lament rich with conventionalized water-associated language that emphasizes his particular character's plight. Later appropriators of the psalms of lament have, in fact, speculated about individuals who might be employing a lament.

As Miller and Menn point out, the templates of biblical laments are filled in by appropriators in the tradition who provide superscriptions identifying the sufferer, for example, David or Hezekiah, and the situation he faces, thus presenting the lament as a personal expression by a particular biblical character.[28] Saul Olyan has urged biblical scholars to look for special nuances, twists, and differences that frame conventions in order to find a "self" in the writings of antiquity.[29] Similarly, Janet Gyatso, a scholar of traditional Tibetan texts, finds a possibility of "personal variation" in the conventionalized autobiographies she studies.[30] Miller has suggested, in fact, that the imagery in Jeremiah's confessions that exemplify the lament in form, content, and language makes sense in the context of the larger book's presentation of supposed biographical information about the prophet's life and trials.[31] As in the case of Jonah, an author links a traditional prayer form with details about his main character's individual situation. Let us look at some of Jeremiah's confessions and then explore the matter of privatization and personalization of the tradition (albeit by an author who may speak for and about Jeremiah). In dealing with this material there are always layers of contributions to complicate the issue of self-representation, even apart from the conventionalized nature of the literature, but we can learn much about modes of self-representation in late-biblical literature by exploring the received text in its current form.

Jeremiah's Confessions

The passages in Jeremiah relevant to our study are 11:18–12:6; 15:10–21; 17:14–18; 18:18–23; and 20:7–13, 14–18. Kathleen M. O'Connor, A. R. Diamond, and a host of excellent commentators on Jeremiah have explored these works from a variety of form-critical, redaction-critical, and source-critical perspectives.[32] The essential form of the lament characterizes all these passages in part or in whole, as many scholars have noted.[33] What interests me, in particular, is the way in which the particular version of the pattern in Jeremiah, as composed and preserved, relates the lament to a representation of the prophet's concerns and contexts.

Thus Jeremiah 11:18–19 refers to Jeremiah's enemies, to the fact that they devise schemes against him, and in 11:20 the prophet asks the deity for retribution in a version of the request to the deity for relief that includes imprecations against the source of the speaker's problem.[34] In Jeremiah, however, that people are scheming against him is revealed to the prophet by the deity himself (11:18), and the request for aid is followed by the deity's own speech. In verses 21–23, specific reference is made to the people of Anatoth, who seek the prophet's life. The conventionalized phrase "to seek" plus "your *nepeš*" (being/life), seen in many of the laments, is thus specified in relation to particular people. Their punishment, moreover, is specifically to die in the coming war by the sword or by famine. In this way, we gain an additional sense of historical and geographic setting and of the people involved. This attention to context, together with the dialogic nature of the lament scene, distinguishes the lament.

Jeremiah 15:10 sets out the prophet's complaint in typical fashion: he declares in first-person speech that he is an innocent man, and yet his enemies curse him. The prophet then quotes the deity's previous promise to intervene for him, but also his plan to punish Israel for her sins by means of the Babylonians.[35] The setting of war, imminent conquest, and exile is clear. In 15:15, the prophet resumes his own self-story. Beginning again with a request to bring vengeance on those who pursue him, he points out that it is because of his commission to deliver the words of God that he suffers reproach or taunting, ḥerpâ, a word found throughout the laments, but here the abuse has occurred specifically because the deity has chosen him to urge acceptance of Babylonian control, a commission, he states, that he accepted with joy. "Your name," he says, "is proclaimed over me" (15:16). He is the deity's, and is identified with God's message, an unpopular one that many deny is in fact the true word of God. In visceral language typical of laments, Jeremiah describes his pain and his wound (15:18) and, Job-like, accuses God of being "a disappointing stream / waters that do not flow true." The passage ends with the deity's first-person response that he will deliver the prophet from the hands of his enemies. The essential motifs of problem or complaint, innocence of speaker, description of taunting enemies, and response or vindication are thus typical of laments, but the pattern is enriched by the autobiographical way in which Jeremiah is shown to describe his own career and the reasons for his suffering, by the clear wartime context in which dislocation and forced migration will be experienced, and especially by the interaction between the lamenter and the deity, who responds. Whereas typical laments explored in the psalms include the motif of hoped-for vindication, the vindicator here speaks himself, responding to the complaint, and this interaction between him and the prophet, who essentially accuses him of disloyalty, of not upholding his side of their relationship, enriches the lament with a high degree of reciprocity and qualities of I-thou discussed earlier in relation to Job. The lament has become privatized and personalized in Jeremiah.[36]

More typical of the psalms is Jeremiah 17:14–18, with its opening imperatives "heal me / save me!" (17:14), its reference to the taunting words of enemies (17:15), the claims of righteousness by the speaker (17:16), and the curse on his enemies, which includes nuances of just deserts: they should be shamed and not he, they should be dismayed and not he. The context of the prophet's career is clear here also, specifying the setting of the lament within the prophet's life and experience as constructed in the collection (17:16).

Jeremiah 18:18–23 is especially interesting in that it begins with a fly-on-the-wall, third-person account of the nefarious activities of Jeremiah's enemies. We hear what they are saying and doing against him: "the plots" (literally, their "thoughts," devices that they think to make). They not only refuse to listen to him, but also plan to bring charges against him, literally, "to strike him with the tongue." Jeremiah asks for help with the imperative "pay attention, Yahweh, to me!" (18:19), speaks of his righteousness mani-fested once again in faithful service to God in the fulfillment of his call, and then follows with a rich and lengthy call for vindication in the form of vengeance against his enemies (18:21–23). The specific curses include all manner of suffering, as in the particularly thorough list in Deuteronomy 28. It is of note, however, that references to dying by the hand of the sword and to young men who are struck down by the sword in battle relate to the other curses involving bereavement and a marauding band of soldiers, all of which suggest wartime experiences appropriate to the Babylonian conquest (18:21–23). Jeremiah's complaint is thus set in a particular kind of historical framework and background narrative.

Perhaps the most exquisitely interpersonal of Jeremiah's laments is Jeremiah 20:7–13. In this passage, the prophet describes the way in which his relationship with Yahweh has alienated him from human beings. The language is of seduction; God has seduced him into prophesying. The same verb is used in Exodus 22:15 to describe a man's seduction of a virgin girl and in the story of Samson, in which the Philistines try to have Samson's woman seduce him into revealing the source of his strength (Judges 14:15; 16:5). Intimacy and deception are implied.

Because Jeremiah has to shout "violence and destruction" (20:8) and has been a faithful spokesman for his god, others deride and mock him (20:7–8). They denounce him and hope for his failure (20:10). The lengthy description of his condition of suffering, a motif typical of the lament, ex-pressed in typical language (*śḥq:* Jeremiah 20:7, Lamentations 3:14; *l'g:* Jer-emiah 20:7, Psalm 35:16; *ḥrp:* Jeremiah 20:8, Psalms 31:13, 69:8, 69:10, 69:20, 109:25), is, as expected, followed by assurance of divine rescue (20:11) in which the enemies will be shamed (20:11). The piece ends with praise to the Lord, the rescuer. The conventional pattern and content, however, have spe-cific, situated qualities. As in several of Jeremiah's confessions, the prophet's suffering, described as well in the moving song of self-curse in 20:14–18, relates to his career. The context is the oncoming war, and the degree of involvement between the speaker and the deity is beyond formulaic, reaching into language of sensuality and seduction.

These texts from Jeremiah are well located in the trajectory we have been tracing. The conventionalized pattern of content, found in a wide array of ancient Near Eastern incantations and specified in the formulaic language and imagery of the psalms characterized as personal laments, is strongly represented in the confessions of Jeremiah. These versions of lament, however, are set within the narrative of the received tradition, which is presented as a collection of the oracles of a particular prophet, whose career takes place within the period of the Babylonian crisis. These laments in the Jeremiah tradition differ from those of Psalms in their degree of specificity about the purported speaker's career, life, and challenges; in the overt reference to a war context; and in the response of the deity addressed for relief, in which the rescuer (who is also the source of the prophet's troubles) interacts with the lamenter in the midst of his confession. At the very least, in dealing with the nature of the literature, we have to conclude that composers are engaged in portraying a specific prophet's self-representation: his emotions, disappointments, fears, and hopes. This is not to say that these confessions were delivered by the real Jeremiah,[37] nor to dismiss the thoughtful redactional suggestions for the development of the confessions by Diamond, O'Connor, Erhard Gerstenberger, David J. A. Clines, David M. Gunn, and others.[38] Rather, we emphasize that in late-biblical literature, and this designation certainly applies to the received form of the tradition, there is a marked interest in self-representation that makes the portrayal of Jeremiah and his words possible and believable, and this portrayal comes much closer to the individualistic, the personal, and the autobiographical in form and perceived function than do the highly formulaic laments of the psalms or the incantations, in which only the illness and the name of the sufferer sometimes fill in the blanks in the conventionalized pattern.

Nehemiah's Memoir

A final example of the lament pattern is offered by the so-called memoir of Nehemiah. The Persian-period book of Nehemiah, no earlier in date than the fifth century BCE, presents a first-person account of a Judean governor appointed by the imperial Persians. The purported speaker, Nehemiah, describes his ethnic and professional background, the emotions he experiences in response to being a member of the Jewish diaspora, his career as the empire's representative in colonial Judea, his challenges, political enemies and rivals, and his (in his view) considerable accomplishments. Such is the stuff of autobiography; a person is pictured as explaining, in this case, in the best possible light, how he became who he is.[39]

Scholars have drawn comparisons between the Nehemiah memoir and a range of ancient texts from the Mediterranean world that provide models for or parallels to Nehemiah's memoir.[40] Most striking from the perspective of this book is the durability of the pattern of the lament, including motifs of problem/suffering/complaint; intervention/appeal to the deity, including a self-justification of the hero; hoped-for or actualized vindication.

The opening of Nehemiah's self-story describes the hero as being in the Persian capital Susa, inquiring of one of his fellow Judeans (literally, his "brothers") about the disposition of those who remained in or returned to Judea and about conditions in the homeland. His first-person account situates him in a geographic location, period of time, and historical setting. When Nehemiah hears about the troubles of his fellows and about the sorry state of Jerusalem, he is overcome by grief. The memoir thus opens with the description of a problem and the speaker's empathic and physical response (Nehemiah 1:1–4). The suffering is specified in geography, chronology, and history. The composition is not necessarily an actual diary by the governor Nehemiah, but the work assumes the quality of a memoir, related in Israelite literary tradition to the form and function of the lament. The allusion to Nehemiah's troubles and their immediate causes is followed by a petition or request for relief from the deity (1:4–11). Nehemiah's supplication alludes to the covenant with Moses (1:8) and to the late-biblical version of the Deuteronomic theology of blessings and curses, promising return from exile for repentance. In contrast to many lamenters' protestations of innocence under the conventional rules of the covenant, Nehemiah admits to his and his "family's" sin—the sin of the people Israel. Nehemiah concludes his petition by providing more of his professional background, reporting that at the time of receiving this news, he was serving as cupbearer to the king of the Persians. Nehemiah 2:1–9 continues his self-story.

Nehemiah recounts that when the king observes the sad demeanor of his faithful servant, he makes inquiry, and Nehemiah describes to him Jerusalem's plight, asking that he be allowed to rebuild the city of his ancestors (2:5). The king agrees and makes arrangements for his loyal servant to undertake the task. The memoir has a strongly narrative quality, revealing an interest in characterization and interaction between characters, a matter of texture and text explored in more detail in chapter seven with reference to Jonah and Ruth. Nehemiah, like Ruth and Jonah, features cameo scenes in which characters reveal inner selves and concerns, for example, the conversations between Nehemiah and his visitor from home and between Nehemiah and the Persian king. The ruler has sympathy for his servant and displays genuine affection, asking how long he will have to do without Nehemiah at court. While the motifs of the lament remain visible in the framework of the memoir, these chapters tell a man's story in his own voice, and it is this quality of narration that moves the conventional pattern of the lament toward the genre of autobiography.

The self-narrative in the first person continues with an allusion to Nehemiah's enemies (2:10), the description of his brave inspection of the city, and his urging of his countrymen to begin rebuilding. Those who oppose Nehemiah's work, resentful of his efforts to establish another power center vying for the favor and resources of the Persian establishment, mock and ridicule him (2:19), playing their role in the lament form. The language used to describe their mockery (*l'g/bzh*) is typical of laments. More reference to the enemies' derisive behavior is found at 3:33–36 (English 4:1–3), when they suggest that even a fox could topple Nehemiah's pathetic wall were the small animal to climb upon it. This taunting is followed by the speaker's petition to the deity that the taunting be turned back upon his enemies, that they suffer exile, and that they be punished for their sins (3:37; English 4:5). Nehemiah thus curses his enemies with nuances of just deserts, as seen in the psalms and confessions discussed above: he asks that the reproach (*ḥerpâ*) be turned on their heads and that they be given as plunder in the land of captivity (3:36; English 4:4). For their part, the enemies continue to plot against him (4:2; English 4:8), and he responds with a petition to the deity (4:7; English 4:13).

Chapter 5 continues Nehemiah's self-story as he highlights his courageousness in the area of economic ethics. The message throughout, typical of the lament, is that he is good and generous, whereas his selfish and mean-spirited opponents are disengaged from the needs of their countrymen and inflicting suffering upon them. Nehemiah projects an image of his own righteousness, as do the monuments of a variety of ancient Near Eastern figures.

In this way, the motifs of the lament are fully and specifically elaborated in a narrative medium. The enemies have names, engage in dialogue, and make reference to the supposed incompetence and ineptitude of Nehemiah and the Judeans in their efforts to rebuild Jerusalem. The imagery of the fox, for example, and the description of Nehemiah's travels, efforts, and motivations capture the particular situation and make the participants seem real rather than conventionalized. Similarly, as Morton Smith has discussed, Nehemiah, as portrayed in his own words, produces an image of his success, providing details concerning his actions, his speeches, and his successes.[41] He is rich, generous, self-denying (5:10, 14–16), and has friends in high places as well as local enemies. As Jacob Wright has noted, Nehemiah is the big man who is able to project and wield power, to make and keep influential friends by commensal means, sharing food resources at his own expense like the lord of a manor (5:17–19).[42] This righteous supplicant is drawn with care that goes beyond the conventional motifs of the lament. We have traced some of this individualization of the traditional form in the confessions of Jeremiah. In Nehemiah, the attention to his characterization and situation is even more detailed and specific.

Particularly interesting within the emphasis on the speaker's righteousness, a common motif in the lament, is the sign act of 5:13, framed by Nehemiah's insistence that the priests take an oath to make economic restoration to those who have, in Nehemiah's view, been taken advantage of by a wealthy aristocracy. Another example of religion as lived, oath taking is an interactive ritual form involving a speech act, a promise, and witnesses. The oath is taken in the sight of God and the community and is presumably enforceable by the deity, peer pressure, and the expectations of the group. The oath is followed by Nehemiah's sign act, a brief performance by him involving the manipulation of a material object, in this case the robe he is wearing. Sign acts are explored in chapter five in connection with a study of material religion as manifested in late-biblical texts and contexts. The scene in Nehemiah anticipates this discussion and points to the cultural role of an individually undertaken, traditional form of symbolic communication. The symbolic actions and the verbal interpretation placed upon them serve both as a predictor of the future and as a guarantor of consequences. Nehemiah shakes out the fold of his garment, turning the action into a promise of retribution and a curse: "Thus will God shake out every man, who does not fulfill this thing, from his house and from his property, and thus he will be shaken out and empty" (5:13). The physical action and object both represent and help bring about events, even while building Nehemiah's projected self-image as a prophetic-style leader. Critical to Nehemiah's self-story is the portrayal of antagonists, continued in Nehemiah 6. Nehemiah describes the way in which his opponents try to undermine him by suggesting there is a plot to kill him and urging him to take refuge in the temple. Their goal, in his view, is to make him look like a coward so that they can taunt him (6:13).

The first-person account in chapter 13 further underscores Nehemiah's accomplishments as a defender of the Sabbath (13:23), a bulwark against intermarriage (13:23), and a leader who cleanses the community from everything foreign (13:30). The final line of the memoir, addressed to God, asks that he remember the leader for good (13:31), closing the narrative in a way evocative of the lament's hope for vindication.

Quoting Karl Weintraub and Georges Gusdorf, Janet Gyatso notes that "the more deviation from the normative 'script of life,' the more the story about oneself achieves the fullest possible potential of autobiographical writing."[43] Within a traditional template "there is room for personal variation"[44] that can "express experiences and realizations."[45] Nehemiah's memoir may or may not, even at its core, be the composition of Nehemiah himself. The author, however, whether the governor or a writer who imagines and constructs him, expertly makes use of a pattern of conventional motifs rooted in tradition that he individuates to suit the figure of Nehemiah, his particular identity, setting, and set of challenges.

Just as Patricia Cox Miller notes that the "touch of the real" may be more characteristic and reflective of attitudes in a particular sort of historical and cultural milieu, so Gyatso asks about the existence of "historical conditions for autobiography or lack thereof."[46] Arnaldo Momigliano notes that "autobiography was in the air in the Persian Empire of the early fifth century, and both Jews and Greeks may have been stimulated by Persian and other oriental models to create something of their own."[47] The setting or "air" in Persian-period Judea was permeated by an awareness of having been conquered, of living in a postconquest, colonialist environment. The writing of autobiography, related in the Judean literary context to the personal lament—a form found in Job, Lamentations 3, the Psalms, Jonah, and Jeremiah—is a valuable means of self-assertion and self-representation in the face of economic, social, and political challenges. Autobiography allows the writer to place his own interpretation on events and actions, what he says he has done and experienced, how he portrays others, and how he presents the world around him. Assuming that Nehemiah himself is the author, Morton Smith suggests that Nehemiah portrays himself as the ideal tyrant, popular with the people, attuned to their physical and spiritual needs, engaged in important reconstruction projects, and successfully negotiating Judea's relationship with its Persian overlords.[48] If instead the author assumes the persona of a Judean governor, his composition portrays, in an eyewitness, participatory, and laudatory way, the point of view of his own particular group, those who work with the Persians, are intensely conservative on social and religious issues of intermarriage and Sabbath keeping, and are liberal regarding the treatment and protection of the poor.

4 The Negotiating Self
Vowing and Personal Religion

Following the revelatory dream at Bethel in which Jacob has a classic visionary experience of a ladder that links heaven and earth (Genesis 28:10–12), he vows a vow to God, his patron deity. If the deity is with him and all goes well with him, that is, if he has food to eat and clothing to wear and returns to his father's house in peace, then, says Jacob, "Yahweh will be for me a god." Moreover, Jacob sets up a stone as a *maṣṣēbâ*, a pillar or standing stone that materially commemorates and represents the deity's presence at this place where heaven and earth have met and where Jacob has witnessed the connection. Jacob, for his part, promises to the deity one-tenth of all that God gives to him, but it is important to note that fulfillment of the promise by the vower, Jacob, depends upon the deity's fulfilling the patriarch's requests. This vow, like many others, thus involves a promise, reciprocity, and expectations of fulfillment for each party involved, and the deal is off if one of the parties fails in his role.

Vows remain a part of contemporary discourse and continue to play a role in our social and ritual lives: marriage vows, Catholic priests' vows of celibacy, monastic vows of silence. Is a New Year's resolution a kind of vow? Is the promise to give something up for Lent? Even this contemporary list suggests that there is a spectrum of vowing according to the seriousness of the vow, the consequences for nonfulfillment, and the parties involved. The psychoanalyst Herbert J. Schlesinger discusses vows in the context of a promise, which he defines as "an explicit statement of one's intention to perform some act at a future time with the proviso that someone relies on the fulfillment of the promise."[1] He views the promise as framed by cultural and social expectations and as having to do with a relationship between the "promiser and promisee."[2] Schlesinger relates promising to morality, noting that the "index of moral and legal weight of a promise is the expected or actual reaction of others to keeping it or breaking it."[3] He writes that "by fulfilling the promise we are relieved of the voluntarily assumed obligation to perform"[4] and sees the promise as a way in which word and deed are united.[5]

Chapter three points to the presence of vows in lament literature, part of a trajectory from incantation to autobiography.[6] The vow in ancient Israel, a stylized promise involving conditions, reciprocity, and consequences, deeply relates to the human being's relationship with the deity, the one to whom laments and confessions are addressed, the one who can rescue the speaker and ameliorate the situation that is the source of his suffering and complaint. Like prayer, the vow is not a late-biblical invention, but a long-standing feature of personal religion in Israel, as noted by the contemporary scholars Jacques Berlinerblau and Tony Cartledge.[7] After a discussion of the vow in ancient Israel with attention to warring contexts, votive offerings, and the status of the Nazirite, I focus on a particularly interesting thread in late-biblical literature involving women and vows, and explore the implications of this material for an appreciation of personal religion in a late-biblical setting. As in the studies of visionary material and literary characterization that follow, a comparison between earlier material and that of the Neo-Babylonian and Persian periods leads to some interesting conclusions about developments in the expression of religious identity in the period following the exile. The study of vows has implications for the ongoing interplay between personal and public, private and institutional dimensions of religion, and for questions about the self and empowerment.

Vows in the Context of War

Formulaic language of vow making, "to vow a vow to the deity," is found in the war contexts of Numbers 21:1–3 and Judges 11:29–40. Each of these passages offers a window into the nature of vowing, its sociological settings, and psychoanalytical underpinnings, and points to the assumptions, motivations, and moods that lie behind the act.

Numbers 21:1–3 begins with a war report. The Israelites appear to be on the brink of defeat and destruction, for the Canaanite king of Arad has met them, fought with them, and taken captives (21:1). Then comes the vow:

"And Israel vowed a vow to Yahweh and said, 'If to give you will give this people into my hand, I will devote their cities to destruction.'" The situation thus involves anxiety, insecurity, fear of defeat and death, and hopes nevertheless to surmount difficulties and achieve victory.

The Israelites, who are indeed subsequently successful in battle, follow through with the vow to utterly destroy the enemies' towns. This act of destruction, with its terminology of *ḥerem*, or "the ban," has deeply sacrificial nuances implying not only the total destruction of inanimate structures but also and especially the killing of everything that breathes, in particular enemy human beings (see, for example, Deuteronomy 2:24; Joshua 6:34; 1 Samuel 15:3, 22:19).[8] References to the ban are found throughout the Hebrew Scriptures, in particular in the books of Deuteronomy and Joshua. The ban figures prominently as well in a non-Israelite victory stele of the Moabite king Mesha, dating from the ninth century BCE. The inscription points to nuances of reciprocity, relationship, and conditionality implicit in vows in general and in the ban in particular. The war vow indicates the way the world is perceived to operate and points to another of the efforts, so typical of lived religion, to gain control of the chaotic and uncontrollable aspects of existence.

Specific language of vowing a vow is not found in the inscription, but that the Moabite king Mesha made a vow in a war context is clear, as are nuances of material and personal religion. Speaking in the first person, the king identifies himself and his lineage. The inscription is situated in a sacred space built by Mesha, a "high place for Kemosh," his god. Emphasizing his relationship to the deity and its importance for political and military success, he declares that the previous subjugation of Moab by Omri, king of Israel, was possible because of Kemosh's anger with Moab (Mesha Inscription [MI] l. 5). At the same time, victory and deliverance from his enemies is made possible by the king's relationship to Kemosh (MI l. 4), and the deity speaks to the king, directing him to seize Nebo from Israel (MI l. 14). The vowing nuance emerges in the language of the ban. Those killed in battle are devoted to 'Ashtar-Kemosh (MI l. 17). This act of "devoting to destruction" is by its very nature a vow to the deity, and those sacrificed are a promised gift offered in exchange for victory. The killing of the entire population of the city 'Atarot is a "satiation for Kemosh and for Moab" (MI l. 12).[9]

In this way, Numbers 21:1–3 and the Mesha Inscription point to certain essentials of vowing: the promise, conditions, the relationship between the one who vows and the one to whom he vows, and the personal aspect of the act. The context in each case is the crisis of war, a high-anxiety situation, and the vow is preserved in national myth in the biblical case and at a sacred location built by the author in the case of Mesha. Personal and public thus intertwine, as do oral and written. The scene imagined in Judges 11 involving the war vow of judge chieftain Jephthah introduces the theme of women, for offering up the daughter of Jephthah in sacrifice turns out to be the fulfillment of the vow's conditions.

Facing battle against the Ammonites, Jephthah is filled with the spirit of the Lord and, in his warrior's frenzy, vows a vow to Yahweh. "If give you will give the sons of Ammon into my hand, it will be: the emerging thing that emerges from the doors of my house to meet me upon my returning in peace from the sons of Ammon, shall be for Yahweh, and I will offer it up as a whole burnt offering" (Judges 11:30–31). The formula pattern parallels that of Numbers 21: the conditional frame language of "if" is followed by the condition (giving the enemy into one's hand), followed by the promise upon fulfillment of the condition that a sacrifice will be offered (the sacrifice of devotion to destruction involving the death of human beings in Numbers 21 or the unspecified emerging living thing which will be offered to the deity in Judges 11). Whereas the scene in Numbers is an efficient and brief transaction, victory followed by the imposition of the ban, Judges 11 includes a longer tale linking myth and ritual. The individual vow of Jephthah relates to a custom shared by Israelites, who in turn participate in this ritual rite of passage on a personal and public level. Jephthah's vow becomes the source of his daughter's experience that relates to the lives of all Israelite young women. As the tale-teller's audiences surely knew, that which emerges from his house is Jephthah's daughter, his only child. Jephthah is horrified, but he and the girl both agree that the vow cannot be undone, for he has "opened his mouth to God" (Judges 11:35, 36). The conditions must be met, the promise kept, for Yahweh upheld his end of the deal, giving Jephthah victory against the Ammonites.

The daughter makes one request: that she be allowed to mourn her maidenhood with a cohort of her friends in the mountains for two months. This custom is to be relived and the story retold in an annual four-day festival celebrated by young women of marriageable age.[10] With the etiology for a custom marking young women's passage from girlhood to womanhood, virginity to marriage, the personal vow meets public religion, and shared community custom is seen to relate to individual religious experience and sensibilities. In these biblical cases, reciprocity between the deity and the human hero is clear, conditions are integral to the vow, and the act of sacrifice is central. The act of offering sacrifice brings us to another relevant set of biblical passages dealing with the votive offering. In making a transition from war texts involving vows to more mundane references to votive offerings, we touch upon biblical polemics against sacrifices to Molech, since these have been related by scholars both to the practice of human sacrifice and to the making of vows.

Human Sacrifice and Votive Offerings

Leviticus 18:21, Leviticus 20:3–5, 2 Kings 23:10, and Jeremiah 32:35 make reference to the offering of children to Molech. Scholars have debated whether the term, rooted in *mlk,* indicates a kind of sacrificial offering or refers to a deity, and if the latter, whether this deity is a chthonic form of Yahweh.[11] A number of Punic inscriptions that have been explored to provide a context in ancient Near Eastern religious thought for the biblical polemics concerning these offerings explicitly refer to vowing one's children to the deity; they are votive offerings.[12] As George Heider concludes about the Israelite evidence in this context, "It is possible that, as was apparently true of the Punic offerings, the sacrifices were performed in fulfillment of vows made to the deity (whether Yahweh, Molek or the ancestors), and one may conjecture that by the nature of the gift and the connections which scholars such as Pope have seen between the cults of love and death, the vows usually had to do with fertility."[13] Heider describes these acts of sacrifice as "irregular" and "voluntary," acknowledging the desperate seriousness of killing one's children and, implicitly, the range of possibilities for vowing. Such life-controlling acts of vowing also point to the objectification of children as virtual possessions that could be promised to the deity, a matter that arises again in the vow of Hannah and the Nazirism of Samuel and Samson, who were dedicated to service and to a particular way of life before their birth.

The votive offerings described below are more ordinary and regular than child sacrifices, and are woven into the fabric of the sacrificial cult that maintains the relationship between people and the deity. While references to these kinds of offerings are not, as in the case of Numbers 21 and Judges 11, surrounded by a narrative or descriptive context, the assumptions behind such references both parallel those that lie behind narrative sources and point to long-held beliefs in ancient Israel concerning the vow. These brief allusions are particularly interesting because of their matter-of-fact, list-like nature. As Jacques Berlinerblau has noted, it is often the banal or offhand reference that tells us the most about cultural "tacit assumptions."[14]

First, we mention the several psalms in which the speaker makes reference to vows performed for the Lord, the one who responds to the petitioner's prayers (Psalm 65:2). The vows are sometimes in poetic parallelism with praises promised to God in response to his protection and his answering of petitions and needs (Psalms 22:26, 61:8). These vows to Yahweh, even if made in private, are often said to be paid in public (Psalms 22:26, 116:14, 116:18). The payment of vows in Psalms is also mentioned in parallel with the giving of burnt offerings (Psalm 66:13). These poetic texts thus point to the integral place of vows and the fulfillment of vows in community ritual and often implicitly relate to the maintenance of the priesthood, which was supported by monetary offerings and sustained by meat from votive sacrifices. It is in the context of community ritual that the many references to vows in Leviticus, Numbers, and Deuteronomy are also to be understood.

Leviticus 7:16, for example, mentions the votive offering in tandem with the free-will offering in order to assert that the food from these offerings is to be consumed on the day of the offering. Leftovers may be consumed the following day, but any remainders must be destroyed on the third day. The votive offering is thus a quite common form of religious expression that often involves animal sacrifice and the communal consumption of meat, an important part of the sacrificial system. A personal vow involving the petitioner's relationship to the deity thus becomes an occasion for more public sharing. As Michael Satlow notes in relation to votive inscriptions, the offering may precede the divine fulfillment of some expressed need, being a means of encouraging the deity to come to one's aid, or the offering may follow an action of the deity perceived to be a fulfillment of the petitioner's request.[15] In either case, the petitioner keeps his promise to give a token of thanks, conditionally made.

Similarly, Numbers 15:2–13 includes the votive offering in a longer list of sacrificial offerings and describes its typical content, along with the accompanying offerings of grain and drink (see also Numbers 29:39, Leviticus 18–23). The goal of all these offerings is to provide "a pleasing odor for Yahweh" (Numbers 15:3). Deuteronomy 12, a text shaped by southern Deuteronomic writers who are interested in the centralization of cult, limiting sacrifice to the place that the deity has chosen, also includes the votive offering in a list of sacrificial offerings (Deuteronomy 12:6, 17, 26). The text mentions monetary votive gifts (Deuteronomy 23:19 [English 18]), but excludes the wages of prostitution from that which can be vowed to Yahweh.[16] Ground rules are set for vowing: payment of the vow cannot be delayed or postponed; if one makes a vow—if it issues forth from the mouth—one must fulfill it (Deuteronomy 23:22–24 [English 21–23]). These texts thus emphasize the spoken and oral dynamics of the vow and its durability.[17] To paraphrase Schlesinger, the moral obligation of the vower is both high and commensurate with the expectation of fulfillment. As Deuteronomy 23:22–23 suggests, if you cannot be sure that you will carry through with your promise, do not vow. The priestly writers of Leviticus 27 acknowledge that vows to the deity of persons, animals, or property may occasionally require release or alteration of the obligation, should a vow, in Carol Meyers's words, "prove unworkable or become an undue hardship."[18] Leviticus 27 sets forth a series of valuations to allow for such redemption, and these valuations are to be assessed by the priest (Leviticus 27:8, 12).

All of the above biblical texts assume a "social relationship" with the deity.[19] And while a vow may well be spontaneous,[20] its fulfillment is framed by shared, institutional, and customary ritual. While a vow, moreover, may be occasioned by a personal situation or be made in private, the fulfillment, in the case of sacrifice, is public and institutionally shared by priests.[21] These poles of private and public, personal and institutional, and the interplay between them arise again in the third corpus under discussion, biblical texts relating to the Nazirite vow and status.

Nazirite Vows

In biblical passages pertaining to the Nazirite vow, we delve more deeply into matters of gender and women's religious identity and expression. References to Nazirite vows suggest two general categories and a trajectory of development. One set of texts deals with special birth and divine selection and treats the Nazirite status of a male child as God's choice or as the mother's vow to the deity to set aside her son for divine service. Numbers 6, however, describes a temporary, self-imposed vow by an adult of either gender. I agree with scholars who view the priestly passage of Numbers 6 as reflecting a later development than the type of Nazirite vow that bound Samson.[22] Numbers 6 reflects an effort to reframe, domesticate, and institutionalize the tradition for reasons that hold significance for women's

vows and larger views of gender. As Berlinerblau notes, vows can be prob-
lematical for the establishment, a matter discussed below.[23]

The story of Hannah in 1 Samuel 1 underscores the role of vow making
in the personal religion of ancient Israelites. The tale begins by introduc-
ing a man, Elkanah, and his two wives, Peninah and Hannah. Peninah has
borne him children and Hannah has not. We learn that the man takes his
family annually to the local shrine at Shiloh to offer sacrifice to God. One
thinks here of Rainer Albertz's and Rüdiger Schmitt's suggestions about
family and local contexts for religious expression.[24] In describing this local
practice, the author soon focuses on more intimate scenes, the stuff of lived
religion.

Elkanah distributes food from the sacrifice and gives his childless wife
a double portion "because he loved her and God had closed her womb."
Nuances of affection and pathos are implicit. The description of Hannah's
mood captures her anguish and desperation. One might translate 1 Samuel
1:6 as "her rival vexed her," but the etymology of the vocabulary suggests
hostility and abuse (rival) and emotions of anger or grief, tinged with anger
(vex). The term for "grief" or "vexation," k's, is found frequently in biblical
language of lament and complaint (Psalms 6:8, 31:10; Ecclesiastes 1:18, 2:23).
Peninah is thus placed in the role of Hagar vis-à-vis Sarah or Leah vis-à-vis
Rachel. The one who is fertile taunts the barren woman, who is nevertheless her husband's favorite. Some would suggest that the fertile wife vexes
Hannah to "make her fret."[25] The term for "fret" is actually more explosive,
rooted in language for "thunder"; "makes her wail loudly with angst" might
be more accurate.[26] One thinks of Rachel's complaint to Jacob, "Give me
children or I will die" (Genesis 30:1).

Family life, ritual pattern, and religious experience intertwine in the
brief cameo scene between Elkanah and Hannah. He asks why she cries
(presumably, instead of enjoying the family festivities) and why she does
not eat (refusing to participate in a commensal custom that binds kin and
links family members to their deity). He wants to know why her heart
is bitter (perhaps especially at this special time and sacred place). Isn't he
more to her than ten sons? The intensely personal interaction in a religious
setting points to lived religion. In this intimate scene, we see the interplay
between human relationships, "the circle of kin" and "bonds of commitment" to which Orsi alludes; a special sacred setting, "their sense of place";[27]
and implicit expectations of the deity, the object of human petition. To reprise Orsi, religion is always "religion-in-action," "religion in relationships

between people,"[28] and it is "situated amid the ordinary concerns of life, at the junctures of self and culture, family and the social world."[29]

In the following scene comes the vow itself. "Bitter of soul," Hannah prays to Yahweh, crying. The formulaic language "to vow a vow" is found, as is the conditional framework, "If . . . , then I will . . ." The approach to the deity during the making of the vow is filled with the woman's self-deprecation. She refers to herself as his servant. Perhaps Yahweh might deign to look upon her, remember her, and give her a son. If the deity does so, she will give the son to Yahweh all the days of his life, and no razor will go across his head.[30] Carol Meyers has noted that the "dialogue and direct speech in the construction of the Hannah story also affords her the measure of visibility and individuality that is a concomitant of reported speech."[31]

The association between a mother's vow and the conception or birth of a special child is suggested by Proverbs 31:2. In the opening of an interesting wisdom speech directed to "King Lemuel," his mother calls him "son of my vow," an epithet suggesting that the existence and perhaps the success of this special man relates to his mother's vow.[32] Hannah's son Samuel, as the Greek version makes explicit and as is implicit in the formulaic language concerning the razor, will become a Nazir, a special sort of hero, dedicated to God. Conditions, reciprocity, and seriousness about the fulfillment of the promise are all present, as in the war vows and votive offerings explored above. Thus, after Samuel is weaned, Hannah takes him to the priest Eli, whom he serves at the Shiloh shrine. A charismatic hero whose very birth from a barren woman is a kind of miracle, the divine response to a vowing process, Samuel goes on to become prophet, priest, and warrior hero. His birth story is thus a marker of future greatness; his Nazirite status, indicated in particular by the hero's long, never-cut hair, is not inherited, earned, or assumed, but a matter decided before his birth, even perhaps before his conception. The annunciation of the hero judge Samson's birth shares similar themes, but the selection of Samson as a Nazir seems to be God's choice rather than the outcome of a vow initiated by a barren mother in the hope of healing her inability to conceive.

Once again, "there was a certain man" whose wife was barren. This opening formulaic language (literally, "there was one man from place-name"), in fact, indicates the origins of a great hero.[33] References to Nazir-ism come in the form of an annunciation. A divine being visits the woman and tells her about the child to be born: he is to be a Nazir, so no razor is to cross his head (Judges 13:5). In preparation for the gestation of this hero, the woman, the wife of Manoah, is to keep kosher and consume no wine or strong drink (13:4, 7, 14). Thus, a promise to follow certain rules of comportment is imposed upon her by the deity, she accepts, and the child is born. The hero promised to his mother then has to keep her promise not to cut his hair in order that his special status remains intact. No explicit language of vowing is found here or in Amos 2:11, in which Nazirism is described as a kind of elevation by the deity. In these cases, God initiates the situation, in a sense, placing the human being under a conditional vow. In the story of Samson, when the Nazir fails to keep his end of the deal and allows his hair to be cut, the deity withdraws support and Samson becomes weak, like other men. The language of vowing is, however, overt in Numbers 6, the description of the Nazirite vow that an individual takes upon himself or herself. This text raises questions about the motivation, role, and implications of vowing in personal religion as presented by a late-biblical contributor.

The passage begins with language that treats the taking of a Nazirite vow by any man or woman as an accepted or common possibility, reminding us of Berlinerblau's urging to pay attention to the matter of fact: "A man or a woman who . . ." or "If/When a man or a woman . . ." The language of vowing (Numbers 6:2) is overt (*nādar neder*), the vow is open to both genders, and it is not a matter of divine selection but of self-imposition, like any other vow.

That women can choose to undertake this vow is of special importance. The traditional Nazirism of Samuel and Samson involves a manly charisma associated with long hair and divine selection. It is the warrior's charisma that the long-haired Absalom, who is ultimately unsuccessful in supplanting his father, seeks to project. It is the *pr*ʿ, the long hair, alluded to in Judges 5:2 and Deuteronomy 32:42, that is associated with this manly status. Hairiness is the purview of certain holy men, such as Elijah (2 Kings 1:8; see also Zechariah 13:4 and Jeremiah 7:29).[34] As noted by Martin Noth and others, the Nazirism of the texts dealing with Samson and Samuel differs considerably from the late-priestly version described in Numbers 6.[35] The participation of women in the Nazirite vow is truly transformative, perhaps reflecting late writers' explicit effort to manipulate this charismatic phenomenon.

The conditions of the temporary Nazirite vow are formalized and specific, seeming to gather together details associated with Nazirism in the narratives of 1 Samuel 1 and Judges 13. Like Samson's mother, who bears a Nazirite chosen by God, the one who places the vow on himself or herself is to drink no wine. With a rabbinic-style extension, not only wine is forbidden, but also other products of the grape listed by name. Not cutting one's hair for the period of the vow is critical, as in 1 Samuel 1 and Judges 13, and the Nazirite is also enjoined not to go near the dead to avoid becoming unclean (Numbers 6:6). The vow moreover is temporary (Numbers 6:5). The person who vows sets a time limit on his or her status.

How does one recognize that a person is a Nazirite of the kind described by Numbers 6? How does he or she signal this set-apart status?[36] If the person, like Samson, never cuts his hair, then he, like a Sikh, clearly signals his status. Samson is said to wear his long hair in plaits. But what of the person whose Nazirism is temporary? How long would hair have to grow until it showed? The term *pr'* is associated with hair that grows long and untamed by a razor, like Samson's, but the term can also mean "let loose," "wild," not neatly done in woven plaits or braids. Could it be that the female Nazirite wears her hair down or uncovered, whereas Numbers 5:18 suggests that under normal circumstances an adult woman would wear her hair up or tied back? Could she leave her hair uncovered, whereas her hair would normally be covered in public? In the eighth-century-BCE Lachish reliefs, captured and exiled Judean women are portrayed with their hair covered, even in such dire conditions. Did men and women who made a Nazirite vow dishevel their hair, as do mourners?

It is possible that for temporary Nazirites, the avoidance of the dead and temperance regarding wine may have been clearer markers to onlookers of their vows than the condition of the hair. To attend to the dead and to share in the drinking of wine are quintessentially social occasions, signals of kinship and community, so that nonparticipation in these events sets the Nazirite apart from quotidian social intercourse. Women are frequently associated with mourning practices and preparation of the dead, and would presumably be precluded from assuming these roles during the period of the vow.[37] It is significant that the conclusion of the description of the vow-ending ritual states not that the person can now treat his or her hair in the customary way, but that "afterward, the Nazirite may drink wine" (Numbers 6:20), implying perhaps that wine drinking returns him or her to mundane and typical social status.

Rules concerning avoidance of wine and the dead in fact associate the sort of Nazirism described in Numbers 6 with priestly status, for the priest is not to drink wine or strong drink before entering the sacred space, the tent of meeting. In this way, he is in a condition of seriousness and sobriety as he attends to his mediating activities linking divine and human, a state of wholeness and holiness (Leviticus 10:8). Moreover, priests are restricted in their contact with the dead, since they need to maintain a state of ritual purity that enables them to perform in the cult (21:1–6). Again, one might ask why the priestly writer is comfortable with women assuming a priestly-like status even temporarily.

Before digging more deeply into the Nazirite vow of Numbers 6 as it relates to women's personal ritual and religious identity, it is important to take stock of the way in which personal and public, peripheral and institutional, official and unofficial categories apply to versions of Nazirite vowing. Hannah's vow is pictured as a private one that nevertheless is made in a local but "official" sacred space, the sanctuary at Shiloh. Her interaction with the officiate at that place, Eli, takes place in private, but his words of blessing again suggest the interplay between unofficial and official religion, personal and institutional dimensions.[38] The vow of Numbers 6, with its ritual and priestly aspects and its carefully articulated regulations, even more strongly challenges these seeming dichotomies, emphasizing, as do Robert Orsi and Meredith McGuire, the interplay between public and private, official and unofficial in lived religion.[39]

This privately made but publically displayed vow involves interaction with religious officials in many ways. At the end of his or her vow period (Numbers 6:13–20), or when the vow and the person's status are prematurely ended by contact with the dead (6:9–12), the Nazirite participates in ritual activity that is directed and controlled by the priest and from which the priest benefits. The ceremony marking an interruption of the vow because of contact with the dead involves the sacrifice of turtledoves or pigeons, one as a sin or purification offering and the other as a burnt offering. The hair is shaved, the vow is voided, the person atones, and the sanctification process of growing hair recommences (6:11) as the person brings a year-old lamb as a guilt or reparation offering. The priest must oversee this ritual. At the successful conclusion of the vow, the hair is shaved and placed on the fire that is under the sacrifice of well-being (6:18). In a sense, the Nazirite offers to the deity a substance that is a part of or contiguous with his or her body, mediating divine and human in a most visceral and material way. The hair, a bodily excrescence, has become infused with holiness and is transferred to the deity, to whom the vow has been made. There are costly offerings of a lamb, a ewe, and a ram, along with bread and cakes, grain and drink offerings. Offerings are placed by the vow maker in the hands of the priest as an elevation offering, "holy for the priest." In other words, the priest is integral to the emergence from Nazirite status and benefits materially from the process. The official shrine is involved, as are official personnel, emphasizing the interplay between private and public, personal and official.[40]

Cartledge emphasizes that the Nazirite vow is a conditional vow in which the condition is not overtly expressed. He sees "the vows offered by 'temporary' Nazirites" as probable "conditional promises offered to God in the prospect of answered prayer rather than unconditional promises of unselfish devotion."[41] He concludes that "a conditional promise of special service" depends upon God's granting the petition.[42] Conditional or not, the deportment that results from the vow to behave like a Nazirite for a certain length of time suggests an assumption of holiness, a denial of the pleasures of conviviality, and a willingness to miss out on the soothing responsibility of caring for the dead, even within one's own immediate family. In closeness to the deity, one assumes a priestly status at the expense of forms of interaction with society and kin. The term "devotion" does not seem out of place. On the other hand, there is status to be gained by exhibiting a self-assumed closeness to the deity. The Nazirite is showing others that he or she is a special devotee of Yahweh for a set period of time. The self-assumed variety of Nazirite status, moreover, is not within reach of marginal members of Israelite society, because of the cost of sacrifices integral to the ritual process. To be a Nazirite of the kind described in Numbers 6 is not only to assume holiness by demeanor and behavior but also to declare that one can afford it. This economic feature perhaps cuts against Berlinerblau's suggestion that vows of various kinds often appeal precisely to those "social groups usually categorized under the rubric popular religion."[43] The vow may offer opportunities for members of peripheral groups or people on the socioeconomic margins to make their own "unofficial" appeals to the deity, but vows that involve sacrifice, interaction with the priestly establishment, and the financial means to fulfill the vow point to the interaction between unofficial and official, private and institutional. Such vows appeal to the wealthy. The promise to praise the deity or to give one's son to the service of God better suits Berlinerblau's concept, but even in these cases, the praise, if public, may spill over beyond the private, personal realm, and the son may serve the "official" religious establishment.

The sociohistorical environment that lies behind Numbers 6 is, I argue, the late-biblical Persian period that is the focus of our larger study. While some priestly material in Leviticus and Numbers relating to ritual personnel and accoutrements may well reflect a culture predating the sixth century BCE, I agree with those who date the final form of priestly literature in Numbers to the Persian period, a time when an important set of leaders hold positions with the support of the colonialist Persian government.[44] This connection to the Persians applies not only to the fifth-century leaders Ezra and Nehemiah, but also to a previous generation of leaders mentioned in prophetic works including Zechariah 1–8, such as Zerubbabel and Joshua (see also Ezra 1–4), not to mention Deutero-Isaiah's enthusiasm for Cyrus the Great, whom he describes as a veritable messianic figure. When considering the temporary Nazirite in this context, we want to ask about who in the Jewish community might have had the motivation and wherewithal to take on a vow of this kind and about what the priestly establishment got out of allowing or encouraging some men and women to assume a holy status reminiscent in some respects of priestly status itself.

Haggai sheds some light on the wealthy members of the return community when he complains about people living in paneled homes who do not contribute initially to the rebuilding of the temple (Haggai 1:4). Zechariah refers to wealthy donors who contribute to the crown of the leader (Zechariah 10–11). It would appear then that early returnees were people of means. Other people of means may have been northern Israelites whose elites also had ties with Persian authorities and who apparently thrived during the exile of southern elites.[45] Some of these well-off members of society, northern and southern, seem to have made alliances with members of the hereditary priesthood as well (see Nehemiah 13:7, 28). Also among the well-off are the "people of the land," the local Judean landed gentry, whose economic and social position may have been enhanced during the absence of the king and his cronies. As discussed in the introduction, the political and economic interests of these groups—early returnees, later returnees, northerners, and landed gentry—would have overlapped or collided depending upon the issue. For any of these people, the assumption of Nazirite status may have held personal and public rewards.

C.-L. Seow offers a glimpse of the Persian period socioeconomic environment in which the appeal of temporary Nazirism makes sense. Seow has made a case for the "boom and bust" nature of economic well-being in the Persian period. Drawing upon a range of biblical and extrabiblical sources, he points to the existence of a new middle class, the lively participation in commerce by its members, and the role of a cash economy.[46] This situation led to new wealth but also to economic instability, since today's newly rich could suffer financial ruin tomorrow. The favor of Persian patrons is part of the mix, and such alliances could be fragile and unreliable. In the face of such heady uncertainty, it is understandable that people nervous about their standing would assume the image of a holy person who could take on the heavy financial responsibilities of sacrificial offerings due at the end of the process—a matter of status demanding others' respect. At the same time, the vow no doubt expresses the hope that an act of devotion will encourage the deity's continued support. That women in the Persian period sought to participate in this projection of status and request for divine favor is not surprising and speaks to the theme of women's vows as they relate to gender, power, periphery, and center.

Christine Yoder has pointed to Proverbs 31 as an indicator of women's economic engagement in the Persian period.[47] This paean to the "woman of valor" describes a capable person engaged in cottage craft (31:13), overseeing her complex and wealthy household's economic needs (31:14, 15) and her commercial activities beyond the household (31:16). She is a counterpart to her husband, an elder who sits in the city gate and whose success relates to his wife's capabilities. That women in this period, as well as in the period preceding the exile, had economic and political power is confirmed by the existence of cylinder seals inscribed with women's names.[48] The seals, which indicate ownership and identity, point to women's economic and political power. It is thus imaginable that an adult woman, like men of her class—a woman of means, perhaps a wealthy widow, or any woman of significant resources—would seek to take upon herself a Nazirite vow, and for the same reasons as men, to project status, to perform an act of devotion to Yahweh, to offer thanks as promised for his munificence, or to engage the deity in continued blessing. Why, however, are the priests who provided us with Numbers 6 comfortable with this phenomenon for men and for women?

Holy people can be a challenge to the establishment. There is no reason to assume that the Persian period saw an end to the appearance of charismatic holy people regarded as Nazirites, perhaps vowed by grateful parents or regarded as chosen by the deity.[49] Such figures can rally marginal members of society or form a power base that is an alternative to the establishment, as did the hairy man Elijah. Indeed, in periods of social change such as the time following the Babylonian conquest, charismatic figures of various kinds may become more prevalent, a vehicle for protest.[50] Charismatic Nazirites who never cut their hair could serve as visible symbols of alterity. The hereditary priesthood, which had a vested interest in a particular kind of stability, may have attempted to co-opt Nazirism by making it just another vow, available to men and to women who could afford its responsibilities. The priests themselves oversaw important concluding ritual aspects of the vow process and benefited from the sacrifices owed. But what about the women?

The priestly writers of the Hebrew Bible are in general not supportive of public displays of female religious power. One thinks here of the priestly version of the portrayal of Miriam's supposed pretentions to power in Numbers 12, a view of the female Levite leader that contrasts with her portrayal as prophet, her mention as one of the three heroes of the exodus account (along with her brothers Moses and Aaron), and her inclusion in their genealogy elsewhere (Exodus 15:20–21, Micah 6:4, Numbers 26:59). Of course, not all priestly tradents are necessarily the same, nor might all be as overtly misogynistic as Ezekiel, who develops imagery of the filthy pot that plays upon imagery of women's menstrual blood and a highly charged metaphor of Israel as a whore. In the priestly creation tale of Genesis 1, woman and man are created simultaneously in the image of God. Yet this tale was placed at the opening of Scripture, perhaps with the knowledge that her status would be short-lived, given what follows in the account about man, woman, and the snake. While the possibility of undertaking a Nazirite vow allows a woman temporarily to assume a special and holy status, the fact that Nazirites could now be female might be seen to diminish the role's importance and significance. Even women could take on a vow to live as a temporary Nazirite.

In this way, the hereditary priests seek to transform Nazirism, offering people options for the expression of deep and sustaining religious devotion in a time of change and instability, even while inserting themselves into the vowing process. The priests thus underscore their own unique, inherited status as those who link divine and human, a lifelong condition of holiness rather than a limited assumption of special identity. Moreover, they domesticate Nazirite status, perhaps seeking to neutralize the lifelong, powerful, charismatic, and manly phenomenon exemplified by a figure such as Samson, whose Nazirism, in fact, stems from his mother's interaction with the deity. It has often been noted, in fact, that it is Manoah's wife who first receives the message about Samson, not Manoah himself. It is she who knows about the condition involving hair and she who understands the angel's presence as a blessing and not something to be feared. The husband is not in the loop.[51] In the priestly traditions of Numbers, however, there are protections for upholding male power in the form of conditions placed on the act of vowing itself, and the Nazirite vow as described in Numbers 6 comes under these controls.

Vows are a quintessential example of "personal" religion, since they can, as Cartledge notes, allow a person an unmediated "channel of access to the deity."[52] For Israelite women, vows could be not only private acts of devotion but also a means of self-assertion, a way to express their own desires and identities, apart from husband or father. In dealing with overbearing fathers or husbands, vows of asceticism or vows not to participate in expected patterns of social behavior could be acts of rebellion or signs of passive-aggressiveness. These forms of revolt are sanctioned by the culture, providing ways in which women could use roundabout means to make a point or obtain a goal without direct confrontation. The priestly tradition, on the other hand, insists on reining in this potential display of power by women.

Numbers 30 begins with the reminder that an oath to Yahweh must be fulfilled and cannot be broken. The remainder of the chapter, however, is occupied with women's vows and with circumscribing women's independence in this arena. In this respect, her relationship with the deity, like much else in her life, is within the purview of the men around her.[53] Exceptions to this control are widows and divorcées (Numbers 30:10), as is true with independence as it relates to other aspects of their lives. And so, if a young woman in her father's household vows a vow or takes an oath upon herself, if the father hears of her vow or oath and says nothing (literally, "is silent,"), then the vow stands and she must fulfill it. If, however, he hears about it and he refuses or restrains or forbids her, then the vow does not stand and the deity will forgive the young woman, not holding her to her obligation under the vow. Once she is married, her husband has the same power, should he hear about the vow, to allow or to cancel it. One type of vow is mentioned in this chapter, the vow of self-abuse, usually understood to mean fasting (30:14 [English 30:13]). One wonders whether perhaps she also could vow to neglect her appearance or to refuse to eat a particular food or to participate in festivals or to have sex. These are all issues that later rabbinic material explores vis-à-vis women's vows, for women's vows present a continuing area of interest and concern in the postbiblical period.[54]

What if the husband or the father somehow did not hear about what his wife or daughter vowed? Might he not notice a less obvious vow until it had gone on for months? Of course, in the light of what we explored above about a woman's self-assertion, would the hidden vow adequately accomplish her goals, or is it possible that a secret act of reciprocity between the woman and the deity might make her feel empowered and better able to deal with the conditions of her life? Does Elkanah learn of his wife's vow concerning their son Samuel only after the birth (1 Samuel 1:22)? He acquiesces in her wishes, in deference to her and, perhaps even more importantly, to the deity who controls all blessing (1:23).[55] Would other husbands refuse to give up a son even if his wife had vowed him to God? There could be not-so-subtle pressures at work, fears of denying God his due. God, after all, fulfilled his end of the vowing process, to provide a son to the previously barren wife.

Vowing is thus a powerful medium, but one with ambiguous limits and ambivalent implications for gender roles and relations. Controls surrounding the vow are somewhat porous, and a woman's vow may well be an arena for tension within families as men and the women of their household vie for control, on the one hand, and a display of independence on the other. Numbers 6 and 30 suggest that the priestly establishment recognizes women's traditional power to place themselves under a vow, but this vow is circumscribed for daughters in their fathers' households and wives in their husbands'. In the view of priests, the vows of such women are generally under the control of their men, although as noted above, there may have been ways to keep the vows a secret or ways to force the men to acquiesce, and thereby to engage in genuinely personal expressions of religion. Adult widows and divorcées have the freedom to make vows without fear of abrogation. Including the Nazirite vow under the heading of vows open to women in fact diminishes the unique status of the long-haired, lifelong, charismatic, and divinely selected holy person whose Nazirism is integral to his maleness but whose status, as in the case of Samuel, may result from the vow of a woman.

5 Material Religion, Created and Experienced

Burial Sites, Symbolic Visions, and Sign Acts

An important theme of this book concerns material aspects of personal religion. The introductory chapter explores the engagement with "household religion," "personal piety," and "family religion" in the work of Carol Meyers, Rainer Albertz, Saul Olyan, Theodore Lewis, Susan Ackerman and others.[1] Major recent volumes by Ziony Zevit, Rainer Albertz and Rüdiger Schmidt, and Assaf Yasur-Landau, Jennie R. Ebeling, and Laura B. Mazow point further to the complex and variegated ways in which Israelites and their neighbors experienced and expressed themselves religiously by partaking of what Patricia Cox Miller calls "a touch of the real."[2] Chapters dealing with Qohelet, Job, and the trajectory from incantation to autobiography take account of images of embodiment and emotional state that inform and project the writers' sense of self. The study of vows points to the bodily and material implications of aspects of vowing: the growing of hair, the avoidance of wine and of the dead, the act of fasting. Subsequent chapters point to the physical aspects of visionary experiences and the embodied, emotional dimensions of characterization in Ruth and Jonah. The material and visceral informed and reflected ancient writers' vital concerns and their orientations to life, and were, no doubt, integral to their religious identities as lived, day by day.

Material religion involves the physical body but also objects and spaces, things manufactured by people and held in the hand, and natural and manmade environments. The material dimension contributed to Israelite religious experience throughout its history and across all social groups. The assemblages of pottery buried with the dead, the variously decorated incense

stands, the figurines—some of the most common of which are the ubiquitous female figurines—the references to sacred groves, the burial caves,
the locations within dwellings or work settings in which items related to
household religion have been found are all important to recognize and consider as we contemplate Israelites' cultural identity, links imagined between
themselves and their deity (or deities), and, more widely, the ways in which
they hoped to affect, experience, and make sense of life. The "material" was
an important component of religion in all biblical periods, but surely it
was a vital source of identity, continuity, innovation, and comfort during a
time of nationally experienced stress. Melody Knowles suggests that pil-
grimages to the ruins of the temple may have become a source of physical
engagement with the site as people underwent the rigors of the trip.[3] Jill
Middlemas wonders whether psalms were recited at the ruins of the temple
by those who remained in the land.[4] Both scholars thus emphasize the
possible importance of interaction with a specific physical place. Ephraim
Stern suggests that the absence of female figurines in Judea and Samaria
indicates a change in material religion;[5] others, noting that burials continued at Ketef Hinnom, point to continuity in aspects material religion.

When we think of material religion in ancient Israel, we think of bric-
a-brac of various kinds, instruments, containers such as bowls or beakers,
the walls and benches of burial tombs, and the objects left there—such as
the famous Ketef Hinnom silver amulets, pieces of silver inscribed with
writing, rolled, and probably originally worn on the body, a form reminiscent of later mezuzot. We might think of drawings on walls or objects.
We also need to think of writing, the materiality of writing—writing on
bowls, sherds, amulets, walls, or scrolls made of skin, lead, or precious met-
als, as in the case of Ketef Hinnom. Such writing is often an important
feature of what we might call applied or practical religion, the goal of the
writing being to control or alter a reality for the benefit of the writer or
the person named in the writing or the wearer of the amulet. And often
these words are directed not only to the physical well-being of a person,
but also against those who would harm him, whether human or demonic.
Here we enter the realm where curse, imprecation, incantation, and execra-
tion meet prayer, lament, and confession. As Tzvi Abusch has pointed out
in his work on Mesopotamian *šuilla*-prayers, magic and religion are not to
be considered separate realms.[6] Some in the past have suggested that the
attempt to control chaos via magic suggests a kind of human agency apart
from the all-powerful deities whose concerns and activities occupy a special

transcendent category, over and above such petty realities and pathetic human machinations.[7] While the power of Yahweh in the Israelite context is not to be doubted, evidence from ancient Israel nevertheless indicates that, as in all cultures, the interplay between what used to be called magic and religion is ongoing. Incantations invoke God by name, as do curses, as Theodore Lewis has shown.[8] The deity is symbolized on incense stands, for example, his indwelling presence invoked by a variety of material objects. In a sense, one can conjure him, appeal to him as a familiar. He appreciates the praises humans vow to him, and a kind of reciprocity is involved. The line between vow, prayer, incantation, and lament is thin indeed. Rather, there is a continuum among these related material forms in words. Even in Job, in which the message is about the absolute power of the deity and the message to Job is that he has no genuine agency, there is incantation.[9]

This chapter explores three case studies. First is the burial tomb of Khirbet Bet Lei, which offers information relevant to our period. Scenes of burials are rich in material religion: artwork in the form of drawings at the site, the architectural layout of the space, the natural environment, the treatment of the bodies of the departed, inscriptions carved into walls, and the actions possibly undertaken by the living at these sites, actions implied by the material evidence. A second example is provided by two visions of Zechariah, the sixth-century-BCE prophet. Material objects are seen by a visionary and interpreted to have significance for a particular future—in fact, seen as helping bring it about. These visions portray ritual actions involving the manipulation of material items. A third study involves the sign acts of Jeremiah and Ezekiel in which the prophets engage in purposeful symbolic actions often involving ordinary objects and materials that they arrange, compose, or create, in a kind of performance art.

Burial Sites: Material Religion at Khirbeit Beit Lei

The inevitability of death and the unpredictability of the life span affect the very nature of human identity, one's sense of self, one's engagement with daily reality, and one's attitude to the supernatural. Death shapes essential questions about the nature of human existence, the quality of divine justice, and the limits of life's worth. Death is such a fundamental concern of lived religions that one might be tempted to conclude no death, no religion. And so the treatment of the departed and actions undertaken after their loss provide an essential window on religious identity. Since death is an exceedingly personal and embodied experience, burial sites provide an excellent case study in material aspects of personal religion.

Archaeologists such as Ephraim Stern and Elizabeth Bloch-Smith provide valuable assessments of the architectural contours of burial spaces and their contents, describe the disposition of human remains, and offer suggestions about the dates of the sites based on the style of burial, typology of the pottery, and other criteria of chronology.[10] Work in the field of epigraphy helps us to understand writing on the objects and walls of such spaces and to date these preserved messages. Those who study symbols and iconography help us to appreciate the message and meaning of art found on walls and of objects such as figurines made of various materials, and they draw conclusions from typologies and materials that help determine the dates of these works at sites associated with the dead. Some of the writing and the drawings may have been spontaneously produced and nonprofessional, whereas other writing and objects may have been manufactured by artisans.

A dimension of these sites sometimes neglected by scholars involves the visceral feelings and sensations evoked by the space, the objects, the drawings, and the writing—what can be smelled, seen, touched, tasted. In his study of the origins of the rural cemetery movement in nineteenth-century America, David Charles Sloane, for example, points to the aesthetic and emotional appeal of Mt. Auburn Cemetery, which was said to embrace the "beauty of nature . . . heightened by the care of man."[11] So too, Kristin Ann Hass points to the interactive, physical dimensions of the Vietnam War Memorial in Washington, D.C., designed by Maya Lin: the way in which the shape of the wall envelops the visitor, the way in which the polished granite allows visitors' own images to reflect back to them, the way in which the dead are invested in the site through the names carved into its surface. Visitors are able to experience the wall in a tactile manner, able to touch the names and, in a sense, make contact with the dead.[12] In her study of fragrance bottles found in Jewish burial sites of late antiquity, Deborah Green urges us to think of the sensual dimensions of material substances, about their effect on the living and possible attitudes implied about the sentience of the dead.[13]

The tomb of Khirbet Beit Lei, located eight miles east of Lachish, is rich in material evidence and offers an excellent case study. We want to consider the features of the space, the disposition of the dead, accoutrements that accompany them, pictorial graffiti, and inscriptions. What does this evidence say about attitudes to the dead and about the experiences of visitors to the tomb—their "moods and motivations," to use a phrase coined by Clifford Geertz?[14] Scholars have dated the tomb to the seventh or sixth century BCE.[15] Joseph Naveh points out that benched burial sites similar to Khirbet Beit Lei "are characteristic of the pre-exilic period."[16] A juglet found at the entrance of the tomb is, however, typical of Persian-period pottery.[17] Frank Moore Cross makes a convincing case for an early sixth-century-BCE date for the inscriptions.[18] We might therefore conclude that the burial site was visited by people of the Neo-Babylonian and Persian periods as a location of ritual activity, although it had been established and used in the previous decades, as would be expected of a family burial space. This continuity is indeed a feature of lived religion.

The tomb is carved out of limestone in the slope of a hill. There may have originally been a "carved entryway,"[19] in addition to the antechamber and two burial chambers, each with three benches. What might descending into the tomb have felt like for the living? Would one brush up against the chalky lime walls and leave the place with residue of having been there? Was it cool and musty under the hill? Did one feel as if one were entering an adumbration of the underworld? The carving-out of rooms and benches suggests a home, a parallel realm where the dead reside. The very existence of this burial chamber suggests that its inhabitants were well-off, for poorer folk would have been buried in a simpler, less structurally intensive way, and evidence of their burial is now lost.[20] The juglet found outside at the entrance might suggest the transporting of scented oil.[21] Was the aromatic a gift for the departed, used in a ritual of remembrance, or was it a means of making the inside of the tomb more bearable for the living?

Remains of the deceased have been found laid out on each bench. Archaeologists have concluded that the dead in the southern burial chamber include an elderly person, "a middle aged woman wearing a bronze earring, and a 16–18 year old wearing a bronze ring on a finger of his right hand." The western chamber houses "a 20–21 year old woman with an 11–13 year old child, a middle-aged woman with a 5–6 year old child, and a 16–18 year old."[22] The bones have not been collected or disturbed; some of the dead are buried with jewelry; and upon two benches are older and younger figures. The jewelry suggests, as Elizabeth Bloch-Smith has noted, that the dead were sent off with some of their possessions,[23] things regularly worn close to the skin, and the shared benches suggest the comfort of being laid to rest with kin, perhaps a mother or grandmother at rest with child or grandchild.

Line drawings and inscriptions located on the wall of the antechamber raise additional questions and may suggest possibilities about the religious orientations of those associated with the tombs. Avraham Faust offers an important initial caution: in the hundreds of Iron Age tombs discovered and explored, the presence of line drawings is very rare, "the exception rather than the rule."[24] And so, in examining evidence from Khirbet Beit Lei as relevant to participants' religious orientation, the term "personal" in personal religion seems especially apt. Data thus far does not support the idea that tombs of this period and earlier regularly included drawings. Someone at some point in the history of the site was moved to embellish the cave with certain forms. Subsequent visitors would then have seen the handiwork of the earlier visitors and responded to them, perhaps emotionally or intellectually. It is impossible to know when the drawings were etched or how many hands were involved. Naveh notes that the two standing figures and the one with headgear admit of quite different styles.[25]

It seems unlikely that the etcher was a professional artist, skilled in reproducing traditional forms with an eye to certain aesthetic or artistic considerations. On the other hand, one need not be a professional singer to accurately chant prayers and be considered liturgically adept. It is the content that counts, knowing that content and producing it. And so it is possible that those who etched these drawings were skilled in reproducing certain traditional or symbolic content important in a cultural and religious sense. It is possible that a family member of a person interred at the site played such a role or that someone was hired to do the etchings, but it is also possible, as Cross has suggested, that the drawings, or some of them, were created quite apart from specific funerary ritual activities.[26] What representational traditions do the graffiti invoke, what may be their symbolic messages and meanings, and what meanings might they hold in this setting?

The drawings are as follows: a figure with muscular legs, feet facing one way, face in profile the opposite direction; he appears to hold a lyre.[27] The image is rough, a vertically oriented line drawing that does not reflect fine artistic or aesthetic sensibilities. A second figure stands in profile with raised arms, etched in a similar thin, vertical, line style; perpendicular crossed lines appear at the right of the head.[28] A third figure faces front, carved with deeper, thicker lines and wearing headgear that looks like ibex horns.[29] There are line drawings of two ships.[30] There are also two closed shapes, one a kind of square in a square, crossed into four quadrants with diagonal lines visible in the top two quadrants, which might have met within the figure; a second, more tentlike, is of a pyramidal shape divided into three sections, lines meeting at the top of the figure, with an *X* drawn at the bottom of the middle section and an additional few lines to the right.[31] What to make of these fairly crude graffiti?

The figure with lyre suggests a symbolic introduction of music into the space. Sitting lyre players are common in the iconography of the ancient Levant, and references to the lyre abound in the Hebrew Bible.[32] In her study of the iconography of drawings at Horvat Teiman (Kuntillet ʿAjrud), Pirhiya Beck points to the popularity of lyre-playing figures,[33] although to be sure the painted, seated figure on a large jar at Kuntillet ʿAjrud (Pithos A), with its ornate headdress and a costume that appears to be decorated with a dotted pattern, is more baroque and finer in detail than the line drawing in the burial cave. The role of the iconography on the large vat and the function of the (probably eighth-century-BCE) site itself are not certain. In the case of the tomb at Khirbet Beit Lei, we know that it was a burial site. Music is frequently associated with the numinous, as in 2 Samuel 10:5, in which Saul is told he will encounter a guild of prophets making music, and in 1 Kings 3:15, in which the prophet Elisha asks for a musician in order that he might receive divine communication. If we entertain the possibility that the drawing relates to the burials at the site, we might speculate that musical accompaniment is imagined to ease the pain of death, to mark a passage for the dead and for those who lost him or her, or to summon the positive energy of the deity to the site of eternal rest.

The figure with raised arms is also a common in iconography and suggests a position of supplication or prayer. Side-view figures with raised hands are also found, for example, at Kuntillet ʿAjrud in the row of figures drawn on a large jar (Pithos B). Is the figure at Khirbet Beit Lei invoking the deity, offering himself to the deity in open pose? Does it express the emotions of mourners, hopes that the deity will be with the departed and comfort him, the projected emotions of the dead now committed into the arms of the deity? These questions cannot be answered, but the least one can say is that some message is attached visually to this place of burial, one that is expressed in conventionalized forms but that may have had special meaning for the individuals involved, those who etched the drawing, who saw it, or who shared the space. The crossed-line graffito next to the figure with raised arms is noteworthy. In exploring later Jewish funerary inscriptions of the first to third centuries CE, Catharine Hezser has pointed to

the suggestion that the sign of the X may well have had magical significance, functioning as an amulet for protection.[34] Perhaps the crossed lines
belong to a lengthy iconographic tradition that reaches back into the Neo-
Babylonian and Persian periods.

The drawings of ships are suggestive of a number of later Jewish burial
sites, including the tomb of Jonathan, described in 1 Maccabees 13:26–29
as having been carved with the imagery of ships; the so-called tomb of
Jason, containing two charcoal drawings of ships;[35] and the tombs at Beth
Shearim dating to the third and fourth centuries CE, where images of two
ships were incised into a wall of the tomb. As David Kraemer notes, it
seems unlikely that the ships point to an actual sea or to an activity of the
tomb dwellers. Rather, it seems likely (and we would suggest the same in
the case of Khirbet Beit Lei) that the ships relate to a journey, the journey
of the dead, the great passage.[36] Faust has suggested that the sea and the
seaward side (the westerly direction, from an Israelite perspective) are associated with the land of the dead. Thus, the passage to death is a seaward
or westward journey—hence, the imagery of ships in burial settings.[37]

The most noticeable feature of the deeply incised figure is the headdress with perhaps horns and a beard. Is this image a fanciful, part-human–
part-ibex figure of the sort encountered in the iconography of the ancient
Levant?[38] Does the headdress suggest the power of the horns as symbols of
fertility, warrior prowess, and royal status, a symbolic power rooted in perceptions of actual horned animals? Horned crowns, which indicate princely
or divine power, marked the corners of altars and the thrones of gods and
kings in the ancient Near East. It is because of the power and status associated with horns that the prophet Zedekiah offers his king bronze horns to
take with him in battle (1 Kings 22:11) and that the prophet Zechariah has
a vision of horns that will subdue Israel's enemies (Zechariah 2:1–4). Horns
are metonymic markers of power and the many mythological themes about
victory associated with them.[39] In a burial site, they may suggest both the
power of death and power in the face of death, power when one is most
weak, power for the dead and for those subdued by the death of a loved one.

The closed forms, the square and the more triangular one, are difficult
to interpret. Pyramidal structures are alluded to in the 1 Maccabees description of the tomb of Jonathan (13:28), and the so-called tomb of Jason has
a pyramidal structure on its top.[40] Naveh, inspired by Yigael Yadin, points
to parallels with images in ninth-century-BCE Assyrian reliefs depicting
military camps and perhaps a tent.[41] One wonders whether the triangu-

lar drawings invoke places for the dead, or whether both closed shapes at Khirbet Beit Lei suggest a kind of magic circle (or square or pyramid), closed spaces of protection. Note that crossed lines appear again in the square.

Suggestions concerning the meaning of the drawings in the burial tomb of Khirbet Beit Lei are speculative to be sure, as must be ideas about their origins, artists, and dates. It is, of course, possible that these drawings have nothing to do with funerary customs, as Cross has noted: "The drawings in the cave, human figures and ships, and what we can best label as 'doodling' are inappropriate tomb decorations and hardly come from the hand of mourners or near kin of the deceased."[42]

We have tried, however, to think in terms of material religion, drawing connections to comparable imagery elsewhere in ancient Israel and the Levant and to the symbolic resonances of horns, lyres, and raised arms as they might relate to funerary spaces, concepts, and practices in the culture of ancient Israel. These drawings are now a part of the burial site. Someone buried loved ones in a cave containing these graffiti without trying to efface them, or else someone created these drawings in a place where the dead were already buried or were to be buried. We have tried to ask what such images might have meant to those who etched them and to those who viewed them. Could the act of etching an image into the wall of a burial tomb be a kind of personal ritual pointing to the passage from life to death? Given that drawings are not usually found in Iron Age tombs, could these artworks, in fact, anticipate a trend that became more common among Jews in subsequent centuries? Did a person or persons do something innovative in a Jewish burial space by etching graffiti there, some of which nevertheless reflect widely shared communal traditions and cultural symbols?

Another important material dimension of the tomb space as it now stands is shaped by words, inscriptions etched on the walls of the tomb. Naveh has noted that the root for curse, 'rr, is found in four words on three walls and must be related to the meaning of curse. He writes, "We may hazard a guess that these inscriptions have a magical purpose and were designed to lay a curse upon somebody, perhaps some enemy."[43] Perhaps those who etched the curse language were protecting the deceased or allowing him, like David (1 Kings 2:5–9), to take leave of this world with words of vengeance against his enemies.

Longer inscriptions found in the tomb have been dated by Cross to the beginning of the sixth century BCE, based on the script's similarity to that of the sixth-century Gibeon jar handles.[44] The content of these poetic and often parallelistic lines is particularly interesting, and like the drawings may or may not be related to the burial functions of the cave. Cross reads a request for deliverance, "Deliver [us] O Lord"; a request for absolution, "Absolve [us] O Merciful God! Absolve [us] O Yahweh"; and an oracle in which Yahweh speaks in the first person.

> I am Yahweh thy God
> I will accept the cities of Judah
> And will redeem Jerusalem.

Cross speculates that these petitions to God and his response may have been left by Judeans fleeing from the troubles of the Babylonian conquest, taking refuge in the cave. Their messages to God, requests for forgiveness from sin, and the prophetic-style oracle that promises redemption are all appropriate to such a situation. These writings, inscribed in a holy space where the dead were buried, suggest the power of incantation and the form of the lament with their admissions of human frailty and their requests for divine intervention. Such messages would not have been inappropriate for the dead who rested in the tomb, for those who visited them, or for those who took refuge with them during difficult times. Hopes for absolution and restoration might well have been bound up with mourning and remembrance. If Cross is correct in seeing the writers as refugees, then leaving the homeland location where fellow Israelites were buried involved cultural loss and dislocation, an awareness of one's sin, the ultimate cause of death, and the need for divine redemption.

In these complex ways, Khirbet Beit Lei points to the material aspects of personal religion: the importance of a designated place with descent, walls, benches; the role of the visual and physical in the laying out of the bodies and jewelry worn on the body, the tactile nature of incised drawings and inscriptions, and the meaning and messages of words; the role and experiences of visitors who may have brought a little jug of perfume or who may have taken refuge in or visited a local tomb before fleeing during a time of war. Material religion also informs a number of the prophetic visions from the sixth century BCE, a medium of divine communication that plays upon objects and actions evoking an array of sensory responses.

Visions: Objects and Actions

In the fourth vision of the prophet Zechariah (Zechariah 3), a priestly leader is seen standing between the angel of Yahweh and the "Adversary," the accusatorial trickster figure who appears in the prose narrative of Job.

The deity's words to the Adversary, the troublemaking member of his divine council (3:2), suggest an act of exorcism: "The Lord rebuke you, Adversary!" As noted by Theodore Lewis, the term for "rebuke," *g'r*, is associated with the ridding of demons and the content of incantations in extrabiblical contexts, including the language that introduces a version of the priestly blessing on one of the two inscribed silver amulets found in the burial cave at Ketef Hinnom. Yahweh is described as "the rebuker of [E]vil" who has been called upon to bless the person to whom the amulet belonged.[45]

In the vision scene, the priest undergoes ritual transformation, effected by the change of clothing from filthy vestments, described with a term associated elsewhere in Hebrew Bible with vomit and excrement, to clean ones, described with a term used for festive garments in Judges 14:19. A clean turban is placed upon his head. This ritual passage is interpreted as a removal of guilt (Zechariah 3:4). These symbolic actions thus involve clothing, material markers of identity and status worn on the body. The stone of Zechariah 3:9, moreover, may be an intriguing reference to a rosette worn on the turban of the high priest (Exodus 28:36–38), "engraved with an engraving" or "inscribed with an inscription."[46] This language suggests an amulet inscribed by the deity himself. In this way, the visionary scene experienced by the prophet Zechariah is essentially a rite of passage and a branding, demarcated by new clothing, a stone inscribed by the deity, and a cleansing of evil through the oral medium of ritualized rebuking. This prophetic medium is strongly visual, interactive, embodied, and material. Another vision of Zechariah, rich in qualities characteristic of representations of personal religion in late-biblical literature, is vision seven, which portrays a female figure who is stuffed into a container (Zechariah 5:5–11).

This passage describes a symbolic vision in which seen objects and actions are interpreted as a comment on Israel's contemporary experience or future expectations. An indication that something suddenly emerges in the seer's range of vision is followed by a question or questions about it that are then answered to provide a response about the objects' and actions' identity and meaning. The next chapter more fully discusses this literary form and the ways in which developments in the form reflect changes in religious and literary sensibilities over the course of Israelite history. For the purposes of this chapter, we take note of ways in which the essential and traditional pattern is filled out.

The prophet sees something, asks an angelic being what it is, and is told that it is an *'êphâ*, a grain measure—or more precisely here, a container that holds this measure of grain. A lead weight covers the container. It is lifted, and a woman is seen within. Then comes the interpretation: the woman is wickedness. The interpreter thrusts the woman back into the container and "thrusts the lead stone against its opening" (Zechariah 5:8). Then the vision continues as two winged women, flying and stork-like, lift off the container and take it to Shinar or Babylonia. Once again the visionary scene involves ritual action, the physical trapping of wickedness, and its removal to be enshrined in the homeland of Israel's enemies. This scene evokes the scapegoat ritual of Leviticus 16, in which the sins of the community are symbolically placed on the goat and sent away. The material and embodied dimension of this prophetic experience is underscored by sight itself and by the physical treatment of the woman who is wickedness, her containment. The act of pressing her down and carrying her away is evocative of imagery in incantations in which evil is encased, bound, sealed, rebuked, removed, divorced, or sent away.[47] In fact, the covered container suggests the use of incantation bowls that may have been buried in the floor upside down to keep the evil contained.[48] In this case, wickedness, contained and sealed, is set on its base and housed in Babylon, serving as a symbol of the evil enemies and a source of continuing curse that resides among them.

Sign Acts: Performance Art

A final set of examples is offered by sign acts of the prophets Jeremiah and Ezekiel. The sign act is a kind of performance art in which the prophet, at the command of the deity, acts out his prophecy through the manipulation or creation of material objects and often through particular engagement of the body, making his very person a part of the symbolic message. Like the symbolic vision, the sign act appears in threads of Israelite literary tradition that predate the crises of the sixth century BCE, for example, Hosea 1–3, in which the prophet is commanded to wed a harlot and to give his children particular names. The sign act, like the symbolic vision, is a visually and dramatically rich medium of prophetic revelation. The physical activities commanded and the everyday objects that are destroyed or constructed or worn are then interpreted to predict a future event or to comment on a present situation. As in the practice of sympathetic magic, the prophet's actions and the verbal comments about their meaning help bring about what is predicted.

Jeremiah 13:1–11, in which the prophet Jeremiah is ordered by God to buy a loincloth, is especially striking from a material perspective. A loincloth is a piece of clothing in intimate contact with the body. Jeremiah is ordered to wear it, to never wash it, to remove it and hide it in the cleft of a rock, and then to dig it up. The soiled inner garment that is now corrupted and useless is interpreted as a symbol of Israel's ruin. Israel, which has been unfaithful to Yahweh, is "like this loincloth," which was supposed to "cling" to one's loins as Israel was supposed to cling to God. The people would not listen and so have been ruined (13:11). The term for "cling," *dbq*, can have nuances of a close relationship between partners or amorous connotations (for example, in Genesis 2:24, 34:3), perhaps suggesting the theme of Israel as an unfaithful wife. Again, imagery and vocabulary suggest intimacy, embodiment, and questions concerning clean and unclean. The scene is visceral, physical, and rich in materiality.

In Jeremiah 19:1–13, the prophet is directed to purchase an earthenware jug. He is then directed by Yahweh to deliver a long monologue in the Valley of Hinnom at the entry of the Potsherd Gate. The message is one of disaster, blamed on acts of apostasy, in particular the burning of children as sacrifices to Baal. Punishment will follow, a sacrifice of Judah and Jerusalem in war whereby they will become a feast for the birds and the beasts in a macabre evocation of the banquet motif that concludes the ancient Near Eastern victory enthronement pattern, found as well in Zechariah 9:15, Jeremiah 46:10, Isaiah 34:5–7, and Ezekiel 39:17–20. In an additional ironic twist, the people are told that conditions of siege will become so dire that they will eat their own children and neighbors—more nuances of a macabre feast. Jeremiah is instructed to break the jug: the people and the city will never be mended. The breaking of the jug, an ordinary object, is a ritual enactment that not only represents and predicts a breaking point but also helps bring about the disaster.

A third example of sign act as performance art that beautifully exemplifies material religion is found in Jeremiah 27–28. Yahweh commands Jeremiah to make himself a yoke of straps and bars and to wear the contraption on his neck. The message is to submit to Babylon. Most interesting about this sign act and the yoke is the way in which the symbolic object becomes a locus for bitter political and theological dispute. The prophet Hananiah, who, unlike Jeremiah, supports resistance to the conquerors and regards submission as treason, takes Jeremiah's yoke and smashes it, predicting that the "yoke" of Nebuchadnezzar will be broken in two years. The divine response delivered through Jeremiah takes up the yoke imagery: the broken wooden bars of Jeremiah will be replaced with bars of iron, so severe and absolute will be the Babylonians' control of the ancient Near East. Jeremiah adds that Hananiah himself will be dead within a year, and the passage concludes with an announcement of that prophet's death, underscoring the validity of Jeremiah's prophecy and the true meaning of the yoke.

The sign act of the yoke, like those of the jar and the loincloth, is a powerful example of material religion. Objects are created or purchased; they are worn or broken or sullied. They represent situations, but their manipulation brings events about. Their creation and their use involve a locus of divine communication. Although quite physical and ordinary, the objects and the actions undertaken with them have wide-ranging cosmic and historical implications and become foci for divine intervention in the course of Israelite experience. Sign acts allow for that touch of the real described by Patricia Cox Miller, in which late-biblical writers appear to be especially interested. Prophecy involves verbal communication but also material and visual representation, cameos drawn from physical and tactile experience.

Like Jeremiah, the book of Ezekiel is rich in sign acts involving objects and the body, suggesting the creative composition of performance art. Ezekiel 4 describes the prophet being asked to create a model of a city under siege (4:1–3). The prophet is directed, moreover, to use his own body, stilled in a prone position, to represent the duration of each stage of the Babylonian siege of Jerusalem (4:4–7). Paralysis is imposed upon the prophet by the deity; the prophet's person becomes a sign. One might be tempted to compare Ezekiel's condition with that of shamans or spirit mediums in a trance state. Much indeed has been written on the psychoanalytical dimensions of such behaviors. What interests us here is the physicality of the mode of religious expression and messaging in which the prophet's very body is objectified and made into a symbol reflecting and affecting the events of war.

A second sign act involves the command to manufacture and cook a barley cake on dung to symbolize and predict the people's future way of life as desperate refugees of war (Ezekiel 4:9–15). Food, its preparation, and its consumption, basic material aspects of life, become markers of critical events on a national historical time line, capturing the depressing and visceral experiences of human beings caught up in that history. The sign act in Ezekiel 5 plays upon the significance of hair as a cultural and personal marker of status and identity. Ezekiel is ordered to pass a razor over his head and beard, making himself bald. Baldness is associated with the state of mourning, a situation of personal loss, but is also associated with the loss of status and self, particularly with the loss of manly status as evidenced by the tale of David's emissaries who are sent back to David in a state of humiliation, their beards shaved by an enemy king (2 Samuel 10:4–5). The shaving of Samson's locks is an unmanning that breaks his status as a Nazirite.[49] The shaving of Ezekiel's hair is, however, only the first part of this sign act. His ritual-like manipulation of the hair itself relates to specific messages about the disposition of the Judeans in the coming conquest. Ezekiel is commanded by God to divide the cut hair into three portions: a third is to be burnt in the fire once the siege is completed, a third is to be struck with the sword, and a third is to be scattered to the wind. Then, from this final portion, the prophet is to keep a small number of hairs and sew them into his robe. Some of these are then to be thrown into a fire that will burst forth against all of Israel. The prophet's hairs thus have a powerful, incendiary capacity, dooming the people while evoking mayhem, the predictable realities of war. The message is one of punishment and utter devastation: a third of the people will die in pestilence or by famine, a third will die by the sword, and a third will be scattered (Ezekiel 5:12). In the context of objects and actions ritually combined, the verbal interpretation of the sign act functions as a veritable curse or imprecation. Material, oral, and performative dynamics combine in these examples of personal religion.

Context

This chapter concludes with a question about the appeal of symbolic visions and sign acts in the later works of the Hebrew Bible. Why do these forms appeal to writers who present and preserve prophecies that deal with the conquest, the exile of elites, and the subsequent aftermath and reconstruction? To be sure, symbolic visions in a simple form are found in Amos 7–8 and Jeremiah 11 and 24, and sign acts are described in the investiture of Jeroboam (1 Kings 11:29–32) and in Hosea 1–3 as well. One would have to assume that like the *māšāl* and other verbal art forms, these symbolic media were features of ancient Israelite expressive culture related to predicting or affecting the future and understanding the present. These forms were available to seers of the central establishment and the periphery: available as means of buoying the establishment, as Hananiah attempts to do in usurping Jeremiah's symbol of the yoke, or as a means of resisting it, as in Samuel's interaction with Jeroboam. It cannot be denied, however, that these forms are developed, densely represented, and written about in traditions surrounding and subsequent to the Babylonian conquests of the sixth century BCE. Various explanations might be offered. National crises lead to cultural loss—perhaps the loss of ancient techniques of poetic composition in which classical prophets were trained—but crisis and chaos can also give rise to new creative forms or to a repurposing of traditional ones available to those who would deliver the word of God. Ellen Davis's study of Ezekiel points to the innovative features of that prophet's compositions.[50] Contextual reasons for the appeal of these traditional forms are as old as Israelite culture. The preference expressed in Numbers 12 for direct-word oracles rather than dream interpretation and other means of communication with God, especially those that smack of divinatory ideas and techniques common in the traditions of the ancient Near East, may have always been the point of view of an elitist minority. With tensions in and transformations of the social fabric in the face of invasion, war, and displacement traditional forms survive and flower, becoming a central feature even of elites' compositions that claim to report experiences of God. That these messages are couched in symbolic media requiring interpretation may also point to beliefs about the hiddenness of God, who departs in the face of the people's sin, a matter taken up in chapter six, dealing with visions and the experiential dimensions of late-biblical religion. On some level, these symbolic media lack the clarity of direct-word oracles, the conventional mode of prophecy in the preserved literature of the classical period. Just as the authors of Job and Ecclesiastes question conventional wisdom, Jeremiah, Zechariah, and Ezekiel employ and experience what are, from an eighth-century-BCE elitist perspective, a nonclassical and unconventional means of divine communication, even though these means are very ancient indeed. These forms are so old they are new. They are visual, dramatic, and participatory, creating material links between this world and the other. Such possibilities have always existed in funerary ritual and burial, in the use of curses and incantations, and in popular religious practice. Here the popular defines the prophetic medium.

6 Experiencing the Divine Personally

Heavenly Visits and Earthly Encounters

Building on the work of Rudolph Otto, who explored the nature of the "numinous," the electric and transformative presence of the divine, Ninian Smart, a scholar of comparative religions, urges students of religion to explore the ways in which human beings experience the divine on emotional, visceral, and intellectual planes.[1] Judaism and its ancient precursors in the biblical tradition are sometimes described as pragmatic and this-worldly in orientation, concerned with behavior and with what Smart would call the ethical dimension of religious orientation. The experiential dimension, however, shimmers in the writings of the Hebrew Bible and undergirds many of its recurring literary forms and the worldviews they express. Most interesting for our study of personal religion is the way in which late-biblical examples of these forms emphasize the individual seer, his response, and his particular experience. A diachronic study of two varieties of vision reports points to these directions and developments.

A study of visionaries and their visions exemplifies the interconnections between official and unofficial religion and between private and public religious expression and points to the conventionalized literary traditions that characterize literary manifestations of personal religion in ancient Israel. Within this framework, we trace two sets of biblical texts: descriptions of visits to God's realm, the divine council, and descriptions of a particular type of vision, the symbolic vision. In each case, a trajectory of texts reveals not only synchronic aspects of Israelite religion but also its diversity. These examples of the experiential dimension reflect patterns and changes in Israelite social, political, and intellectual history as well as aesthetic and theological developments that point to the ancient writers' interests in the representation of individual experience.

As Susan Ackerman noted in her 1992 monograph on popular religion in sixth-century-BCE Judah, it has long been axiomatic in biblical studies to draw a sharp contrast between the religion of the commoners and the religion of the elite, a position that Ackerman deftly contests.[2] Similarly problematic is a related dichotomy between "official" and "unofficial" religion suggesting, for example, that during the Judean monarchy, the official Jerusalem cult was centralized, whereas praxis at other sacred spaces exemplified unofficial religion, or that the institutional religion professed by priestly sources was strongly aniconic, whereas examples of unofficial or popular religion may suggest the use of icons. Some biblical polemics have been seen as condemnations of popular religious practices viewed as renegade by "mainstream" or official biblical writers. As Ackerman, Peter Brown, Arnaldo Momigliano, and others have emphasized, however, and as our work with incantations, vows, sign acts, and other media have indicated, the boundary between official and unofficial, popular and institutional, vulgar and elite, is a porous and artificial one.[3] To suggest a clear demarcation is to deny the overlap and synergy between and the diversity among modes of religious expression in ancient Israel. Then as now, popular and even peripheral practices influenced and informed "central" ritual, and elites or representatives of the central religious leadership in turn influenced and no doubt participated in popular beliefs and practices. Biblical polemics may well reveal the views of the few, preservers of particular biblical texts. Israelite religion as lived, however, may have included the very beliefs and behaviors condemned by the writers. By the same token, many key features of worldview and practice were, no doubt, shared by Israelites, rural and urban, commoner and aristocrat, those outside of the power structure and political insiders.

Biblical descriptions of divine realms and encounters present a paradox. On the one hand, they appear to reflect unique, individual, powerful experiences. On the other, they partake of culturally shared conceptions of such religious experiences. Reports of visions or descriptions of a divine realm reveal and reinforce socially embraced expectations concerning the otherworldly. Moreover, imagery, events, and responses are expressed in conventionalized or formulaic language. They are products of culture and of tradition.

In exploring religious symbols, Gananath Obeyesekere emphasizes the complex ways in which the personal intertwines with the public and the cultural. For a female mystic he interviewed in Sri Lanka, her long matted hair is "personal" and has to do with her life experience, her "anxieties," "psychology," and "idiosyncrasies."[4] Social context, however, is also critical to the meaning of the hair; if there were not certain assumptions and expectations concerning hairstyle in Sri Lanka, where the mystic lived and developed, her personal response to her own hair might differ considerably.[5]

The workings of religious symbols, patterns, and language thus reveal an interplay between the personal and the sociocultural. A symbol such as the divine throne, an image of the deity or an angel, a chain of events such as an initiation process, and the words in which these may be described by the seer, as well as the words he or she may hear in the vision, all have personal meaning. They are mediated through individual consciousness, emotions, and life experiences. But in the language employed, the imagery created, and the constellations of motifs assembled, the individual experience is also mediated through culture and tradition.

When reading a biblical vision text that is rich in the experiential, for example, we do well to ask about the emotional and personal experience of the seer as well as the cultural media that make such an experience believable to him and to the audience that receives his report. This suggestion raises other, related questions. Did ancient Yahwists believe in the possibility of vision experiences? Do the biblical writers consider their reports to be of "real" visionary events? Or rather, do composers and receivers of these now-literary traditions agree that such vision forms are conventionalized and staged media used to frame certain kinds of meanings and messages? I think we can assume that reports of having had such experiences were culturally believable, even while the contours of those experiences and the reports of them were shaped by conventions of content, language, and plot.[6]

The closest many of us come to experiencing visionary experiences in our daily lives may be in dreaming. Even for contemporary, rationalistic post-Freudians, dreams can be powerful, transformative, intensely personal experiences that immerse the dreamer in an alternate reality that may shed light upon and influence waking experience. In the cultures of the ancient Near East, dreams were accorded varying degrees of respect as divinatory and prophetic media. As with religious symbols, the contents of dreams are rooted in individual life experience, in the very nature of human psychology, and in the dreamer's culture. Symbols and scenes recur in people's dreams, leading ancient scholars of Assyria, Egypt, and elsewhere to prepare lists of dream omens. The interpretation of dreams became a divinatory science, as was reading the flight patterns of birds, the entrails of animals, and the shapes of rising smoke.[7] Specific techniques of interpretation include idea association and word association; in this way, dream interpretation shares a border with the later rabbinic activity of midrash, whereby the words and imagery of biblical texts provide a medium to be decoded. One sees glimpses of this mantic activity in tales of Joseph, a wise man who has dreams that relate to his future and the future of his family and who has the ability to interpret the dreams of others. In the beautifully composed bildungsroman about Joseph, dreams have an important narrative function, both foreshadowing the hero's career and leading directly to his elevation as pharaoh's vizier and as savior of his own people. To dream and to understand dreams are presented in a positive light, signs of God-sent wisdom and a special connection to the deity who makes possible both the dreams and the capacity to interpret them. This set of stories, which is in the "official" canon, reflects general beliefs about the efficacy and usefulness of dreams in popular cultures, ancient and modern. Abraham, venerable patriarch, is pictured in Genesis as receiving God-sent messages and visions in a divinely induced deep sleep, a trancelike state (14:12). Jacob receives important information from God via dreams (Genesis 28:12, 46:2). Positive assessments of dreams as having prophetic content and indicating communication with the deity are, however, not uniform in the Hebrew Scriptures. And as one might expect, dreams share a conceptual border with visions that are received in a waking state, phenomena we might call paranormal experiences or events. Both mark a boundary between reality and meta-reality, the earthly and the divine, and both are sudden intrusions into the mundane, uncontrollable in content, often richly symbolic in meaning, and open to interpretation. There is also a thread of biblical texts that belittles or condemns dreamers, dream interpreters, and visions. Attitudes to visionary experiences, in fact, reveal interesting ambivalences and tensions among ancient Israelite writers.

Numbers 12:6–8 serves in context as propaganda in favor of the levitical power of Moses, whose status is said to transcend that of Aaron and his descendants and of priestly groups claiming descent from Miriam, the female levitical sibling. A message about leadership is intertwined with one about forms of revelation. Speaking "face to face," as God does with Moses in direct-word oracles, is preferable to other forms of divine communication, that is, messages mediated by dreams and visions, visual rather than auditory media. Implicitly, overt messages are preferable to symbolic content, to "riddles" (literally, that which is turned aside or indirect, dark speech), visions, and dreams, which are grouped together as media that need to be interpreted in order to be understood. The direct-speech mode of experiencing the divine dominates in the preserved oracles of the classical prophets, who speak in richly formulaic speech and patterns of content. Dreams and visions, however, are not entirely rejected. Warnings to beware of these visual forms of divine communication suggest, in fact, their cultural vibrancy and currency throughout the history of Israel. Criticisms are leveled by biblical writers against the improper use of dreams and visions, singling out those whose visions and dreams reveal only their own imagination or mind (literally, their "heart") rather than the message of God (Jeremiah 23:16; Ezekiel 13:2, 17). False seers produce vapor or delude (Jeremiah 23:16 [New Revised Standard Version]). Their message is wrong, that is, it does not reflect the critic's own view of God's wishes (Jeremiah 27:9). Their dreams misinform: "In falsehood they prophesy to you in my name. I did not send them." (Jeremiah 29:8; see also Ezekiel 13:6, 7).

Deuteronomy 13:2, 4, 6 equates the prophet with the dreamer: If this person, prophet, or diviner of dreams tempts you to go after other gods, you must not follow. These dreamers and prophets are deserving of death for speaking treason (13:6), but their worthiness entirely depends on the content of the dream and its application. The scene in 1 Kings 22:19–23 underscores some of these matters concerning true and false prophecy as they emerge in a vision experience. The spectrum that spans the official and the unofficial, the individual and the cultural, and the unique and the formulaic, is also at play in this passage, an example of the visit to the divine council, a case study in experiencing the divine.

Case Study: The Divine Council

One important set of biblical materials dealing with the experiential dimension describes the physical presence of a human being inside the realm of the sacred; he has somehow been transported to the divine throne room, where he observes and interacts with holy beings, including some manifestation of the deity himself. Divine-council scenes are common stock in the epic literature of the ancient Mediterranean world. In its most frequent form, the chief deity, who makes decisions regarding groups and individuals, war and peace, is surrounded by fellow celestial beings, including his advisers and sometimes his adversaries or rivals. This cross-cultural constellation of motifs, including the king-like figure, his retainers, the conversation, and actions, is specified in an Israelite prophetic medium. The seer, a human being, is transported to the heavenly realm, where he observes the scene or hears the conversation and often participates in the action. Isaiah 6, Ezekiel 1–4, and Daniel 7 offer a chronological trajectory from the eighth to the second centuries BCE. The accounts in 1 Kings 22 and Exodus 24 are more difficult to date, but all these texts present a shared type, and increasing complexity comes to characterize the style of datable versions. Certain variations and trends emerge in views of the deity and the experience of the seer or human participant.

The simplest (though not necessarily earliest) version is found in Exodus 24:9–11, in which Moses, Aaron, Nadab, Abihu, and seventy of the elders ascend to the divine realm after the escape from Egypt and the formative scene at Sinai. Exodus 24:9–11 alludes to a banquet, an appropriate motif to conclude the victory-enthronement pattern that characterizes the escape from Egypt, the defeat of the Egyptian enemy, and the enthronement on the mountain, "God's sanctuary," as described poetically in Exodus 15. This same pattern is found in ancient Near Eastern creation epics such as the Mesopotamian *Enuma Elish* and the Ugaritic tale of Baal and Anat, in which the enemy is death or chaos and the new order is celebrated by a gathering of deities and feasting. In Exodus 24, the world of God is "above"—one ascends (24:9). The deity is visible—he has feet (24:10)—and the human guests behold him. The seeing is described in two verbs (24:10, 11), one of which, *ḥzh*, is related to an ancient term for "prophet," as suggested by the biblical author at 1 Samuel 9:9. The environment appears to be tactile, though more luminously pure than anything on earth—"like the image of sapphire tile-work," like the "very substance of heaven" (24:10). A feast is provided as the guests commune with God in an important symbolic representation of their relationship. The deity, the powerful warrior seen in the electric, volcanic presence at Sinai, where the people and even ritually pure priests are warned to keep their distance lest he lash out against them, here welcomes the feasters. The author emphasizes that God does not lay a hand upon them, although they are in his very realm. Indeed no supramundane counselors are present. Human beings play the role of those invited to dine at God's behest, but this is no randomly selected set of people; they are leaders, people of inherited status. The image and role of the elites, Levites and elders, is thereby asserted and enhanced. Such establishment authors may well lie behind this particular use of the traditional scene.

The divine council appears in 1 Kings 22:19–23 in a more theatrical version. An auditory as well as visual dimension is included, and the narrator is not the anonymous biblical voice but the prophet himself, who is lifted into the scene depicting the deity surrounded by heavenly beings, and who reports what he observes. This version of the type, as contextualized, points to the sliding scale between central and peripheral, establishment and anti-establishment, as it emerges in descriptions of the experiential.[8]

The author pictures a contest between royal prophets—who predict victory and urge the Israelite king Ahab and his southern ally, Jehoshaphat, to go to war against the Aramaeans—and the outsider Micaiah, who predicts military failure. Micaiah establishes his divinatory credentials by revealing an experience of the divine council in which he learns about the inevitable defeat. The experiential thus validates his message. The council scene is clearly imagined to be culturally recognizable and believable by all who hear the report; the vision is a source of spiritual capital and has efficacy. There is no bifurcation between "popular religion" and "official religion." Ahab at first resists hearing from the prophet Micaiah, and as the king had feared, the scene provides the prophet's bona fides. He is a "fly on the wall" who observes the archetypal king-deity enthroned, surrounded by his heavenly courtiers, the hosts or armies of heaven to his right and left. In the scene, the spirits speak, revealing the divine plan to entice Ahab to his final battle via a lying spirit placed in the mouth of the king's prophets. The message of the vision suggests that prophets such as Zedekiah, whom Ahab trusts and wants to believe, are wrong. The king will be defeated and will die in battle. Micaiah's vision experience both accurately predicts the future and, in a sympathetically magical way, helps bring it about. As in the case of dreams and visions, not all prophecies are accurate. God may send miscues in order to fulfill his larger purpose. While validating the role of the peripheral prophet Micaiah, whom the royal leaderships hates, the vision as a whole casts doubt on the prophetic enterprise itself. There is no sure way to know the will of God. The connection with the divine realm is always tenuous and fraught with uncertainty.

In Isaiah 6, the divine-council experience serves as the eighth-century-BCE prophet's initiation as a seer of God. This more expansive version of the scene outlined for Exodus 24 and 1 Kings 22 includes a dateline and seeing the anthropomorphized deity sitting on his throne, the train of his robe filling the temple or palace. His courtiers are six-winged seraphim who cover his (or their) face and feet, and fly. They call to one another in divine song. There is loud noise, smoke, and vibration, and finally a purification ceremony in which the prophet is cleansed of his sin via a burning coal put to his mouth. He then volunteers to deliver the deity's message of doom. A human being not only provides a first-person report of the vision and serves as a witness, as in 1 Kings 22, but also participates in the activities of the divine realm. The divine realm and the heavenly leader evoke not only the powerful fiery forces of nature but also the architecture, dress, and retinue of earthly monarchs. Human institutions thus parallel the divine, and the heavenly realm gives validation to the earthly; special people are acknowledged to be immersed in the very essence of the heavenly realm. The scene is more baroque than those in Exodus 24 and 1 Kings 22, and a greater role is provided for the human participant. Pietistic and mystical experience is implicit. The prophet has been personally transformed: this eighth-century vision provides a perspective on personal religion represented in the First Temple period. These traits are even more pronounced in Ezekiel 1–4, the vision of the sixth-century-BCE prophet-priest Ezekiel.

The traditional pattern of content seen in Isaiah 6 recurs. There is a dateline (Ezekiel 1:1), a rubric indicating an encounter with the divine (1:3), a vision of the deity enthroned (1:26), a description of his courtiers and surroundings (1:4–28), a commission (2:1–7), and a ritual initiation or transformation (2:8–3:3). The prophet speaks in the first person, an important marker of works we are exploring within the framework of personal religion. The author, as in Isaiah 6, is overtly self-referential, assuming a self-representational voice. The recurring core of the vision that opens Ezekiel not only reflects a shared tradition but also is flexibly adapted to suit the prophet's sixth-century-BCE message and aesthetics, his individual experience and personal orientation to life. Ezekiel's use of this form reflects and shapes a particular view of the prophetic role and an attitude to the relationship between the divine realm and the human realm.

The scene is altogether more baroque than previous examples. God's chariot throne is described in mesmerizing, mystical detail, and understandably becomes an iconic focus of later Jewish mystical speculation. We hear the chariot's rumbling wheels and see them whirling, the rims full of eyes (Ezekiel 1:18, 3:13). The divine courtiers are similarly described in detail, wings brushing (3:12–14), mysteriously moving, associated with fire and shiny materials such as burnished bronze; alternatively, the wings sound like mighty waters, thunder, an army (1:24). Sounds are more lushly described and less controlled than the artful singing in Isaiah. The author revels in metaphor and simile. The creatures are imaginative combinations of beings, dreamlike and reminiscent of ancient Near Eastern iconography. God is tactile and felt (3:14, 8:3). Emotion and the experiential dimension are enhanced. At the sight of a kind of magnificent splendor that the prophet identifies with "the appearance of the likeness of the glory of the Lord," Ezekiel falls on his face, seemingly overcome (1:28). A spirit enters his body and stands him up. He can feel and hear it (2:2). He is physically lifted up, and behind the glory of the Lord he hears loud noise, the sound of the wings of the creatures that surround the divine chariot, the iconic representation of divine presence. He mentions "bitterness in the heat of my spirit, the hand of the Lord being strong upon me" (3:14). These are visceral descriptions of the experiential, how things look and feel physically and emotionally. At the same time, paradoxically, the divine realm is more transcendent and distant from human cognition and capacity to comprehend. The vision reveals "something like four living creatures" (1:5), the wheels have "an appearance like the gleaming of beryl" (1:16), above the dome over the heads of the living creatures was "something like a throne," and above the likeness of a throne is "something that seemed like a human form" (1:26). All is indefinite: something like, something having the appearance of, something that looked like. As Robert R. Wilson has noted, this very indefiniteness is central to Ezekiel's worldview.[9] There is no direct encounter as in Exodus 24, 1 Kings 22, and Isaiah 6. Rather, the sacred realm is seen through a glass darkly; it is utterly "Other," distant, a metahistorical reflection of reality. The prophet's immersion in this other world has a trancelike quality. God is farther away from human comprehension, and the son of man can only obliquely describe the ineffable quality of the heavenly realm, reporting the encounter in the pathetic and limited medium of human perception and speech. Even so, he interacts with the scene, becoming part of this mythic reality.

This trajectory of visions that picture the divine council beautifully reinforces suggestions gleaned from studies of the experiential dimension of religion explored at the opening of the chapter. The constellation of motifs is rooted in a formulaic, conventionalized set of material, and yet each contributor to the tradition draws upon this set creatively, adapting it to his message in the context a particular sociohistorical situation. Thus, we see Ezekiel reflecting the uncertainty of the period of the exile of elites such as himself; the Babylonian threat is perceived by him as punishment and alienation from God. God is harder to perceive than ever. The enhanced emotional dimension reflects a different aesthetic from that of the eighth-century-BCE prophet; a more baroque aesthetic is at play, and a more personal engagement. The narrative dimension of the visionary experience is deepened by descriptions of the place where the prophet sees the vision (Ezekiel 1:1–3) and by the windswept, stormy setting of the scene (1:4). The physicality of being lifted up (3:12), of feeling God's hand (3:14), of experiencing emotions of awe (1:28) and bitterness (3:14), point to the way in which the tradition is rendered personal and internalized.

There is, moreover, no divide between official and unofficial religion throughout the use of this form. Exodus 24 pictures the quintessential community leaders mystically taken up, the kings of 1 Kings 22 fear and implicitly believe what the peripheral prophet Micaiah sees, the eighth-century-BCE Isaiah, a central prophet with close ties to the monarchy, offers his bona fides in a visionary report, and Ezekiel, a priest of the Jerusalem establishment, receives the most baroque and otherworldly vision of all. The medium itself thus spans dichotomies between official and unofficial religion, unique and formulaic, and personal and cultural, even while serving as a mirror of the history of ideas reflected in and shaped by Israelite literary tradition. A similar trajectory characterizes texts in the form of the symbolic vision.

Symbolic Visions

An essential pattern of content characterizes symbolic visions, one rooted in a larger ancient Near Eastern tradition of divination, means by which people on earth discern the future planned by the divine powers. Texts from the eighth-century-BCE Amos, the sixth-century-BCE prophet Jeremiah, the late-sixth-century-BCE Zechariah, the second-century-BCE Daniel, and a host of postbiblical pseudepigraphic works include shorter and longer versions of the following motifs: an indication of a vision experience involving language of seeing or showing; a description of certain objects or images; questions asked about what is seen; and a response that explicitly interprets or more obliquely comments on the significance of sights in the opening vision. This trajectory of texts, however, offers a similar challenge to the dichotomies posited to lie between official and nonofficial religion, elite and popular religion, discussed in connection with the divine-council scenes, and also points to the spectrum from personal to cultural, unique to formulaic, that encompasses and frames the broader visionary tradition. The increasingly emotive, baroque, and narrative qualities of these examples of the experiential dimension point to the aesthetic and sociohistorical developments seen in our first case study. A key theme is the increasing hiddenness of God and the accompanying election of the seer and his group, who are uniquely and selectively allowed knowledge of the machinations of the divine realm as they apply to the future of the cosmos.

The pattern of this literary form exhibits stages from simpler to more complex. Amos 8:13 provides a good example of a simplest stage (see also Amos 7:7–9, Jeremiah 1:11–12, Jeremiah 24). God is the interlocutor in this version; he asks the question, allowing the seer to repeat the description of the seen objects, and God provides the interpretation. The seen objects are simple, everyday items, in this case, a harvest basket or a basket of summer fruit, and the interpretation is achieved via the divinatory technique of wordplay, since the term for "summer," an end point in time, plays upon the word for "end," a cutoff point in time: "Come has the end to my people Israel" (8:2). Repetition of language is dense in the brief format, the style economical. The interpretation of the vision helps, in a sympathetically magical way, bring about its prediction; meanings are clear, and the symbols correspond directly to their interpretation.

Zechariah 6:1–8, exemplifying a second stage in the development of this form, introduces further complexity and important nuances.[10] Questions and answers play a role, but now an angelic interpreter is introduced. The seer, more interactive than Amos, asks the questions. The reader is thus drawn to the person of the seer, to his voice and concerns. What is initially seen, moreover, is no mere mundane basket, as in Amos 8:1–3, or plumb line, as in Amos 7:7–9, or basket of figs, as in Jeremiah 24, but dramatic, motion-filled horse-drawn chariots coming forth from cosmic mountains of bronze (Zechariah 6:1). These are interpreted to be synonymous with the four winds of the earth, which "wait upon the Lord of the whole earth," a phrase suggestive of the divine council. Whereas Isaiah 6 and Ezekiel 1–3 suggest an ascent to the divine council, Zechariah 6 suggests the descent of divine emissaries to earth. Having been given leave, they go forth to traverse the world and set down God's spirit in the land of the north, a possible reference both to actual historical enemies and to a more mythical nether land. The seer thus describes his hopes for a rehabilitated Judean kingdom, made possible by the defeat of Babylonia and the return of elites to the holy land in the late sixth century BCE. He pictures himself made aware of the activities of divine servants in the cosmos, and he interacts with an angelic messenger. The relationship between symbol and meaning is integral and deeply mythological in the way that the Mesopotamian goddess Tiamat in the *Enuma Elish* is the sea.

Daniel 7 and 8 exemplify the most ornate version of this form in the Hebrew Scriptures and anticipate late usages in works such as 2 Baruch and 4 Ezra. The opening symbols of Daniel 7 provide not merely a cameo scene but also a cosmogonic narrative in which dreamlike beasts emerge from a troubled sea. The beasts are metahistorical representations, some of which scholars have linked to a shared stock of ancient Near Eastern astrological and other iconic symbols.[11] The visionary is immersed in a divine-council scene at verse 9, so symbolic vision and divine-council scene combine as anticipated in the visions of Zechariah. Once again, we see the deity on a throne. As in Ezekiel 1–3, motifs of fire and wheels are present, and the deity, pictured in Daniel as a white-haired Ancient One, reminiscent of El, head of the Canaanite pantheon, sits in judgment surrounded by his thousands of minions.[12]

The beasts are interpreted to mean four kingdoms, a stock motif found as well in ancient Persian and Greek sources.[13] The passage of kingdoms describes a historical trajectory leading down to the time of the text's composition. It is a fiction of the past, since Daniel 7, a work of the Hellenistic era, assumes a date as if anticipating the coming of each of these historically antecedent kingdoms. It is important for our purposes to note, however, that the given interpretation of the vision's scenes of enthronement and judgment is as difficult to understand as the dream symbols; correspondences between symbol and interpretation are not simple or direct. The message of the symbolic vision is even more encoded than those in Amos and Zechariah; the interpretation raises as many questions as it answers. Who exactly are the holy ones, for example (Daniel 7:18, 22, 25, 27)? The increasingly complex symbols and difficult-to-comprehend interpretations are a filtering medium suggesting great distance between the unknown and the knowable. Meanwhile, narrative detail and emotional dimensions are greatly enhanced. The dream nuance becomes more explicit when compared with the brief mention of seeing in the night in Zechariah, and this nuance provides a more detailed setting for the narrative. The seer, moreover, expresses fear, describing his anxious spirit and his state of dismay (7:15). He concludes his account, "As for me Daniel, my thoughts greatly alarmed me and I went pale, but the matter I kept to myself" (7:28). Similarly, after the visionary description in chapter 8, the author concludes, "I, Daniel, was exhausted and was ill for day. Then I arose and did the king's business, but I was appalled by the vision and did not understand it" (8:27). It is important that the seer reiterates his name, "As for me, Daniel," "I, Daniel." One begins to get a sense of the lead character in this narrative, his daily activities, his shock in response to the mysterious vision, his feelings of emotional and physical depletion. The vision thus incorporates and extends a motif of theophany, an ancient experiential form.

The symbolic vision form clearly exists in its simplest version in classical prophecy and becomes a much more common medium in postexilic material, dominating Zechariah and playing an important role in Daniel and a number of postbiblical examples, including 2 Baruch and 4 Ezra. Why and how this particular revelatory medium became so popular in the Second Temple period and beyond reflects changes in setting, worldview, and aesthetic sensibilities, and an accompanying attention to the individual.

The symbolic vision emphasizes that God is distant; visual messages must be decoded to be understood. As in the divine-council scene of Isaiah 6, the seer himself becomes part of the vision. He takes a role in the drama, a character in this visionary narrative, and the narrative becomes complex and elaborate, allowing him to play a large part. The mythic realm implicit in the scene is present and visceral. In the latest examples we explored, from the book of Daniel, only the select few receive these visions. Rather than shout forth revelation, as in the case of the classical prophets, the seer keeps the matter in his mind (Daniel 7:28) or is told explicitly to "seal up the vision" (8:26). The message is for the saved alone, and Israel is no longer perceived as a whole community that rises or falls together. The real Israel that receives revelation is thus perceived as more and more circumscribed as symbolic visions become the medium of apocalyptic.

The trauma of exile as experienced by elites, the perceived potential of God to hide himself, increasing sectarianism in Israelite self-definition, an increasing emphasis on the religious experience of individuals, and perhaps also a loss of those institutions that supported the passing-down of techniques of creating classical poetic oracles all lead to the popularity and preservation of symbolic visions. As noted above, even the most ornate versions of the symbolic vision are not a wholly new form. They are a medium found in the writings of the classical prophet Amos and reach back into forms of divination practiced in a variety of ancient Near Eastern cultures over a lengthy period of time. Divination in certain forms was the purview of learned elites, but we would be mistaken if we saw any of the visionary material shaped and preserved by scribal elites as merely reflecting their own circumscribed worldview without reference to ancient Israelite religion as lived by ordinary people.

The texts were contoured within a written, literary tradition preserved by the few, but they testify to a host of general perceptions of the divine world and its relationship to the lives of people across the social spectrum who participate in and contribute to Israelite culture. There is a heavenly realm that parallels in many ways the sacred spaces created by human beings on earth. God is not alone in that realm but has a retinue. Seers are capable of envisioning the heavenly throne room and of experiencing divinely sent visions on earth. Some visions, like the many biblical theophanies, divine appearances on earth, are nonsymbolic, whereas others require interpretation in order to be understood, and the interpretative technique is related to the use of dream omens to divine the future, a specialized skill, but one about which all Israelite dreamers were no doubt aware. There is, moreover, a large fund of culturally shared, traditional patterns and motifs: the way that vision experiences go, the sorts of symbols that have meanings. The council scenes, the symbolic visions, and their contents are pancultural communicative phenomena. In exploring genres in the experiential dimension, we thus point to a border shared by popular and elitist cultural threads, by uniquely individual sensibilities and socially shared expectations. These forms allow us to trace theological and intellectual currents among the framers of the Hebrew Bible while pointing to shared aspects of Israelite belief. The vision forms may be, at the same time, both radical and conservative, built as they are on long-standing, traditional motifs and patterns of thought, and they provide another case study in representations of the individual.

7 Characterization and Contrast
Dynamics of the Personal in Late-Biblical Narration

In their reports of experiential events, the visionaries of late-biblical texts express emotions and more fully become characters than do earlier seers. Several examples of late-biblical narration that fall more clearly under the heading of story, exhibiting a plot that moves from problem to solution, reveal additional important nuances relevant to the discussion of personal religion and the representation of individuals. We begin with the book of Ruth, a work related to and revealingly different from the tale of Tamar in Genesis 38.

Ruth and Tamar: Contrasts

To appreciate the special engagement with characterization in Ruth, it is useful to employ the tale of Tamar as its foil, paying special attention to the quality of its language, its texture, and the pieces of content that the language expresses, its text. In content, the tale of Tamar shares a good deal with the story of Ruth.[1] Both women are young childless widows who take their futures into their own hands and find a male protector to father their children, thereby integrating themselves into a secure patriarchal setting, and both successfully bear children, thereby reinforcing and enhancing their position in the clan. The link between the women is made explicit in Ruth when the people and elders at the gate offer Boaz, her husband-to-be, a blessing that says in part, "May your house be like the house of Perez whom Tamar bore to Judah" (4:12). Whether or not the author of Ruth explicitly based his story on that of Tamar, Ruth is a homage to tradition, including a conscious comment on the Davidic genealogy; the two tales and the two women are linked. It is striking, however, how different these stories are in texture, tone, and religious orientation. While the tales share certain views of gender, a typical biblical agrarian setting, and aspects of plot, a comparison of the two narratives points to the ways in which Ruth, in particular, relates to the study of personal religion in the Persian period.

The date of the composition of Ruth has been debated by scholars for decades, and we begin with some comments on the work's probable socio-historical setting. Arguments about dating have been made on the basis of vocabulary and linguistics—for example, the presence of supposed Aramaisms or archaisms—and on the basis of content and theme, for example attitudes to Moabites, views of intermarriage, and questions about the levirate law. While some, like Edward L. Campbell, argue for a date during the monarchy, others, such as André Lacoque and Bernard M. Levinson, date Ruth to the Persian period.[2] The two essential positions and the evidence are nicely outlined in the recent commentary on Ruth by Tamara Cohn Eskenazi and Tikva Frymer-Kensky. They conclude that the consensus of contemporary scholars supports a Persian-period date but that earlier or later dates cannot be ruled out with absolute certainty.[3] I agree with the consensus regarding a late date for Ruth, but what I find most interesting and revealing falls under the headings of texture and text, that is, style, the very way language is used, and content, that is, the way scenes are framed, characters are created, plots progress, and information is provided in Genesis 38 versus the book of Ruth.

Genesis 38 provides an excellent example of the trickster tale. The protagonist, Tamar, finds herself in a marginal condition, a childless widow who has been denied the benefits of levirate marriage. She is in this desperate situation because of wrongdoing by her first husband, now dead, and by the brother-in-law who was to raise children in his deceased brother's name (see Deuteronomy 25:5). The former is simply described as evil and as having been killed by God. The wrongdoing of the second son is avoidance of the obligation to father his brother's sons, a custom designed both to keep the deceased brother's name and essence alive and to provide a patriarchal connection and protection for the woman he had taken as wife.[4] God punishes the second son also with death, leaving Tamar without husband or child. Judah, her father-in-law, sends her back to her own people, promising to arrange for her marriage to his third son at some later time. He is perhaps understandably reluctant to let his only remaining son wed a twice-made widow, and he delays fulfilling the levirate obligation.

Tamar addresses her situation of marginality via deception and disguise. She dresses as a prostitute, appropriately stationing herself at a crossroads, and attracts Judah's attention. He avails himself of her services, leaving as a pledge of payment his staff, his seal, and the rope that holds the seal. Like Cinderella's glass slipper, these are recognition tokens, and are brought forward by the heroine when, pregnant by Judah, she is accused of adultery and sentenced by him to death. The tokens prove that he is the source of the pregnancy, and he admits his own culpability in not providing his remaining son as groom. Tamar's position in the clan is regularized and her status established as she gives birth to twins. The trickster content pattern consisting of marginalized state, trickery, and, finally, increase in status is clear.

The structure of the narrative reflects a formulaic and conventionalized traditional plot. A creative author employs the trickster pattern to convey his own messages. He is perhaps a northern writer who paints a negative and mocking portrait of the ancestor hero of the Judeans. His account reinforces the important place of the levirate law in a patriarchal culture that accepts that one lives beyond death only through one's children. He strongly points to divine control over the lives of humans, portraying a deity who punishes evil with a scary, predictable immediacy. The tale also reflects a variety of gendered literature in which women use roundabout means to enforce their rights within the contours of a world ruled by men.

As in folktales worldwide, characterization is sketched in short strokes, conventionalized and predictable, and this economical predictability is part of the story's communicative strength. Listeners know who to root for and how they will succeed. Tricksters deceive, dupe those who have power over them, and gain a fragile improvement in their lot. The author does not describe the characters' inner thoughts. You are what you do. Tamar is resourceful; Judah is self-serving and impulsive, a villain who, in the folklorist Vladimir Propp's terms, becomes a helper.[5] The characterizations, indeed, take on identity and substance through their links with counterparts throughout the tradition and by means of the creative variations upon these traditional motifs with which audiences are familiar.[6] In the particular medium of Genesis 38, language is minimalist, characterized by brief dialogues and economic repetition of syntax and vocabulary. Necessary and required information about events, actions, and characters unfolds in brief staccato phrases.

The opening lines of the tale unceremoniously and in a typical biblical medium describe Judah's acquisition of a wife—travel, seeing a woman, taking her as wife, and having sex with her (38:1–2). Then follows the birth of his sons and their names—all in rapid succession—with repetition in frame language. The wife becomes pregnant, gives birth, and Judah names the boy (38:3–5). Judah takes a wife named Tamar for the eldest son (38:6). Repetition again marks the demise of the two sons (38:7, 10) providing a sense of the swiftness of divine judgment. The father's response is to send the girl back. Here we have a little insight into his motivation and inner thoughts: "for he said, 'Lest he die too like his brothers,'" but the commentary is about events, about what might happen next, not about emotions or feelings. We can fill in the blanks: he was filled with anxiety or fear and reeling from the deaths of the two husbands of Tamar, his sons. The representation of the self is kept at a minimum, however, implicit and reflected in action.

The interaction between the disguised Tamar and Judah is achieved in brief phrases of exchange, as is the conclusion, "he went into her and she became pregnant" (38:18). The revelation about Tamar's condition results in no conversation at all between the patriarch and his daughter-in-law. Instead, upon hearing the news, he says, "Bring her out and burn [her]." This exchange, of course, beautifully reveals the negative side of Judah's character, but again impressions are achieved by action. She, in turn, immediately brings forth the recognition tokens, echoing the language of the earlier exchange at the crossroads. The naming of the twins involves wordplay and a folk etymology.

Drawing upon a classic essay by Erich Auerbach, Barry Holtz points to "the laconic nature" of biblical literature: "The Bible is loath to tell us the motivations, feelings, or thoughts of characters. Rarely giving us descriptive details either of people or places, it is composed in a stark, uncompromising style."[7] While not all traditional biblical literature is characterized by the particular laconic style of Genesis 38, the tale of Tamar beautifully exemplifies the qualities to which Auerbach points, particularly as they relate to representations of self. Hermann Gunkel has also taken stock of this style in Genesis, contrasting it with tales of Joseph, for example, which allow for longer speeches and displays of emotion, however stylized.[8] Even in the tales of Joseph, however, revelations concerning the interiority of characters are muted. Emotions are basic, and the characters emerge through their actions. Cultural cues supply a sense of characters' interiority, thus making the medium exquisitely communicative to its intended audience, participants in tradition, but this is a different sort of communication from the kind one finds in Ruth.

Brief Excursus: Tales of Joseph

Genesis 37:3, 4 declares Jacob's special love for the son of his old age and the brothers' resentment of their father's preference, but the emotions of the parent and the older sons are presented simply as love and hate. Jacob's emotions emerge in an action, his provision of the special coat. The brother's hatred emerges in an intended action: "Let's kill him" (37:19). The dreams throughout the narrative are, to us, perhaps subconscious indicators of their characters' emotions, for example, Joseph's narcissism or the pharaoh's fears, but the author means them to be concrete divinatory media. To be sure, Reuven's words upon finding that Joseph is missing from the pit, "The boy is gone, and I where can I go" (37:30), are filled with pathos, as is Jacob's declaration that he will go down to his son, mourning, to Sheol (37:35). His mourning is more fully marked, however, in ritual actions: he tears his clothes and puts sackcloth on his loins and mourns for many days. Pharaoh expresses fear in response to his dreams, and the sons "fear" when they find the silver in their packs. They acknowledge guilt at 44:16, but this is not exactly the same as being eaten up by guilt. They realize that their current troubles may well be related to what they did, again in a concrete way. When Joseph recognizes his brothers, he "speaks harshly to them," thus evidencing anger and resentment, but again through action (42:7). Even his self-revelation to the brothers is not filled with self-representation. The Joseph story, of course, famously includes scenes of weeping: at 42:7, when Joseph privately weeps apart from his brothers; at 45:1, 5, when he cries out loud, wailing so that all hear him before he reveals his identity; and at 45:14, when he and Benjamin weep in each other's arms. The last case is in fact an example of expected ritual behavior when long-parted kin are reunited—found as well, for example, in the reunion between Jacob and Esau (Genesis 33:4).[9] Joseph is a more emotionally interiorized character than Judah or Tamar, but it is a matter of degree that marks this more baroque aesthetic. The story of Ruth is different.

Ruth

In Ruth, conversations and settings suggest intimacy. Direct attention is paid to the interiority of characters, and their own comments reveal their motivations and their views of the significance of their actions. Moreover, the author includes information that is not necessary for the progress of the plot but that adds richness to the narrative. To his credit, Campbell notes what I might call "lived religion" aspects of the narrative: typical people; ordinary events as loci for divine action; characters who have "a certain individuality" and are not "just two-dimensional."[10] Campbell, however, finds Genesis 38 and the book of Ruth to be comparable kinds of literature. I disagree.

The book of Ruth begins with famine as a cause for migration, and with the names of the characters: a husband, wife, and two sons. The husband dies, the sons take wives, also named, and then the young husbands die, leaving the women alone. Some of this sort of information is common at the opening of biblical tales, and the information in Ruth 1:1–5 is framed in formulaic language of the variety that introduces many biblical tales (Judges 19:1; Genesis 12:10, 14:1, 26:1; Exodus 2:1). In Ruth, however, more of this typical information is included, so the scene is drawn more fully than is usual in biblical tales. There are also unnecessary but enriching details about the period, the time of the judges, the geographic setting (Moab), and the passage of time, ten years after the elder husband's death.

Hearing that the famine has eased in Judah, the land of her birth, the wife, Naomi, decides to return to her homeland. The conversation that follows between the older woman and her daughters-in-law suggests a relationship, reciprocity, graciousness, and a particular religious orientation that sees the deity in small everyday matters, in the personal pathways of individual lives.

Naomi urges the young women to return to their mother's houses (note the emphasis on the feminine). She expresses the hope that Yahweh will show *ḥesed*, a special kindness and loyalty, to them as they did to her. When they initially refuse to leave her, she articulates at some length how she feels and why she thinks as she does about the situation. She is, she says, too old to start over with a husband and newborn sons. Even were she able to start a new family, could her daughters-in-law realistically wait until the boys grew up and were able to serve as levirate redeemers? She concludes about her own situation: "For it is very much more bitter for me than for you because the hand of Yahweh has gone forth against me" (1:13).

The display of emotion by the women is spontaneous and immediate rather than ritualized (1:9, 14). Ritual action, of course, can be genuinely emotional, fed, as Clifford Geertz would say, by moods and motivations that are culturally informed and personally felt.[11] Whereas tears shed at the reunion of Joseph and Benjamin are in the latter category, Naomi and the young women cry in the moment because they are about to part, and we are observers of intimate cameo scenes punctuated by expressions of feelings.

Orpah finally is convinced to return to her people, but Ruth "clings" to Naomi (1:14). The well-known speech that follows is part of a dialogue between Ruth and Naomi, who urges Ruth to do as Orpah has done and return to her people. Like Naomi, Ruth reveals her inner feelings in a way that emphasizes relationship and reciprocity between the two women. The language is poetic, partaking of the parallel constructions typical of Hebrew poetry, but the choice of words and the patterns of syntax are not conventionalized or formulaic.

> Do not entreat me to leave you,
> to turn back from following after you,
> for where you go, I go,
> and where you lodge, I lodge,
> and your god, my god.
> Where you die, I die,
> and there I will be buried.
> Thus may Yahweh do to me
> and thus may he add,
> even if death separates me from you.
> *Ruth 1:16–17*

The relationship between the women is emphasized, and a relationship with Yahweh is confirmed by Ruth. She invokes the deity in an oath formula that underscores her devotion and promises to her mother-in-law.

When they arrive in Bethlehem, Naomi's words further allow us to understand her state of mind, lending interiority to her characterization. In a scene she shares with the townspeople, who acknowledge her return, her wordplay on her own name is revealing. In another of these intimate encounters in an ordinary everyday village setting, she tells her neighbors not to call her Naomi, a name rooted in the word "pleasant," but Mara, rooted in "bitterness." She says, "For Shaddai has greatly embittered me" (1:20). She elaborates further, providing information or commentary not necessary to the plot but important to the overall theme of the narrative, dealing with the contrast between emptiness and fullness, crushing disappointment and restoration.[12] Her words are evocative of the personal lament, in which the lamenter in the first person bemoans his or her current, diminished state.[13]

Dialogue, relationship formation, and commentary on actions and be-havior continue as Ruth encounters Naomi's kinsman Boaz. She has gone out to the fields to glean and happens to find herself in the kinsman's field. Such happenstance, of course, lies at the heart of romance narratives, an-cient and modern. Boaz spies her and asks one of the lads who she is. The lad tells Boaz that she is the Moabite girl who returned with Naomi and describes how hard and long she has been working to gather foodstuffs for herself and her mother-in-law (2:6–7). Again, information is provided to enhance characterization, one person's admiration for another. We see her through his eyes. Boaz speaks directly to Ruth, and their exchange is another intimate cameo scene in which a relationship is formed through conversation and interaction, each speaker's overt expression of apprecia-tion for the others' qualities of character (2:8–14). Ruth asks Boaz why he is being so generous to a stranger like herself, and he comments on her kindness and loyalty to her mother-in-law. Gaining impressions of Ruth, Naomi, and Boaz through their own eyes and words contributes to the formation of characterization in the narrative.

Naomi's subsequent advice to Ruth to wash, anoint herself, change her clothes, and surreptitiously go to Boaz at the threshing floor, after he has eaten and drunk his fill, suggests an intimate encounter between the younger woman and her elder, who describes herself as seeking security for the girl (3:1). Naomi, who knows human nature, says that Boaz "will tell you what you should do." Ruth responds, "All that you say I will do." The interactive quality of the scene is strong.

The meeting at the threshing floor is also intimate and interactive. As happened earlier in the narrative, Boaz comments on Ruth's fine qualities as a person (3:9–15). For his part, he makes sure to keep their encounter away from gossips and prying eyes (3:13, 14). There is, as it turns out, an-other potential redeemer, one closer in kinship ties to Naomi than Boaz. At the gate in a gathering of town elders, the rival explains why, ultimately, he cannot afford to raise up children in the name of his dead kinsman, son of Naomi. He repeats the point twice, disclosing the thought process that informs his decision. Even a minor character is shown to think out loud about his reason for refusing to take on a particular role. Attention is thus paid to characters' states of mind, to their views of themselves and their needs.

The characters in Ruth are thus beautifully drawn, with attention to self-revelatory disclosures about motivation and feeling, intimate encounters between characters created by dialogue, relationship and reciprocity, and the inclusion of detail unnecessary to the plot but richly contributory to the creation of characterization. The author explores and represents people, their own views of their experiences and responses to life, and the relationships that they form with one another and with God. This variety of characterization simply differs from the equally exquisite style found, for example, in the tale of Tamar, in which metonymically informed expectations of authors and audiences frame variations on particular traditional typologies of character. Such characters, described in brief, are what they do rather than what they reveal and represent about themselves.

Jonah

A second case study in characterization is provided by the book of Jonah, the tale of a prophet who attempts to flee from God aboard a ship rather than accept his commission to chastise the inhabitants of Nineveh, frightening them into repentance as the deity commands. Contemporary scholarly approaches to Jonah typically grapple with one or more of the following points: the place of the book in the larger biblical collection of the twelve prophets and possible intertextual links among these works;[14] questions concerning true versus false prophecy;[15] comparisons and contrasts with other prophets,[16] in particular Joel[17] and the seventh-century Nahum, who also prophesies against Assyria but who, in contrast to the author of Jonah, presents the foreigners in a completely negative light and with the utmost animus; discussions of satire, irony, and humor in the work.[18] My own interests are in characterization and how this work, like the book of Ruth, might illuminate its author's engagement with the interiority of his characters, their emotions, their self-revelations and self-representations. Do descriptions of motivations and information go beyond the desire to move the plot along? Are relationships formed and revealed in the narrative? Are we allowed to see intimate scenes of interaction that go beyond ritual or conventionalized formulas? Are we given an author's glimpse into his notion of everyday religion as lived? How does the author play upon the tradition or invoke it to say something unique?

As discussed in relation to the "confessions" of Jeremiah, prophetic literature offers particular opportunities to explore questions pertaining to personal religion and representations of the individual. Prophets' very roles as intermediaries between God and Israel involve conversation and complaint, exhortation and rejection, commissioning, visits to the divine realm, and first-person reports of experiences. We have argued that Jeremiah or, perhaps more accurately, the authors who present the prophet and his messages enhance the representations of self via the tone and content of his confessions. It is clear, moreover, that the author of Jonah draws upon the larger prophetic tradition in creating his tale of the prophet.[19] Does not Elijah give up and go off in 1 Kings 19? Does not Baruch, disciple of Jeremiah, complain about his status and role (Jeremiah 45:3–5)? Nevertheless, the book of Jonah differs significantly from other prophetic books. Rather than a collection of oracles that may include some sort of time line or narrative framework, background information, and cameo scenes with their own plots, the book of Jonah is a narrative that moves from an initial problem to complications and finally to a degree of resolution, at least from the perspective of the controller of the plot, Yahweh.[20]

From Yahweh's perspective, the problem is Nineveh's sin. Yahweh wants to send its inhabitants a warning via the prophet Jonah so that they can repent and be saved from destruction. The problem from Jonah's perspective is that they might indeed repent, something we learn only near the end of the tale. In an attempt to flee from this commission, Jonah runs away to sea, whereupon God in his displeasure sends a massive storm, unnerving the innocent crew. Jonah, the cause of the life-threatening storm, is eventually and reluctantly thrown overboard by the sailors. He is then swallowed by the divinely sent big fish and disgorged after three days, whereupon he grudgingly bends to God's will and warns the Assyrians. The inhabitants of Nineveh do repent, in an exaggerated display of mourning that includes putting sackcloth on the animals, and the deity relents. God's problem is solved, but Jonah feels that he has been made a fool by being forced to predict a doomsday that now need not come about. The tale ends with God justifying his actions. As in Job, he always wins the argument, but we do not hear again from Jonah.

A close look at the scenes on the ship, at Jonah's expression of anger, at his use of the lament, and at his interaction with the deity points to matters of characterization and personal representation that distinguish this example of late-biblical literature. The scene on the vessel relates beautifully to questions about the interiority of characters, their emotional responses, the relationships between characters, and their motivations. Dialogue reveals characters' thoughts, provides background information, and invokes the quality of actual interactions between people.[21]

When the storm rages, for example, the sailors are fearful, call to their various deities, and try furiously to lighten the load on the boat to prevent it from sinking. Details are thus provided concerning demeanor, personal religious action, and realistic activity in the face of life-threatening danger. The narrator contrasts this buzz of activity with Jonah's inaction—he is sound asleep in the hold of the ship. The first face-to-face interaction (or noninteraction) of the narrative takes place between the captain and Jonah: "What's with you, [slug/sluggard, slumberer, dead-beat]? Get up, call to your god. Maybe the god will give a thought to us and we will not perish" (1:6).[22] The captain receives no response from Jonah, a sulking, silent fellow. The captain's words, however, reveal his own thoughts about the situation; he responds in a genuine human way to the possibility of drowning.

The sailors take action, drawing lots to find out the source of the trouble. Who among them has drawn divine wrath? The lot falls upon Jonah, and another interaction ensues: "Tell us, please, on account of what is all this 'bad' upon us? What is your occupation and from where do you come, and what is your land, and from what people are you?" (1:8). The query about origins is formulaic language found as well in the encounter between Eliezer and Rebecca (Genesis 24:16–18), Jacob and the shepherds (Genesis 29:4), Joseph (feigned) and his brothers (Genesis 42:7), and the host and the Levite (Judges 19:17).

These examples of formulaic usage reveal the way in which the author of Jonah creates characterization. In the cases involving Eliezer and Rebecca as well as Jacob and the shepherds, the query about origins merely leads to the next scene. Joseph's posing of the question heightens the drama, since we know that Joseph is only feigning his desire for information; he knows very well who the sojourners are. The query posed by the hospitable sojourner in Gibeah is interesting as well in that it leads the Levite to dissemble about the full nature of his journey. In all four cases, however, the encounter serves to reveal or comment on certain bonds of kinship between the participants in the encounter—between cousins, brothers, or those who share status and ethnicity. In Jonah, the men have nothing in common other than the storm and their shared danger, making relationship formation all the more striking and the role of formulaic language more than a comment on what has happened and what follows.

Jonah responds that he is a Hebrew, a fearer of Yahweh, God of heaven, who has made the sea and the dry ground, an evocation of creation in Genesis 1. The narrator indicates, moreover, that Jonah has revealed to the sailors that he is fleeing from the Lord (1:10). The men become even more fearful after hearing about Jonah's situation. They ask him, "What shall we do with [literally, "to/for"] you?" to quiet the sea (1:11). They seek his advice and earnestly interact with him in the midst of a disaster. He asks them to toss him overboard and satisfy the deity in order to quiet the storm and save their lives, but they do not want to do as he asks. The words of 1:13 suggest decent people in an extreme situation trying to do the right thing. As in the case of Ruth, the author portrays the way in which religious sensibility includes an ethical orientation that guides actions in everyday life and in crises. The sailors try to avoid killing Jonah and finally ask Yahweh to forgive them for throwing him overboard. Their respect for Yahweh's power intensifies, and they offer him sacrifice and make vows, an important manifestation of personal religion, rich in ideas of reciprocity.[23]

The lament, which serves as Jonah's prayer while in the fish, is typical of the late-biblical psalms explored earlier in the trajectory from incantation to autobiography. The inclusion of this piece contributes significantly to the representation of self in the narrative. To be sure, as discussed in chapter three, such psalms are conventionalized and formulaic in form and content, and some would suggest that Jonah 2 is not merely traditional but derivative, consciously based on the psalms. Nevertheless, here as in the psalms of lament, the voice in the first person, the emotional crying, the complaint, and the hope for deliverance provide a mechanism for self-expression. Images of death as drowning, typical in such laments, are a good fit for the content of the narrative.[24]

Jonah's response to Yahweh after the Ninevites repent and the deity relents lends depth and interiority to his character. The troubled relationship between Jonah and his god is well sketched. One might translate Jonah's initial response to God's mercy, "A really bad feeling came upon Jonah and he was filled with anger," literally, "It became bad to Jonah, a great badness, and he became angry" (4:1). He is absorbed by negativity, an impression beautifully conveyed by the idioms themselves. Jonah's subsequent prayer, which shares language with the excursus in the ten commandments at Exodus 20:5–6 and divine words to Moses at Exodus 34:6–7, reveals his argument with God and finally why it was that he tried to flee to Tarshish: "Ah Lord, was this not what I said when I was on my own land? For this reason I came to flee to Tarshish because I knew that you are a gracious and compassionate god, slow to anger and full of kindness, and one who thinks better of inflicting adversity" (4:2).[25] Paradoxically, the deity's loving patience is the cause of Jonah's anger. Indeed, he is so miffed that he wishes to die, saying to the deity, "Take, please, my life from me because better is my death than my life" (4:3).

Other biblical protagonists are portrayed as prepared to die and as expressing this willingness. Moses offers his life in place of the people's well-deserved punishment after the events of the golden calf (Exodus 32:32) and, once again, when he is seemingly fed up with another of the people's many complaints concerning conditions during the wilderness trek (Numbers 11:5). David offers his life after the people are struck by a divinely sent plague, punishment for his undertaking a census (2 Samuel 24:17). Elijah's situation is perhaps closest to that of Jonah in that his depression relates to his role as a prophet. Jezebel, patroness of the Baal cult in the northern kingdom, seeks his life, and he seems to give up. He is tired and emotionally deflated. He has done his best and feels as if it is over. He says, "Take my life, for I am no better than my ancestors." While Jonah is as dispirited as Elijah, in contrast to Elijah, he is not upset because his mission in some sense has failed. Elijah is outnumbered, on the periphery, but Jonah has succeeded in making people change their ways—the Assyrians of Nineveh have repented. Is this not the true mission of the doomsday prophet? Jonah, however, takes it the wrong way, and personally. Because his prediction of doom has failed to materialize, he feels he has been made to look like a fool, a lying prophet. He is suffused with anger, narcissistic. It is all about him. He feels he has been made to look like a fool because of the deity's capacity for forgiveness. The interior dimensions of his character are critical to the narrative, and his response to God is intensely personal and expressive. The final scene of the tale, involving shade, a bush, and the death of the plant, leads to one more conversation with the deity, which further builds characterization.

The deity is also a character. He responds to Jonah's tirade with the question "Is it good to be angry?" or perhaps one might translate these words as a statement: "If it pleases, be angry" (4:4).[26] Jonah again takes off to a position east of the city and builds himself a booth to shelter himself from the sun. The deity provides a planting to shade him, and Jonah, content, "rejoices over the planting a great joy" (4:6). But then the deity, just as serendipitously, causes the plant to wither and die, and again Jonah asks for his own death, deep in depression.

The deity reframes Jonah's complaint, suggesting that Jonah is upset about the bush's death—a plant that he had not toiled over or even sown, a plant that existed only between one night and another and then was gone. And yet, God says, Jonah could not take pity on the many humans in Nineveh, not to mention the animals! Jonah, of course, does not care about the plant as a living creation that has died, but about his own comfort in the heat. He misses the shade. Yahweh is pictured as accusing Jonah of having empathy for a plant in the absence of human empathy, and there the story ends. Even in this amusing and somewhat curious conclusion, the capacity for empathy, human relationships, and the personal response to difficult situations figure prominently.

Conclusion

Religion, on some level, is always personal, immediate, and fluid, even in official contexts and even when we are in the midst of fellow believers, all participating in liturgy at the same place and time. As we follow the Torah reading in the synagogue or sing prayers aloud with the rabbi and congregation, however determined our concentration and however strong our appreciation for the community, we each experience different levels and forms of engagement, different emotional experiences rooted in our personalities, memories, problems, or sources of happiness. In this series of essays, we have explored the conscious emphasis placed by late-biblical writers on individual experiences of religious engagement and personal religious identities.

I make the case that extraordinary creativity accompanies the heightened sense of crisis following the Babylonian invasions and conquest and the subsequent Persian domination. All the forms of religious expression explored in this work have precursors in ancient Near Eastern traditions, and specifically in Israelite tradition, whether they are sayings, prayers, laments, vows, burial customs, visions, or narratives. The late material, however, displays a particular interest in individuals and portrayals of self. This engagement is manifested in a variety of ways and is illuminated by ideas offered by sociologists of religion who write about religion as lived, personal, and material. I argue that late-biblical texts such as the confessions of Jeremiah, the soliloquies of Job, and the social critiques of Qohelet, the characterizations of and interactions between characters in Ruth and Jonah portray individuals' emotions, disappointments, and doubts with greater attention to detail and urgency than do classical texts. We are invited by these texts to observe some of the intimate scenes and special ways in which religious idioms are employed, those aspects of religion as lived to which Robert Orsi and Meredith McGuire point. Conventionalized forms become more specified as attention is paid to particular personalities and life challenges, so that a trajectory from the lament leads to something approaching the autobiographical in Nehemiah. In this way, religious ideas and expressions are privatized and personalized, albeit always within the contours of traditional content, structures, and turns of phrase. We also explore the material aspects of religious life and expression in considering a physical burial site, a cave that not only housed the departed but also served the living in various ways. We take stock of the role of material objects in prophetic media such as the sign act and the symbolic vision and pay special attention to the embodied aspects of verbal and nonverbal media.

A variety of features recur in these case studies, so that each chapter anticipates and reaches back to the others: the use and significance of first-person speech and related autobiographical nuances; imagery of embodiment; the concern with individual responsibility for one's conditions in life; the often radical challenge to conventional wisdom about suffering, righteousness, and sin; the emotional dimensions of the words attributed to first-person speakers; the interiority in depictions of narrative characters; the portrayal of everyday, ordinary actions that have to do with profound matters of worldview; enactments of self-imposed ritual. Expressions of lived religion in a range of media are always both conservative and innovative. The border, moreover, between sacred and profane blurs, and the interplay is lively between self and tradition, individual and cultural identities.

I have tried to avoid the simpler suggestions of earlier generations of scholars, who suggest that somehow exilic writers discover the individual or invent the self, whereas earlier biblical writers emphasize community and shared culture. Overt and explicit manifestations of personal religion, however, are preserved in noticeably large numbers in the written tradition in the period following the Babylonian troubles, and are transformed. The pattern of the lament, for example, not only is popular among postexilic psalmists, but also moves in new, more individuated directions in the self-portrayals of Jeremiah and Nehemiah. The symbolic vision, so rich in qualities of material religion, is a traditional Israelite form of prophetic expression, but there are many more of these visions preserved in the writings of

Zechariah than in earlier prophetic books, and then an explosion of them in Daniel and postbiblical Jewish works. Similarly, the classical prophet Hosea employs sign acts, but in Jeremiah and Ezekiel these forms of prophetic communication are more densely represented, a kind of performance art. Even Nehemiah employs a sign act to reinforce an oath under which he places members of the community. We have discussed possible reasons for the popularity of these forms in the literature of the sixth century BCE and later. We have also engaged in diachronic work, comparing, for example, the Genesis tale of Tamar and the tale of Ruth. The narratives share important content and themes, but the book of Ruth employs intimate cameo scenes, self-revealing speeches, expressions of emotion, and indications of personal motivation that provide the later narrative with individualized portrayals of its heroes and heroines and insight into their personal religion. Additional diachronic work reveals that prophetic vision forms become more elaborate over time and that, in later examples, the characterization of the prophet's emotions and responses to his visionary experiences are elaborated; the prophets emerge more fully as characters.

Integral to thinking about personal religion is materiality, the visual, tactile, physically experienced dimensions of lived religion. The material in turn relates to embodiment: in the self-portrayals of Job, whose body bears the physical evidence of his undeserved suffering, and in the laments of the psalms that describe the embodied nature of the speaker's alienation and deterioration. In a discussion of the burial cave of Khirbet Beit Lei, attention has been paid to the physical environment of the space, to the way in which bodies are laid out, to the objects they wear, to an object found nearby, and to the drawings and inscriptions etched into the wall. Important questions concern what sort of impressions these features may have made on the living, how they may indicate visitors' participation in marking the passage to death, and whether the dead were regarded as able to appreciate the space and its design. We have considered who might have prepared the rough drawings, and the significance of their aesthetic or artistic shortcomings, paying attention to what seems to be conventional in the drawings and in particular to the version of a horned being or a lyre player. We have asked how this site relates to religious experience and how it might have affected anyone who took refuge in the cave during the Babylonian invasions. Material aspects are also critical to symbolic visions and sign acts, which involve the seeing or purposeful creating of certain objects and scenes, and the participation of the seer or actor. Sign acts function as religious performance art that links God and human, the present and the future.

The vow is another traditional form as old as Israelite religion. This means of negotiating with the deity or, better, of seeking to influence him with promises of praise or sacrifice is a particularly useful means of tracing ways in which late writers of the Hebrew Bible present personal religion. The act of vowing requires no official context, is self-motivated and self-generated, arises out of individual needs or hopes, and assumes a personal relationship with the deity based upon reciprocity. At the same time, the act of vowing is framed by communal expectation and culturally shared formulaic language and actions, and sometimes the vow is undertaken in the context of an official sacred space or an officially sanctioned holy occasion.

The nature of the temporary Nazirite vow described in the Persian-period priestly passage of Numbers 6 is a fascinating indicator of developments in personal religion. In contrast to the manly lifelong status of Samson and Samuel, Nazirites from birth, the Nazirism in Numbers 6 is a temporary status that one takes upon oneself. In contrast to the content of Amos 2 and Judges 16, the deity does not select the Nazirite, nor does his mother promise him, as in 1 Samuel 1. And this vow is available to men and to women. Like Numbers 6, the long excursus in Numbers 30, largely concerned with women's vows and when they can be overridden by their men, suggests an interest among members of the priestly establishment in taking charge of and controlling vowing, an important form of personal religious expression. Could it be that the difficult period following the conquest, characterized by destabilization, factionalism, the movement of populations, and the power of colonialist overlords, led to the increasing rise of charismatic holy men claiming to be Nazirites from birth and to an increase in the act of vowing as a means by which people hoped individually to bargain with or gain favor from the deity in times of particular challenge? By tying Nazirism to a time-limited vow, one available only to those with the means to offer expensive sacrifices upon completion of the vow, and by making it open to men and women, its force as a charismatic phenomenon is reduced. Similarly, Numbers 30 reflects an interest in reducing most women's control over the powerfully personal aspect of the act of vowing, except in the case of women of independent means, for example, widows, who are not under the sway of husband or father.

The effort by late writers to circumscribe vowing is one more example of the creative response to the challenges of the sixth century BCE and beyond. As seen in each of the case studies, Numbers 6 and 30 reveal ways in which the innovative use of traditional media is informed by intense preoccupation with the self in context. The quotation of a proverb about sour grapes and the lament placed in the mouth of a prophet, the physical characteristics of a burial place such as Khirbet Beit Lei and the performance art of the sign act, stories about little things and ordinary people such as Ruth, and the preoccupation with vows all point to the complicated interplay between personal and cultural self-definition. I have sought throughout to explore the connections between patterns of culture, perceived to be ancient or timeless, and human beings' capacity to renew, appropriate, and adapt traditions to suit the realities of a particular sociohistorical setting. Complex relationships between continuity and change, the formulaic and the specific, the communal and the individual, the material and the metaphysical, underlie and frame self-expression within the context of religion as lived.

Notes

Introduction

1. See Moshe Greenburg, *Biblical Prose Prayer as a Window in the Popular Religion of Israel* (Berkeley: University of California Press, 1983); Samuel E. Balentine, *Prayer in the Hebrew Bible: The Drama of Divine-Human Dialogue* (Minneapolis: Fortress, 1993); Rodney Werline, *Penitential Prayer in Second Temple Judaism: The Development of a Religious Institution* (Atlanta: Scholars Press, 1998).

2. Carol Meyers, "The Family in Early Israel," in Perdue, Blenkinsopp, Collins, and Meyers, 38–39; Joseph Blenkinsopp on "religion in ordinary time," ("The Family in First Temple Israel," in ibid., 78–83); Rainer Albertz, "Personal Piety," in Stavrakopoulou and Barton, *Religious Diversity in Ancient Israel and Judah,* 135–46; Albertz, "Family Religion in Ancient Israel and Its Surrounds," in Bodel and Oylan, *Household and Family Religion in Antiquity,* 89–112.

3. For an important study of changing worldviews in the Second Temple period that focuses on attitudes to death and related ideas about the individual, see Shannon Burkes, *God, Self, and Death: The Shape of Religious Transformation in the Second Temple Period* (Leiden: Brill, 2003).

4. Meredith B. McGuire, *Lived Religion: Faith and Practice in Everyday Life* (Oxford: Oxford University Press, 2008), 3.

5. Ibid., 4.

6. Ibid.

7. Ibid., 5.

8. Robert Orsi, "Is the Study of Lived Religion Irrelevant to the World We Live In?" *Journal for the Scientific Study of Religion* 42 (2003): 169.

9. Ibid., 170.

10. Ibid., 172.

11. Ibid.

12. Ibid.

13. McGuire, *Lived Religion;* see also Colleen McDannell, *Material Christianity: Religion and Popular Culture in America* (New Haven, Conn.: Yale University Press, 1995), 4–8.

14. McDannell, *Material Christianity,* 1.

15. Ibid., 2.

16. Ibid., 14. On the language of embodiment as it relates to constructions of self-hood in the Qumran literature, see Carol A. Newsom, *The Self as Symbolic Space: Constructing Identity and Community at Qumran* (Leiden: Brill, 2004), 92, 95–99, 150. Newsom's attention to the way in which the language of 1QS deals with the body and its regulation in a sectarian context is richly informed by the theories of Michel Foucault.

17. McGuire, *Lived Religion,* 85.

18. See Carol Meyers, "Family in Early Israel," 38–39; Beth Alpert Nakhai, "Varieties of Religious Expression in the Domestic Setting," in *Household Archaeology in Ancient Israel and Beyond,* ed. Assaf Yasur-Landau, Jennie R. Ebeling, and Laura B. Mazow (Leiden: Brill, 2011), 347–60.

19. McDannell, *Material Christianity,* 1, 7–8, 16.

20. Patricia Cox Miller, "Shifting Selves in Late Antiquity," in *Religion and the Self in Antiquity,* ed. David Brakke, Michael L. Satlow, and Steven Weitzman (Bloomington: Indiana University Press, 2005), 17.

21. Blenkinsopp, "Family in First Temple Israel," 78–82.

22. Melody Knowles, *Centrality Practiced: Jerusalem in the Religious Practice of Yehud and the Diaspora in the Persian Period* (Atlanta: SBL, 2006), 55–71.

23. Ibid., 4.

24. Frank Moore Cross, "The Cave Inscriptions from Khirbet Lei," in *Near Eastern Archaeology in the Twentieth Century: Essays in Honor of Nelson Glueck,* ed. James A. Sanders (Garden City, N.Y.: Doubleday, 1970), 302, 304.

25. Knowles, *Centrality Practiced,* 103; see also Erhard S. Gerstenberger, *Israel in the Persian Period: The Fifth and Fourth Centuries BCE* (Atlanta: Society of Biblical Literature, 2011), 120.

26. Orsi, "Study of Lived Religion," 172.

27. See also Jill Middlemas concerning "a cult of lamentation as part of a continuation of Yahwistic practice in Judah" (*The Troubles of Templeless Judah* [Oxford: Oxford University Press, 2005], 122–26).

28. David Brakke, Michael L. Satlow, and Steven Weitzman, eds., *Religion and the Self in Antiquity* (Bloomington: Indiana University Press, 2005), 1.

29. Ibid., 5. For an excellent discussion of the self, the construction of "subjectivities," and questions concerning the individual voice, community, culture, and tradition, see Newsom, *Self as Symbolic Space,* 191–92, 198–204.

30. Brakke, Satlow, and Weitzman, *Religion and the Self,* 5.

31. Ibid.

32. Saul M. Olyan, "The Search for the Elusive Self in Texts of the Hebrew Bible," in *Religion and the Self in Antiquity* (Bloomington: Indiana University Press, 2005), 44, 47.

33. Janet Gyatso, *Apparitions of the Self: The Secret Autobiographies of a Tibetan Visionary* (Princeton, N.J.: Princeton University Press, 1998), xii.

34. Ibid., 108.

35. Ibid., 112.

36. Ibid., 114.

37. Stephen T. Katz, "The 'Conservative' Character of Mystical Experience," in *Mysticism and Religious Traditions*, ed. Steven T. Katz (Oxford: Oxford University Press, 1983), 5–6.

38. John Miles Foley, *Immanent Art: From Structure to Meaning in Traditional Oral Epic* (Bloomington: Indiana University Press, 1991).

39. Shemaryahu Talmon, "The Old Testament Text," in *Cambridge History of the Bible*, ed. P. R. Ackroyd and C. F. Evans (Cambridge: Cambridge University Press, 1970), 1:159–99.

40. Oded Lipschits, *The Fall and Rise of Jerusalem: Judah under Babylonian Rule* (Winona Lake, Ind.: Eisenbrauns, 2005); Avraham Faust, "Settlement Dynamics and Demographic Fluctuations in Judah from the Late Iron Age to the Hellenistic Period and the Archaeology of Persian-Period *Yehud*," in *A Time of Change: Judah and Its Neighbors in the Persian and Early Hellenistic Periods*, ed. Yigal Levin (London: T&T Clark, 2007), 23–51; Kenneth Hoglund, "The Material Culture of the Persian Period and the Sociology of the Second Temple Period," in *Second Temple Studies III: Studies in Politics, Class and Material Culture*, ed. Philip R. Davies and John M. Halligan (Sheffield, UK: Sheffield University Press, 2002), 14–18; Charles E. Carter, *The Emergence of Yehud in the Persian Period: A Social and Demographic Study* (Sheffield, UK: Sheffield Academic Press, 1999); Jeffrey R. Zorn, "Tell en-Nasbeh and the Problem of the Material Culture of the Sixth Century," in *Judah and the Judeans in the Neo-Babylonian Period*, ed. Oded Lipschits and Joseph Blenkinsopp (Winona Lake, Ind.: Eisenbrauns, 2003), 413–47; Ephraim Stern, *Material Culture of the Land of the Bible in the Persian Period, 538–332 B.C.* (Warminster, UK: Aris and Philips, 1982).

41. Amichai Mazar, *Archaeology of the Land of Israel* (New York: Doubleday, 1992), 548; Gabriel Barkay, "The Iron Age II–III," in *The Archaeology of Ancient Israel*, ed. Amnon Ben-Tor (New Haven, Conn.: Yale University Press, 1992), 372; Hans M. Barstad, "After the 'Myth of the Empty Land': Major Challenges in the Study of Neo-Babylonian Judah," in *Judah and the Judeans in the Neo-Babylonian Period*, ed. Oded Lipschits and Joseph Blenkinsopp (Winona Lake, Ind.: Eisenbrauns, 2003), 3–20; Lipschits, *Fall and Rise of Jerusalem*, 197, 210, 216, 248, 271; Zorn, "Tell en-Nasbeh," 438; Middlemas, *Troubles of Templeless Judah*, 234.

42. Carter, *Emergence of Yehud*, 320–21; Kenneth G. Hoglund, *Achaemenid Imperial Administration in Syria-Palestine and the Missions of Ezra and Nehemiah*

(Atlanta: Scholars Press, 1992), 6–29; David S. Vanderhooft, "New Evidence Pertaining to the Transition from Neo-Babylonian to Achaemenid Administration in Palestine," in *Yahwism after the Exile: Perspectives on Israelite Religion in the Persian Era*, ed. Rainer Albertz and Bob Becking (Assen, Netherlands: Royal Van Gorcum, 2003), 219–35; Faust, "Settlement Dynamics," 42.

43. Barstad, "'Myth of the Empty Land'"; Hoglund, "Material Culture of the Persian Period," 18; Faust, "Settlement Dynamics," 44.

44. Ephraim Stern, "The Religious Revolution in Persian-Period Judah," in *Judah and Judeans in the Persian Period*, ed. Oded Lipschits and Manfred Oeming (Winona Lake, Ind.: Eisenbrauns, 2006), 199–205.

45. William M. Schniedewind, *How the Bible Became a Book: The Textualization of Ancient Israel* (Cambridge: Cambridge University Press, 2004), 165–72, 181. Compare the views of Ehud Ben-Zvi, who draws a contrast between early and later Persian periods ("The Urban Center of Jerusalem and the Development of the Literature of the Hebrew Bible," in *Urbanism in Antiquity: From Mesopotamia to Crete*, ed. Walter E. Aufrecht, Neil A. Mirau, and Steven W. Gauley [Sheffield, UK: Sheffield Academic Press, 1997]), 194–209.

46. Carter, *Emergence of Yehud*, 287–88; Raymond L. Person, *The Deuteronomic School: History, Social Setting, and Literature* (Atlanta: Society of Biblical Literature, 2002), 60–63, 79.

47. Middlemas, *Troubles of Templeless Judah*.

48. Joseph Blenkinsopp, *Judaism: The First Phase; The Place of Ezra and Nehemiah in the Origins of Judaism* (Grand Rapids, Mich.: Eerdmans, 2009), 10. Compare Jeremiah W. Cataldo, *A Theocratic Yehud? Issues of Government in a Persian Province* (London: T&T Clark, 2009).

49. Jon L. Berquist, *Judaism in Persia's Shadow: A Social and Historical Approach* (Minneapolis: Fortress, 1995); Berquist, "Psalms, Postcolonialism, and the Construction of the Self," in Berquist, *Approaching Yehud*, 195–202; see also Jean-Pierre Ruiz, "An Exile's Baggage: Toward a Postcolonial Reading of Ezekiel," in Berquist, *Approaching Yehud*, 117–35.

50. Daniel L. Smith, *The Religion of the Landless: The Social Context of the Babylonian Exile* (Bloomington, Ind.: Meyer-Stone, 1989); and "The Politics of Ezra: Sociological Indicators of Postexilic Judean Society," in *Second Temple Studies I: Persian Period*, ed. Philip R. Davies (Sheffield, UK: Sheffield Academic Press, 1991), 73–97.

51. Gary N. Knoppers, "Revisiting the Samarian Question in the Persian Period," in *Judah and the Judeans in the Persian Period*, ed. Oded Lipschits and Manfred Oeming (Winona Lake, Ind.: Eisenbrauns, 2006), 265–89.

52. Vanderhooft, "New Evidence," 227, 231, 233.

53. Ibid.; Ingo Kottsieper, "'And They Did Not Care to Speak Yehudit': On Linguistic Change in Judah during the Late Persian Period," in *Judah and the Judeans in the Fourth Century BCE*, ed. Oded Lipschits, Gary N. Knoppers, and Rainer

Albertz (Winona Lake, Ind.: Eisenbrauns, 2007), 95–124; Frank Polak, "Sociolinguistics and the Judean Speech Community in the Achaemenid Empire," in *Judah and the Judeans in the Persian Period*, ed. Oded Lipschits and Manfred Oeming (Winona Lake, Ind.: Eisenbrauns, 2006), 589–628; Schniedewind, *How the Bible Became a Book*; Schniedewind, "Aramaic, the Death of Written Hebrew, and Language Shift in the Persian Period," in *Margins of Writings, Origins of Cultures*, ed. Seth L. Sanders (Chicago: Oriental Institute, 2004), 141–51.

54. Morton Smith, *Palestinian Parties and Politics That Shaped the Old Testament* (London: SCM Press, 1987).

55. James Watts, ed., *Persia and Torah: The Theory of Imperial Authorization of the Pentateuch* (Atlanta: SBL, 2001).

56. See, for example, L. S. Fried, "The Political Struggle of Fifth Century Judah," *Transeuphratène* 24 (2002): 9–21.

57. David Daube, *Collaboration with Tyranny in Rabbinic Law* (London: Oxford University Press, 1965).

58. Brent A. Strawn, "'A World under Control': Isaiah 60 and the Adapana Reliefs," in Berquist, *Approaching Yehud*, 85–116.

59. Morton Smith, *Palestinian Parties and Politics*; Paul D. Hanson, *The Dawn of Apocalyptic* (Philadelphia: Fortress, 1975).

60. Knowles, *Centrality Practiced*, 10, 13–14.

61. See Thomas J. King, *The Realignment of the Priestly Literature: The Priestly Narrative in Genesis and Its Relation to Priestly Legislation and the Holiness School* (Eugene, Ore.: Pickwick, 2009); Thomas Römer, ed., *The Books of Leviticus and Numbers* (Leuven, Belgium: Peeters, 2008).

62. Yigal Levin, ed., *A Time of Change: Judah and Its Neighbors in the Persian and Early Hellenistic Periods* (London: T&T Clark, 2007), xvi; see also H. G. M. Williamson, *Studies in Persian Period History and Historiography* (Tübingen: Mohr Siebeck, 2004), 3–7; Carter, *Emergence of Yehud*, 36–37.

63. Unless otherwise indicated, all translations are the author's.

64. Edward L. Greenstein, "Jeremiah as an Inspiration to the Poet of Job," in *Inspired Speech: Prophecy in the Ancient Near East; Essays in Honor of Herbert B. Huffmon*, ed. John Kalter and Louis Stulman (London: T&T Clark International, 2004), 107.

65. Choon-Leong Seow, "The Social World of Ecclesiastes," in *Scribes, Sages, and Seers: The Sage in the Eastern Mediterranean World*, ed. Leo Perdue (Göttingen: Vandenhoeck & Ruprecht, 2007), 193.

Chapter 1. Sour Grapes, Suffering, and Coping with Chaos

1. The Masoretic Text (MT) includes two words with nuances of "advantage," a noun and a verb, so that one might translate the line literally "the advantage for

giving success is wisdom" (so Brown, Driver, Briggs). The term for "wisdom" can be understood as "skill" in military contexts (e.g., Isaiah 10:13) or in contexts requiring technical expertise (e.g., Exodus 28:3). The Septuagint (LXX) reads "and wisdom is the advantage of the human."

2. Carole R. Fontaine, *Traditional Sayings in the Old Testament* (Sheffield, UK: Almond Press, 1982), 247.
3. The opening portion of this section is included in my discussion of proverbs and context in "Twisting Proverbs: Oral Traditional Performance and Written Context," in *Discourse, Dialogue, and Debate in the Bible: Essays in Honour of Frank H. Polak,* ed. Athalya Brenner-Idan (Sheffield, UK: Phoenix, 2014) 125–28.
4. See Susan Niditch, *Folklore and the Hebrew Bible* (Minneapolis: Fortress, 1993), 86.
5. Fontaine, *Traditional Sayings,* 247.
6. Barbara Kirshenblatt-Gimblett, "Toward a Theory of Proverb Meaning," in *The Wisdom of Many: Essays on the Proverb,* ed. Wolfgang Mieder and Alan Dundes (New York: Garland, 1981), 11–120; Alan Dundes, "Proverbs and the Ethnography of Speaking Folklore," in *Analytic Essays in Folklore* (The Hague: Mouton, 1979), 35–49.
7. Alan Dundes, "Who Are the Folk," in *Interpreting Folklore* (Bloomington: Indiana University Press, 1980), 9.
8. Fontaine, *Traditional Sayings,* 243.
9. Robert A. Oden, *The Bible without Theology: The Theological Tradition and Alternatives to It* (Cambridge, Mass.: Harper and Row, 1987).
10. Whereas Paul M. Joyce emphasizes the collective aspect of guilt in Ezekiel 18 (*Divine Initiative and Human Response in Ezekiel* [Sheffield, UK: JSOT Press, 1989], 36), Michael Fishbane emphasizes nuances of individual responsibility ("Sin and Judgment in the Prophecies of Ezekiel," *Interpretation* 38 [1984]: 141–42). On Ezekiel's interest in individual responsibility, and for suggestions about developments over time in Israelite attitudes, see Leo G. Perdue, "The Household, Old Testament Theology, and Contemporary Hermeneutics," in *Families in Ancient Israel,* ed. Leo G. Perdue, Joseph Blenkinsopp, John J. Collins, and Carol Meyers (Louisville, Ky.: Westminster John Knox, 1997), 237. On the relationship between individual and collective guilt, see Norman Gottwald, *All the Kingdoms of the Earth* (New York: Harper and Row, 1964), 309; on the intertwining of concepts of self and community, see Gordon H. Matties, *Ezekiel 18 and the Rhetoric of Moral Discourse* (Atlanta: Scholars Press, 1990), 148–49, 150. For an overview of views concerning collective and individual responsibility for sin, see Jurrien Mol, *Collective and Individual Responsibility: A Description of Corporate Personality in Ezekiel 18 and 20* (Leiden: Brill, 2009), 222. For a discussion of Jeremiah 31:29–30 and transformations in views of personal responsibility and Israelite identity in response to the Babylonian conquest, see

Bob Becking, "Sour Fruit and Blunt Teeth: The Metaphorical Meaning of the *Māšāl* in Jeremiah 31, 29," *Scandinavian Journal of the Old Testament* 17 (2003): 7–21. In exploring Ezekiel 18 in its context of conquest and trauma, Bernard M. Levinson suggests that Ezekiel's treatment of the proverb challenges and critiques views of inherited sin that had been valorized and endorsed in the ten commandments (Exodus 20:5–6) ("'You Must Not Add Anything to What I Command You': Paradoxes of Canon and Authorship in Ancient Israel," *Numen* 50 [2003]: 26–36). In Levinson's view, the prophet "censure[s] a text whose infrangible authority is precisely the problem" (30). For a nuanced approach suggesting that the contrast between corporate and individual responsibility is often overdrawn by scholars, see Joel S. Kaminsky, *Corporate Responsibility in the Hebrew Bible* (Sheffield, UK: JSOT Press, 1995), 116–37; Kaminsky addresses ways in which this observation applies to the proverb in Ezekiel 18 (177) and Jeremiah 31 (154).

11. See, for example, the discussions by Joyce, *Divine Initiative*, 38, and Barnabas Lindars, "Ezekiel and Individual Responsibility," *Vetus Testamentum* 15 (1965): 452; Levinson suggests that "the formula for individual liability in civil and criminal" contexts provided Ezekiel "a legal and literary precedent" as he attempted to "bring theological justice into conformity with secular justice" ("'You Must Not Add,'" 34).

12. See, for example, Rodney R. Hutton, "Are the Parents Still Eating Sour Grapes? Jeremiah's Use of the *Māšāl* in Contrast to Ezekiel," *Catholic Biblical Quarterly* 71 (2009): 279, 281–84.

13. See, for example, discussions by Matties, *Ezekiel 18*, 147, and Jacqueline E. Lapsley, *"Can These Bones Live?": The Problem of the Moral Self in the Book of Ezekiel* (Berlin: de Gruyter, 2000), 74.

14. Lapsley, *"Can These Bones Live?,"* 74–75.

15. Lindars, "Ezekiel and Responsibility," 462.

16. Fishbane, "Sin and Judgment," 141–42.

17. Joyce, *Divine Initiative*, 35.

18. Wolfgang Mieder, *"Proverbs Speak Louder than Words": Folk Wisdom in Art, Culture, Folklore, History, Literature, and Mass Media* (New York: Lang, 2008), 13.

19. See, for example, Kaminsky, *Corporate Responsibility*, 13; Burkes, *God, Self, and Death*, 24.

20. See Kaminsky, *Corporate Responsibility*, for an interesting discussion of the context of and concept behind Deuteronomy 24:16 (127–37), and on Achan, (67–95).

21. Clifford Geertz, "Religion as a Cultural System," in *The Interpretation of Cultures* (New York: Basic Books, 1973), 108.

22. Ibid., 100.

23. Ibid., 106.

24. Fontaine, *Traditional Sayings*, 250–51.

25. Geertz, "Religion as a Cultural System," 104.
26. Ibid., 105.
27. Levinson suggests that for Ezekiel, "the new principle [is] immediately to re-place the rejected one" concerning inherited sin ("'You Must Not Add,'" 32).

Chapter 2. Personal Religion in Ecclesiastes and Job

1. Edwin M. Good suggests "irony" (*Irony in the Old Testament* [Sheffield, UK: Almond Press, 1981], 176–83).
2. See the discussion of quotation by Robert Gordis, *Koheleth: The Man and His World; A Study of Ecclesiastes* (New York: Jewish Theological Seminary of America, 1951), 100; also R. N. Whybray, *Ecclesiastes* (London: Marshall, Morgan and Scott Publications, 1989), 20–21. Whybray notes that some proverbs are quoted with approval, whereas others are quoted with complex nuance, even if the inherited wisdom is not utterly rejected ("The Identification and Use of Quotations in Ecclesiastes," in *Congress Volume: Vienna, 1980,* ed. J. A. Emerton et al. [Leiden: Brill, 1981], 445–47). For a discussion of the way in which conventional proverb patterns are ironically filled in by the author of Ecclesiastes and for an analysis of the radical framing of proverbs that reflect conventional wisdom, see Niditch, *Folklore and the Hebrew Bible,* 68–71.
3. Michael V. Fox, *Qohelet and His Contradictions* (Sheffield, UK: Almond Press, 1989), 11.
4. Choon-Leong Seow, *Ecclesiastes: A New Translation with Introduction and Commentary* (New York: Doubleday, 1997), 39.
5. Ibid., 38–43. See also Whybray, *Ecclesiastes,* 17–18. For a discussion of tensions, redaction-critical approaches, and interpretative possibilities that allow for an integrated whole, see Thomas Krüger, *Qoheleth: A Commentary* (Minneapolis: Fortress, 2004), 14–19.
6. Carole Fontaine, "Wounded Hero on a Shaman's Quest: Job in the Context of Folk Literature," in *The Voice from the Whirlwind: Interpreting the Book of Job,* ed. Leo G. Perdue and W. Clark Gilpin (Nashville, Tenn.: Abingdon, 1992), 71.
7. David Penchansky, *The Betrayal of God: Ideological Conflict in Job* (Louisville, Ky.: Westminster John Knox, 1990). On tensions between and within characterizations see also H. L. Ginsberg, "Job the Patient and Job the Impatient," in *Congress Volume: Rome, 1968* (Leiden: Brill, 1969), 88–111.
8. Fontaine, for example, sees the poetic and prose portions of Job as "symbiotic" and the work as a whole as a "poeticized folktale" ("Wounded Hero," 71–72). Edward L. Greenstein "seek[s] to read the book as it has been constituted, allowing for the possibility that outlooks and perspectives may shift in the course of reading" ("The Problem of Evil in the Book of Job," in *Mishneh Todah: Studies in Deuteronomy and Its Cultural Environment in Honor of Jeffrey H. Tigay,* ed. Nili Sacher Fox, David A. Glatt-Gilad, and Michael J. Williams [Winona

Lake, Ind.: Eisenbrauns, 2009], 338–39; on the speeches from the whirlwind, see 353. Norman C. Habel makes a case for narrative integrity (*The Book of Job: A Commentary* [Philadelphia: Westminster Press, 1985], 35–39). Marvin H. Pope points to the variousness of material found in Job and notes that the work "in its present form can hardly be regarded as a consistent and unified composition by a single author"; he points nevertheless to "a considerable degree of organic unity despite the inconsistencies" (*Job: Introduction, Translation, and Commentary* [Garden City, N.Y.: Doubleday, 1965], xxx). Carol Newsom thoughtfully reviews previous approaches to cohesion and disparity in Job and provides her own complex response, rooted in issues of genre and voice and influenced by the work of Mikhail Bakhtin. Newsom engages in questions about ways in which the work communicates, focusing on "the fundamentally dialogic nature of the composition, as each genre and voice opens up additional aspects of a complex cultural conversation about the moral nature of reality" (*The Book of Job: A Contest of Moral Imagination* [Oxford: Oxford University Press, 2003], 17. Penchansky writes, "Although Job is not a unified whole, as many have claimed, it now stands as a single narrative unit; first by intention . . . and second by virtue of the reading" (*Betrayal of God*, 43).

9. Carleen Mandolfo explores the ways in which Job's "friends represent normative values of their society" ("A Generic Renegade: A Dialogic Reading of Job and Lament Psalms," in *Diachronic and Synchronic: Reading the Psalms in Real Time; Proceedings of the Baylor Symposium on the Book of Psalms*, ed. Joel S. Burnett, W. H. Bellinger Jr., and W. Dennis Tucker Jr. [London: T&T Clark, 2007], 59).

10. Greenstein, "Problem of Evil," 336, 338–39.

11. Seow, *Ecclesiastes*, 38.

12. Fox, *Qohelet*, 151.

13. Whybray, *Ecclesiastes*, 12–14.

14. Seow, *Ecclesiastes*, 11–36.

15. For a good overview of these opinions, see Krüger, *Qoheleth*, 21–22; see also Fox, *Qohelet*, 16–17.

16. John Gray, *The Book of Job* (Sheffield, UK: Sheffield Phoenix Press, 2010), 35.

17. Robert Gordis, *The Book of God and Man: A Study of Job* (Chicago: University of Chicago Press, 1965), 216.

18. Pope, *Job*, xl.

19. Avi Hurvitz, "The Date of the Prose Tale of Job Linguistically Reconsidered," *Harvard Theological Review* 67 (1974): 17–34.

20. Gordis, *Book of God*, 216.

21. Pope, *Job*, 24–25; see also Penchansky, *Betrayal of God*, 66.

22. See Burkes, *God, Self, and Death*, 57–59, 76–80.

23. See Fox, *Qohelet*, 94; Seow, *Ecclesiastes*, 176.

24. Geertz, "Religion as a Cultural System," 100.

25. Ibid.

26. Kyle R. Greenwood, "Debating Wisdom: The Role of Voice in Ecclesiastes," *Catholic Biblical Quarterly* 74 (2012): 476–91.

27. Ibid., 491.

28. Ibid., 479.

29. Eric S. Christianson, *A Time to Tell: Narrative Strategies in Ecclesiastes* (Sheffield, UK: Sheffield Academic Press, 1998), 40.

30. Ibid., 41. On the multifaceted nature of the pronoun "I," see the discussion by Newsom, *Self as Symbolic Space,* 198–99.

31. Christianson, *Time to Tell,* 177.

32. Ibid., 174–78.

33. Ibid., 194.

34. See the translation as "venom" and a comment by Pope (*Job,* 50).

35. Christianson, *Time to Tell,* 177.

36. See Robert Doran, *The Stewards of the Poor: The Man of God, Rabbula, and Hiba in Fifth-Century Edessa* (Kalamazoo, Mich.: Cistercian Publications, 2006).

37. Seow, *Ecclesiastes,* 55–56.

38. Krüger, *Qoheleth,* 197–98.

39. Fox, *Qohelet,* 294.

40. See Susan Ackerman, "The Queen Mother and the Cult in Ancient Israel," *Journal of Biblical Literature* 112 (1993): 385–401.

41. Seow, *Ecclesiastes,* 356.

42. Ibid., 358–59.

43. See Fox, *Qohelet,* 288.

44. Ibid., 293.

45. See, for example, ibid., 191.

46. For example, Lamentations 3:30 and Isaiah 50:6. On references to the impaired or punished body and lament literature, see Amy Erikson, "'Without My Flesh I Will See God': Job's Rhetoric of the Body," *Journal of Biblical Literature* 132 (2013): 303, and see, for example, Psalms 6:7 (6:8 English) and 31:10–11 (31:9–10 English).

47. Taking account of the deeply embodied language in Job, Erikson argues that Job's speeches subvert traditional imagery of the body. Job "separates his broken body from his contention that he is innocent" ("'Without My Flesh,'" 296). Job accepts that according to conventional wisdom, the condition of the body marks guilt or innocence, but he insists upon "a disjunction between what is written on the body and the essence of one's character, as righteous or wicked" (299).

Chapter 3. From Incantation and Lament to Autobiography

1. These links as well as connections to patterns in a wider range of ancient Near Eastern literatures have been explored by Joseph Blenkinsopp, "The Nehemiah

Autobiographical Memoir," *Language, Theology, and the Bible: Essays in Honour of James Barr,* ed. Samuel E. Balentine and John Barton (Oxford: Clarendon, 1994), 204–8; Ulrich Kellermann, *Nehemiah: Quellen, Uberlieferung und Geschichte* (Berlin: Töpelmann, 1967), 84–88; Kathleen M. O'Connor, *The Confessions of Jeremiah: Their Interpretation and Role in Chapters 1–25* (Atlanta: Scholars Press, 1988); Patrick D. Miller, "Trouble and Woe: Interpreting Biblical Laments," *Interpretation* 37 (1983): 40–45; Walter Baumgartner, *Jeremiah's Poems of Lament,* trans. David E. Orten (Sheffield, UK: Almond Press, 1988). For good studies of the literary form of the lament, see Baumgartner, *Jeremiah's Poems,* 19–40; Claus Westermann, *Praise and Lament in the Psalms,* trans. Keith R. Crim and Richard N. Soulen (Atlanta: John Knox, 1981), 64–81; Tony W. Cartledge, "Conditional Vows in the Psalms of Lament," in *The Listening Heart: Essays in Wisdom and the Psalms in Honor of Roland E. Murphy, O. Carm.,* ed. Kenneth G. Hoglund, E. Huwiler, J. Glass, and R. Lee (Sheffield, UK: JSOT Press, 1987), 77. Cartledge also discusses comparatively the role of the vow in ancient Near Eastern prayer, a motif frequently found in the pattern of the lament; see his *Vows in the Hebrew Bible and the Ancient Near East* (Sheffield, UK: Sheffield Academic Press, 1992), 74–136. See also the careful comparisons drawn by Alan Lenzi between Mesopotamian prayer forms and the Israelite personal lament in "Invoking the God: Interpreting Invocations in Mesopotamian Prayer and Biblical Laments of the Individual," *Journal of Biblical Literature* 129 (2010): 303–15; Tsvi Abusch, "Prayers, Hymns, Incantations, and Curses: Mesopotamia," in *Religion of the Ancient World: A Guide,* ed. Sarah Iles Johnston (Cambridge, Mass.: Belknap Press of Harvard University Press, 2004), 355. For a recent treatment of Akkadian prayer forms and valuable bibliographic data, see Alan Lenzi, ed., *Reading Akkadian Prayers and Hymns: An Introduction* (Atlanta: SBL, 2011).

2. See Theodore J. Lewis, "Job 19 in the Light of the Ketef Hinnom Inscriptions and Amulets," in *Puzzling out the Past: Studies in Northwest Semitic Languages and Literatures in Honor of Bruce Zuckerman,* ed. Marilyn J. Lundberg, Steven Fine, and Wayne T. Pitard (Leiden: Brill, 2012), 110.

3. Ibid., 100–101.

4. James A. Montgomery, *Aramaic Incantation Texts from Nippur* (Philadelphia: University Museum, 1913); Charles D. Isbell, *Corpus of the Aramaic Incantation Bowls* (Missoula, Mont.: SBL, 1975); Joseph Naveh and Shaul Shaked, *Amulets and Magic Bowls: Aramaic Incantations of Late Antiquity* (Jerusalem: Magnes, 1985); Naveh and Shaked, *Magic Spells and Formulae: Aramaic Incantations of Late Antiquity* (Jerusalem: Magnes, 1993).

5. See Isbell, *Aramaic Incantation Bowls,* bowls 28, 38, 59.

6. Ibid., bowls 19:4, 20:6–7, 22:4.

7. Compare views concerning the way in which the bowl functions in Isbell, *Aramaic Incantation Bowls,* 13–15, and Naveh and Shaked, *Amulets and Bowls,* 15.

8. For language of "pressing," see Naveh and Shaked, *Amulets and Bowls,* bowl 3:4, and Isbell, *Aramaic Incantation Bowls,* bowl 11:1. For "cover," see Isbell, *Aramaic Incantation Bowls,* bowl 5:1.

9. Jan Van Dijk, Albrecht Goetze, and Mary I. Hussey, *Early Mesopotamian Incantations and Rituals* (New Haven, Conn.: Yale University Press, 1985), 21–22.

10. Carleen Mandolfo points to the generic relationship between the laments and Job, but also points to important differences in "the rhetorical goals of each text" and to the ways in which Job "as character and text diverges from standard practice in ways that pose a grave threat to the theological status quo" ("Generic Renegade," 54).

11. Isbell, *Aramaic Incantation Bowls,* 19–20.

12. For classic discussions of form and context, see Hermann Gunkel, *Introduction to Psalms: The Genres of the Religious Lyric of Israel,* completed by Joachim Begrich, trans. James D. Nogalski (Macon, Ga.: Mercer University Press, 1998), 123; Sigmund Mowinckel, *Psalmenstudien: ʾAwan und die individuellen Klagepsalmen* (Kristiana, Norway: SNVAO, 1921), 1:137–54. For a good overview of scholarly discussions concerning context and tradition, and matters involving the identity of the purported speaker and his foes, see Patrick D. Miller, "Trouble and Woe," 32–45; on literary convention and appropriation, see Esther M. Menn, "No Ordinary Lament: Relecture and the Identity of the Distressed in Psalm 22," *Harvard Theological Review* 93 (2000): 301–41. Menn is especially interested in the "productive tension … between the primary liturgical function of the Psalms and the more recent palimpsest of historicizing interpretation," evidenced early on by biblical superscriptions that precede individual psalms (302). She calls attention to the "shifting identity of the 'I' of Psalm 22" (303), tries to understand possible contexts for its recitation (304–8), and is attuned to the role and significance of "stereotypical metaphors and imagery (that) offer a means of connecting the idiosyncratic, personal distress of the individual with cultural archetypes of affliction and restoration" (309).

13. On recurring language and imagery in the laments, see Claus Westermann, *Praise and Lament,* 64–81; Baumgartner, *Jeremiah's Poems,* 19–40; and Patrick D. Miller, "Troubles and Woe," 34–35, 38–45. For a review of scholarly suggestions for the identity of the enemy, see Miller, "Troubles and Woe," 34.

14. Cartledge, "Conditional Vows," 78–83.

15. Patrick D. Miller, "Trouble and Woe," 34.

16. Moshe Greenberg, *Biblical Prose Prayer as a Window in the Popular Religion of Israel* (Berkeley: University of California Press, 1983), 40.

17. Menn, "No Ordinary Lament," 308.

18. Greenberg, *Biblical Prose Prayer,* 6.

19. Menn, "No Ordinary Lament," 303.

20. Ibid., 306.

21. Gunkel, *The Psalms: A Form-Critical Introduction,* trans. Thomas M. Horner (Philadelphia: Fortress, 1967), 16.

22. Greenberg, *Biblical Prose Prayer.*
23. For a good discussion of contrasts that scholars have drawn between "prose prayers" and "poetic prayers" as they relate to matters of style, content, and context, and a distinction between formulaic official religious expression and individual expression, see Marc Zvi Brettler, "Women and Psalms: Towards an Understanding of the Role of Women's Prayer in the Israelite Cult," in *Gender and Law in the Hebrew Bible and the Ancient Near East,* ed. Victor H. Matthews, Bernard M. Levinson, and Tikva Frymer-Kensky (Sheffield, UK: Sheffield Academic Press, 1998), 45–56. In exploring women's prayer in the Hebrew Bible, Brettler discusses the interplay and overlap between categories of official and unofficial, set prayer forms and spontaneous expression, and finds analogies in the Yiddish *tkhines,* a type of women's prayers usually composed by men.
24. I agree with Jack Sasson's translation choices concerning the tense of the verbs, employing "the English present to translate ... where the Hebrew has the perfect, but also the imperfect"; see Sasson, *Jonah: A New Translation with Introduction, Commentary, and Interpretations* (New Haven, Conn.: Yale University Press, 1990), 163–64.
25. Ibid., 171–74, 192.
26. Ibid., 164.
27. Erving Goffman, *The Presentation of Self in Everyday Life* (Garden City, N.Y.: Doubleday, 1959).
28. Patrick D. Miller, "Troubles and Woe," 36–37; Menn, "No Ordinary Lament," 303.
29. Olyan, "Search for the Elusive Self," 44, 47.
30. Gyatso, *Apparitions of the Self,* 112.
31. Patrick D. Miller, "Troubles and Woe," 43–45.
32. O'Connor, *Confessions of Jeremiah;* A. R. Diamond, *The Confessions of Jeremiah in Context: Scenes of Prophetic Drama* (Sheffield, UK: JSOT Press, 1987); Mark S. Smith, *The Laments of Jeremiah and Their Contexts: A Literary and Redactional Study of Jeremiah 11–20* (Atlanta: Scholars, 1990). For particular emphasis on references to "heart" (*lēb*) and "inner being" (*nepeš*) in Jeremiah and the use of first-person speech, discussed above in chapter two, see Timothy Polk, *The Prophetic Persona: Jeremiah and the Language of the Self* (Sheffield, UK: JSOT Press, 1984).
33. See, for example, Diamond, *Confessions of Jeremiah,* 74–75; Patrick D. Miller, "Troubles and Woe," 40–45; Robert C. Culley, "The Confessions of Jeremiah and Traditional Discourse," in *"A Wise and Discerning Mind": Essays in Honor of Burke O. Long,* ed. Saul M. Olyan and Robert C. Culley (Providence, R.I.: Brown Judaic Studies, 2000), 69–81; Mark S. Smith, *Laments of Jeremiah,* 2.
34. For a discussion of various approaches to the revenge motif, see Michael Avioz, "The Call for Revenge in Jeremiah's Complaints (Jer XI–XX)," *Vetus Testamentum* 55 (2005): 429–38. Avioz treats the request for vengeance in theological

terms as "a means of measure for measure," pointing to God as judge and the prophet as his messenger deserving of protection (438).

35. For a discussion of text-critical and translation challenges posed by Jeremiah 15:13–14, see Erhard Gerstenberger, "Jeremiah's Complaints: Observations of Jer 15:10–21," *Journal of Biblical Literature* 82 (1963): 395–96. Mark S. Smith regards 15:10–15 as a separate unit from the lament, a curse text (*Laments of Jeremiah*, 2).

36. Diamond discusses nuances of bitterness and irony that might be seen to distinguish Jeremiah's use of the pattern (*Confessions of Jeremiah*, 75). Gerstenberger, concentrating on the redaction history of the piece, concludes that an essential lament form, dealing with individual suffering, has been expanded in stages to theologically frame and explain "the agony of the people," who face the geopolitical realities of the Babylonian conquest ("Jeremiah's Complaints," 408).

37. Robert P. Carroll, alluding to the work of Timothy Polk (*The Prophetic Persona*), employs the phrase "the created persona of the prophet" (*Jeremiah: A Commentary* [Philadelphia: Westminster, 1986], 278; see also 280, 336).

38. Diamond, *Confessions of Jeremiah*; O'Connor, *Confessions of Jeremiah*; Gerstenberger, "Jeremiah's Complaints"; David J. A. Clines and David M. Gunn, "Form, Occasion and Redaction in Jeremiah 20," *Zeitschrift für die alttestamentliche Wissenschaft* 88 (1976): 390–401.

39. See Gyatso, *Apparitions of the Self*, 108.

40. See Blenkinsopp, "Nehemiah Autobiographical Memoir," and, for example, the so-called autobiography of the Egyptian architect Nekhebu and that of Pepinakht called Heqaib in Miriam Lichtheim, *Ancient Egyptian Autobiographies Chiefly of the Middle Kingdom: A Study and an Anthology* (Gottingen: Vandenhoeck & Ruprecht, 1988), 11–16.

41. Morton Smith, *Palestinian Parties and Politics*, 96–112.

42. Jacob L. Wright, "Commensal Politics in Ancient Western Asia," pts. 1 and 3, *Zeitschrift für die alttestamentliche Wissenschaft* 122 (2010): 333–52.

43. Gyatso, *Apparitions of the Self*, 111.

44. Ibid., 112.

45. Patricia Miller, "Shifting Selves," 17; Gyatso, *Apparitions of the Self*, 104.

46. Gyatso, *Apparitions of the Self*, 114.

47. Arnaldo Momigliano, *The Development of Greek Biography* (Cambridge, Mass.: Harvard University Press, 1993), 37; see also Blenkinsopp, "Nehemiah Autobiographical Memoir," 201.

48. See Morton Smith, *Palestinian Parties and Politics*, 107–9.

Chapter 4. The Negotiating Self

1. Herbert J. Schlesinger, *Promises, Oaths, and Vows: On the Psychology of Promising* (New York: Analytic Press, 2008), 4.

2. Ibid., 2.

3. Ibid., 5.

4. Ibid., 19.

5. Ibid., 20.

6. Cartledge explores in detail the role of the vow in the lament form ("Conditional Vows") and the link between incantations, prayers, laments, and vows in an ancient Near Eastern context (*Vows in the Hebrew Bible,* 74–136).

7. Jacques Berlinerblau, *The Vow and "Popular Religious Groups" in Ancient Israel* (Sheffield, UK: Sheffield Academic Press, 1996); Cartledge, *Vows in the Hebrew Bible;* see also A. Wendel, *Die israelitische-jüdische Gelübde* (Berlin: Philo Verlag, 1931).

8. See Susan Niditch, *War in the Hebrew Bible: A Study in the Ethics of Violence* (Oxford: Oxford University Press, 1993), 28–77.

9. See the translation and discussion by Kent P. Jackson, "The Language of the Mesha Inscription," in *Studies in the Mesha Inscription and Moab,* ed. Andrew Dearman (Atlanta: Scholars Press, 1989), 111–12.

10. Peggy L. Day, "From the Child Is Born the Woman," in *Gender and Difference in Ancient Israel,* ed. Peggy L. Day (Minneapolis: Fortress, 1989).

11. See the discussion in John Day, *Molech: A God of Human Sacrifice in the Old Testament* (Cambridge: Cambridge University Press, 1989), 4–14.

12. See ibid., 5–7; for a range of evidence, see George Charles Heider, "The Cult of Molek: A New Examination of the Biblical and Extra-Biblical Evidence (PhD diss., Yale University, 1984), 94–193; Heider, *The Cult of Molek: A Reassessment* (Sheffield, UK: JSOT Press, 1985).

13. Heider, *Cult of Molek,* 406. Note that others argue that *mlk* refers not a deity named Molek but to a kind of sacrifice; see, for example, Heath D. Dewrell, "Child Sacrifice in Ancient Israel and Its Opponents" (PhD diss., Johns Hopkins University, 2012).

14. Berlinerblau, *Vow and "Popular Religious Groups,"* 38, 44–45.

15. Michael L. Satlow, "Giving for a Return: Jewish Votive Offerings in Late Antiquity," in *Religion and the Self in Antiquity,* ed. David Brakke, Michael L. Satlow, and Steven Weitzman (Bloomington: Indiana University Press, 2005), 94.

16. Karel van der Toorn juxtaposes this prohibition with Proverbs 7:14–20, in which a wayward wife mentions having just offered sacrifices to pay for her vow. Van der Toorn concludes that women often prostituted themselves to cover the cost of expensive vows ("Female Prostitution in Payment of Vows in Ancient Israel," *Journal of Biblical Literature* 108 [1989]: 197–201). This idea has been rejected by a consensus of scholars (see, for example, Hennie J. Marsman, *Women in Ugarit and Israel: Their Social and Religious Position in the Context of the Ancient Near East* [Leiden: Brill, 2003], 598–99 and references). More plausibly, Tikva Frymer-Kensky emphasized the connection implicitly drawn in the woman's words between meat eating (made possible by sacrifice) and uncontrolled, socially destructive passion (lecture, Mt. Holyoke College, fall 1981).

17. See also Berlinerblau, *Vow and "Popular Religious Groups,"* 83.

18. Carol Meyers, "Procreation, Production, and Protection: Male-Female Balance in Early Israel," *Journal of the American Academy of Religion* 51 (1983): 585.

19. See Satlow, "Giving for a Return," 95.

20. See Satlow's discussion of Berlinerblau's interest in the "tension between spontaneous and institutionalized religious expression and its control" ("Giving for a Return," 97).

21. See Satlow, "Giving for a Return," 91, 97; Berlinerblau, *Vow and "Popular Religious Groups,"* 67, 145.

22. See Tony W. Cartledge, "Were Nazirite Vows Unconditional?" *Catholic Biblical Quarterly* 51 (1989): 411–12.

23. Berlinerblau, *Vow and "Popular Religious Groups,"* 103.

24. See Rainer Albertz and Rüdiger Schmitt, *Family and Household Religion in Ancient Israel and the Levant* (Winona Lake, Ind.: Eisenbrauns, 2012), 53; see also Carol Meyers, "The Hannah Narrative in Feminist Perspective," in *"Go to the Land I Will Show You": Studies in Honor of Dwight W. Young,* ed. Joseph E. Coleson and Victor H. Matthews (Winona Lake, Ind.: Eisenbrauns, 1996), 123–24.

25. See, for example, the entry in Francis Brown, S. R. Driver, and Charles A. Briggs, *A Hebrew and English Lexicon of the Old Testament* (Oxford: Clarendon Press, 1968), 494–95.

26. On nuances of the language and the medium of "self-address," see J. Gerald Janzen, "Prayer and/as Self-Address: The Case of Hannah," in *A God So Near: Essays on Old Testament Theology in Honor of Patrick D. Miller,* ed. Brent A. Strawn and Nancy R. Bowen (Winona Lake, Ind.: Eisenbrauns, 2003), 124–25.

27. Orsi, "Study of Lived Religion," 169.

28. Ibid., 172.

29. Ibid.; see also Meyers, "Hannah Narrative," 125.

30. Susan Ackerman suggests that Hannah may have taken on a temporary Nazirite vow, reflected in her insistence to Eli that she has not been drinking wine or strong drink (1 Samuel 1:15). Ackerman grapples with variations in the manuscript traditions regarding Hannah's taking of food and wine, pointing out that 1 Samuel 1:15 (MT) might be seen to contradict 1 Samuel 1:9 (MT), which mentions drinking (without an object). While I am not convinced that Hannah is a female Nazirite, nevertheless Ackerman beautifully points to the ritual dimensions of her appearance at the shrine and of the request made, and to the place of these interactions in portrayals of women's religion (*Women and the Religion of Ancient Israel* [New Haven, Conn.: Yale University Press, forthcoming], ch. 5).

31. Meyers, "Hannah Narrative," 122.

32. See the discussion in Marsman, *Women in Ugarit and Israel,* 224, 597. The advice of Lemuel's mother has to do with avoiding the wrong sort of women (who "destroy kings"), embracing temperance, and defending the marginal members

of society; it is followed by the ode to the woman of valor, the ideal wife, discussed in this chapter in connection with the Nazirite vow and female status.

33. See Susan Niditch, "The Challenge of Israelite Epic," in *A Companion to Ancient Epic*, ed. John Miles Foley (Oxford: Blackwell, 2005), 282; Yaira Amit, "'There was a man . . . and his name was': Editorial Variations and Their Tendenz" [in Hebrew], *Beth Mikra* 30 (1984/85): 388–99.

34. See Susan Niditch, *"My Brother Esau Is a Hairy Man": Hair and Identity in Ancient Israel* (Oxford: Oxford University Press, 2008), 81–94.

35. Martin Noth, *Numbers: A Commentary*, trans. James D. Martin (London: SCM Press, 1968); Morris Jastrow Jr., "The 'Nazir' Legislation," *Journal of Biblical Literature* 44 (1914): 266–85.

36. For a discussion of hairstyles for men and women and questions about the visual impact of a temporary Nazirite vow, see Niditch, *"My Brother Esau,"* 93–94.

37. See Philip J. King and Lawrence E. Stager, *Life in Biblical Israel* (Louisville, Ky.: Westminster John Knox, 2001), 373.

38. See Meyers, "Hannah Narrative," 125.

39. See also Francesca Stavrakopoulou, "'Popular Religion' and 'Official' Religion: Practice, Perception, Portrayal," in *Religious Diversity in Ancient Israel and Judah*, ed. Francesca Stavrakopoulou and John Barton (London: T&T Clark International, 2010), 37–59.

40. Compare Berlinerblau's emphasis on the way in which vowing can "circumvent" official religion (*Vow and "Popular Religious Groups,"* 153); see also Cartledge, who notes that "regulations concerning vows may be seen as an attempt to keep the practice within the confines and control of the official cultus" (*Vows in the Hebrew Bible*, 31).

41. Cartledge, *Vows in the Hebrew Bible*, 23.

42. Cartledge, "Were Nazirite Vows Unconditional?," 410.

43. Cartledge, *Vows in the Hebrew Bible*, 16; see also 33, 103, 125, 154–55.

44. See Erhard Blum, "Issues and Problems in the Contemporary Debate Regarding the Priestly Writings," in *The Strata of the Priestly Writings: Contemporary Debate and Future Directions*, ed. Sarah Shectman and Joel S. Baden (Zürich: TZV, 2009), 31–44. For an excellent summary of positions concerning the date and complexity of priestly literature in Numbers, see Adrianne B. Leveen, "Variations on a Theme: Differing Conceptions of Memory in the Book of Numbers," *Journal for the Study of the Old Testament* 27 (2002): 206–7n11, 218n30.

45. See Knoppers, "Revisiting the Samarian Question," 265–89.

46. Seow, "Social World of Ecclesiastes."

47. Christine Roy Yoder, "The Woman of Substance (אשת-חיל): A Socioeconomic Reading of Proverbs 31:10–31," *Journal of Biblical Literature* 122 (2003): 427–47.

48. Nahman Avigad, "The Contribution of Hebrew Seals to an Understanding of Israelite Religion and Society," in *Ancient Israelite Religion*, ed. Patrick D.

Miller, Paul D. Hanson, and S. Dean McBride (Philadelphia: Fortress, 1987), 205–6.

49. See Niditch, *"My Brother Esau,"* 89, 101, and the discussion of Jeremiah 7:29 and Zechariah 13:4.

50. See Robert R. Wilson, *Prophecy and Society in Ancient Israel* (Philadelphia: Fortress, 1980), 69–73, 306–8.

51. See Susan Niditch, *Judges: A Commentary* (Louisville, Ky.: Westminster John Knox, 2008), 145–46 and references.

52. Cartledge, *Vows in the Hebrew Bible,* 31; see also Berlinerblau, *Vow and "Popular Religious Groups,"* 101.

53. See Susan Niditch, "The Wronged Woman Righted: An Analysis of Genesis 38," *Harvard Theological Review* 72 (1979): 145–46.

54. A vow to make an offering to the Queen of Heaven on the part of a wife might well disturb her more orthodox husband, as it does Jeremiah (Jeremiah 44:15–30), although the men described in Jeremiah 44:15 are, in fact, supportive of their wives' relationship with the Queen of Heaven. Husbands presumably have the right to intervene and cancel such vows, which were probably regarded as having power even when the enforcer was a deity other than Yahweh. On baking cakes to the Queen of Heaven, status, and women's religion, see Susan Ackerman, "'And the Women Knead Dough': The Worship of the Queen of Heaven in Sixth-Century Judah," in *Gender and Difference in Ancient Israel,* ed. Peggy L. Day (Minneapolis: Fortress, 1989), 109–24.

55. On Elkanah's response and its implications, see Marsman, *Women in Ugarit and Israel,* 240, 619; see also Meyers's discussion of Hannah's vow (1 Samuel 1:11), Elkanah's vow (1:21), the fulfillment of Hannah's vow (1:27), and the possible significance of manuscript variations ("Hannah Narrative," 123, 125).

Chapter 5. Material Religion, Created and Experienced

1. Carol Meyers, "Household Religion," in *Religious Diversity in Ancient Israel and Judah,* ed. Francesca Stavrakopoulou and John Barton (London: T&T Clark International, 2010), 118–34; Albertz, "Personal Piety" and "Family Religion in Ancient Israel"; and three contributions to *Household and Family Religion in Antiquity,* ed. John Bodel and Saul M. Olyan (Oxford: Blackwell, 2008): Saul M. Olyan, "Family Religion in Israel and the Wider Levant of the First Millennium BCE," 113–26; Theodore Lewis, "Family, Household, and Local Religion at Late Bronze Age Ugarit," 60–88; Susan Ackerman, "Household Religion, Family Religion, and Women's Religion in Ancient Israel," 127–58.

2. Ziony Zevit, *The Religions of Ancient Israel: A Synthesis of Parallactic Approaches* (New York: Continuum, 2001); Albertz and Schmitt, *Family and Household Religion;* Assaf Yasur-Landau, Jennie R. Ebeling, and Laura B. Mazow, eds., *Household Archaeology in Ancient Israel and Beyond* (Leiden: Brill, 2011); Patricia Cox Miller, "Shifting Selves."

3. Knowles, *Centrality Practiced,* 120.

4. Middlemas, *Troubles of Templeless Judah,* 122–26.

5. Stern, "Religious Revolution in Persian-Period Judah," 199–205.

6. Abusch, "Prayers, Hymns, Incantations"; Abusch, "The Demonic Image of the Witch in Standard Babylonian Literature: The Reworking of Popular Conceptions by Learned Exorcists," in *Religion, Science, and Magic in Concert and in Conflict,* ed. Jacob Neusner, Ernest S. Frerichs, and Paul Virgil McCracken (New York: Oxford University Press, 1989), 27–58.

7. See Bronislaw Malinowski, *Magic, Science and Religion, and Other Essays* (Garden City, N.Y.: Doubleday, 1954), 88–90.

8. Theodore J. Lewis, "Athartu's Incantations and the Use of the Divine Names as Weapons," *Journal of Near Eastern Studies* 70 (2011): 207–27.

9. See Lewis, "Job 19," 99–113.

10. Elizabeth Bloch-Smith, *Judahite Burial Practices and Beliefs about the Dead* (Sheffield, UK: Sheffield Academic Press, 1992); Stern, *Material Culture of the Bible.*

11. Comment by a nineteenth-century commentator, cited in David Charles Sloane, *The Last Great Necessity: Cemeteries in American History* (Baltimore: Johns Hopkins University Press, 1984), 46.

12. Kristin Ann Hass, *Carried to the Wall: American Memory and the Vietnam Veterans Memorial* (Berkeley: University of California Press, 1998), 14, 21, 30.

13. Deborah Green, "Sweet Spices in the Tomb: An Initial Study of the Use of Perfume in Jewish Burials," in *Commemorating the Dead: Texts and Artifacts in Context,* ed. Laurie Brink and Deborah Green (Berlin: de Gruyter, 2008), 145–73; see also David Kraemer, *The Meanings of Death in Rabbinic Judaism* (London: Routledge, 2000).

14. Geertz, "Religion as a Cultural System," 94–98.

15. Bloch-Smith, *Judahite Burial Practices,* 230. Ziony Zevit suggests a date from the ninth to seventh centuries BCE, based upon his assessment of the "typological context" (*Religions of Ancient Israel,* 406).

16. Joseph Naveh, "Old Hebrew Inscriptions in a Burial Cave," *Israel Exploration Journal* 13 (1963): 75.

17. Ibid., 75; Bloch-Smith, *Judahite Burial Practices,* 230; Stern, *Material Culture of the Bible,* 78.

18. Cross, "Cave Inscriptions from Khirbet Lei."

19. See Bloch-Smith, *Judahite Burial Practices,* 230.

20. Ibid., 149–50.

21. Ibid., 149.

22. Ibid., 230; see also N. Haas, "Human Skeletal Remains in Two Burial Caves," *Israel Exploration Journal* 13 (1963): 93–96.

23. Bloch-Smith, *Judahite Burial Practices,* 148.

24. Avraham Faust, private communication to the author, July 9, 2013.

25. Naveh, "Old Hebrew Inscriptions," 78.

26. Cross, "Cave Inscriptions from Khirbet Lei," 304.

27. See Naveh, "Old Cave Inscriptions," 77, fig. 4; Zevit, *Religions of Ancient Israel*, 412, fig. 5:15. Note that Zevit considers the figure to be female and seated on a low-backed chair whose line contours are visible in the see-through figure of the player (410–12); cf. Naveh, "Old Cave Inscriptions," 77.

28. See Naveh, "Old Cave Inscriptions," 78, fig. 5; Zevit, *Religions of Ancient Israel*, 428, fig. 5:26.

29. See Naveh, "Old Cave Inscriptions," 79, fig. 6; Zevit, *Religions of Ancient Israel*, 416, fig. 5:20. Zevit identifies the headgear as a warrior's feathered headdress or horns (416).

30. See Naveh, "Old Cave Inscriptions," 80, fig. 7; Zevit, *Religions of Ancient Israel*, 434, fig. 5:32.

31. See Naveh, "Old Cave Inscriptions," 82, fig. 10; Zevit, *Religions of Ancient Israel*, 409, fig. 5:12.

32. See P. King and L. Stager, *Life in Biblical Israel*, 291–94.

33. Pirhiya Beck, "The Drawings From Horvat Teman (Kuntillet ʿAjrud)," *Tel Aviv* 9 (1982): 31–36. For a more recent treatment, see Zeʾev Meshel, *Kuntillet ʿAjrud (Horvat Teman): An Iron Age II Religious Site on the Judah-Sinai Border* (Jerusalem: Israel Exploration Society, 2012), 61–69.

34. Catherine Hezser, *Jewish Literacy in Roman Palestine* (Tübingen: Mohr Siebeck, 2001), 219–23.

35. For a discussion of the drawings, see Dan Barag, "The Tomb of Jason Reconsidered," in *"Follow the Wise": Studies in Jewish History and Culture in Honor of Lee I. Levine* (Winona Lake, Ind.: Eisenbrauns, 2010), 152–53; see also Rachel Hachlili, *Jewish Funerary Customs, Practices, and Rites in the Second Temple Period* (Leiden: Brill, 2005), 94, 148–50. Hachlili suggests that "ships already appeared in funerary art in the Land of Israel at the end of the eighth century BCE" (150).

36. David Kraemer, *Meanings of Death*, 17–18, 55.

37. Avraham Faust, "Doorway Orientation, Settlement Planning and Cosmology in Ancient Israel during Iron Age II," *Oxford Journal of Archaeology* 20 (2001): 140, 143; and private communication to the author, July 9, 2013.

38. See E. Douglas Van Buren, "Concerning the Horned Cap of the Mesopotamian Gods," *Orientalia* 12 (1943): 318–27. Some have identified the figure as a warrior wearing a feathered hat, others as a Bes figure. Zevit points to problems and ambiguities that make the interpretation of the figure challenging. He indicates the importance of the figure's arms in a petitioning pose, but cautiously avoids drawing conclusions as to identity (*Religions of Ancient Israel*, 416–17).

39. See Susan Niditch, *The Symbolic Vision in Biblical Tradition* (Chico, Calif.: Scholars Press, 1980), 121–24.

40. See Barag, "Tomb of Jason," 148–49.

41. Naveh, "Old Hebrew Inscriptions," 76n5. Zevit suggests that the drawing is a map of Lachish (*Religions of Ancient Israel*, 410).
42. Cross, "Cave Inscriptions from Khirbet Lei," 304; see also Zevit, *Religions of Ancient Israel*, 407.
43. Naveh, "Old Hebrew Inscriptions," 81.
44. Cross, "Cave Inscriptions from Khirbet Lei," 302–3; Zevit, along with Naveh and Lemaire, dates the paleography to ca. 700 BCE (*Religions of Ancient Israel*, 420).
45. Lewis, "Job 19," 107, 107n40 for references to the use of *gʿr* at Qumran.
46. For a thorough discussion of imagery of the "stone," see Carol L. Meyers and Eric M. Meyers, *Haggai, Zechariah 1–8* (Garden City, N.Y.: Doubleday, 1987), 204–11.
47. See, for example, the language of the magic bowls in Naveh and Shaked, *Amulets and Bowls*, 125 (bowl 1:11–12), 135 (bowl 2:8), and 147 (bowl 3:4–5).
48. Ibid., 15.
49. See Niditch, *"My Brother Esau,"* 95–103.
50. Ellen F. Davis, *Swallowing the Scroll: Textuality and the Dynamics of Discourses in Ezekiel's Prophecy* (Sheffield, UK: Sheffield Academic Press, 1989), 30–31, 41, 45, 70–71.

Chapter 6. Experiencing the Divine Personally

This chapter is a revised and reframed version of an essay originally published in *Religious Diversity in Ancient Israel and Judah*, ed. Francesca Stavrakopoulou and John Barton (London: T&T Clark International, 2010), 11–22.

1. Ninian Smart, *Worldviews: Crosscultural Explorations of Human Beliefs* (New York: Scribner's Sons, 1983), 8, 62–78.
2. Susan Ackerman, *Under Every Green Tree: Popular Religion in Sixth-Century Judah* (Atlanta: Scholars Press, 1992), 1–3, 213–17.
3. Ackerman, *Under Every Green Tree*; Peter Brown, *The Cult of the Saints: Its Rise and Function in Latin Christianity* (Chicago: University of Chicago Press, 1981), 19; Arnaldo D. Momigliano, "Popular Religious Beliefs and Late Roman Historians," *Studies in Church History* 8 (1971): 18; Lester Grabbe, *A History of the Jews and Judaism in the Second Temple Period:* vol. 1, *Yehud: A History of the Persian Province of Judah* (London: T&T Clark, 2004), 253; Gananath Obeyesekere, *Medusa's Hair: An Essay on Personal Symbols and Religious Experience* (Chicago: University of Chicago Press, 1981).
4. Obeyesekere, *Medusa's Hair,* 7, 37, 40.
5. Ibid., 11–12.
6. See Brakke, Satlow, and Weitzman, *Religion and the Self,* 5; Olyan, "Search for the Elusive Self," 40–41; Steven T. Katz, "'Conservative' Character of Mystical Experience," 5–6; Foley, *Immanent Art.*

7. See Niditch, *Symbolic Vision*, 15–16.
8. See Wilson, *Prophecy and Society in Ancient Israel*.
9. Robert R. Wilson, "Prophecy in Crisis: The Call of Ezekiel," *Interpretation* 38 (1984): 117–30.
10. See also the other visions in Zechariah 1–8 for variations on this stage.
11. See Niditch, *Symbolic Vision*, 203–4.
12. See ibid., 196.
13. Ibid., 207–9.

Chapter 7. Characterization and Contrast

1. Edward F. Campbell Jr., *Ruth: A New Translation with Introduction, Notes, and Commentary* (Garden City, N.Y.: Doubleday, 1975), 5–6; Gillian Feeley-Harnik, "Naomi and Ruth: Building Up the House of David," in *Text and Tradition*, ed. Susan Niditch (Atlanta: Scholars Press, 1990), 170–1.
2. See the overview by Susan Niditch, "Legends of Wise Heroes and Heroines," in *The Hebrew Bible and Its Modern Interpreters*, ed. Douglas A. Knight and Gene M. Tucker (Chico, Calif.: Scholars Press, 1985), 451–52; Campbell, *Ruth*, 23–28; André La Cocque, *Ruth: A Continental Commentary* (Minneapolis: Fortress, 2004); Levinson, "'You Must Not Add'"; Avi Hurwitz, "On the Term שלף נעל in Ruth 4:7," in *Shnaton I: An Annual for Biblical and Ancient Near Eastern Studies*, ed. Jonas C. Greenfield and Moshe Weinfeld (Jerusalem: Israel Bible Company / Tel Aviv: M. Newman, 1975), 45–49.
3. Tamara Cohn Eskenazi and Tikva Frymer-Kensky, *Ruth* (Philadelphia: Jewish Publication Society, 2011), xvi–xix; see also Jack M. Sasson's discussion of dating and his decision not to suggest a date (*Ruth: A New Translation with a Philological Commentary and a Formalist-Folklorist Interpretation* [Baltimore: Johns Hopkins University Press, 1979], 240–52).
4. See Niditch, "Wronged Woman Righted," 143–49.
5. Vladimir Propp, a Russian formalist, notes how the villain in a folktale sometimes changes roles, providing the hero with vital information or other assistance; see *Morphology of the Folktale*, trans. Laurence Scott (Austin: University of Texas Press, 1968), 46–48.
6. See Campbell, *Ruth*, 5.
7. Barry W. Holtz, "Midrash," in *Back to the Sources: Reading the Classic Jewish Texts*, ed. Barry W. Holtz (New York: Summit, 1984), 180; see also Hermann Gunkel, *Reden und Aufsätze* (Göttingen: Vandenhoeck & Ruprecht, 1913), 65–92.
8. Hermann Gunkel, *The Legends of Genesis: The Biblical Saga and History* (New York: Schocken, 1964), 37–87.
9. For approaches to ritual crying from perspectives of comparative religion, see Kimberley Christine Patton and John Stratton Hawley, eds., *Holy Tears: Weeping in the Religious Imagination* (Princeton, N.J.: Princeton University Press,

2005). Patton and Hawley note that crying "can be ethical, releasing communal tensions or reinscribing necessary ethical boundaries" (3), and they attend to qualities of rite of passage, spontaneous versus scripted qualities of crying, and private versus public crying (5–8). On the possibility that "ritualized weeping" in particular contexts is "is a culturally choreographed act, a stylized not spontaneous expression of emotion," see also Gary L. Ebersole, "The Poetics and Politics of Ritualized Weeping in Early and Medieval Japan," in Patton and Hawley, *Holy Tears,* 25.

10. Campbell, *Ruth,* 5–6.

11. Geertz, "Religion as a Cultural System," 94–98.

12. See Feeley-Harnik, "Naomi and Ruth," 176.

13. On the lament in Job and Jeremiah as they relate this passage, see Campbell, *Ruth,* 83.

14. See Carolyn J. Sharp, *Irony and Meaning in the Hebrew Bible* (Bloomington: Indiana University Press, 2009), 185; Alan Cooper, "In Praise of Divine Caprice: The Significance of the Book of Jonah," in *Among the Prophets: Language, Image and Structure in the Prophetic Writings,* ed. Philip R. Davies and David J. A. Clines (Sheffield, UK: Sheffield Academic Press, 1993), 144–63.

15. See Sasson, *Jonah,* 241n6.

16. See Gershom Scholem and Eric T. Schwab, "On Jonah and the Concept of Justice," *Critical Inquiry* 25 (1999): 353, 356; Cooper, "In Praise of Divine Caprice."

17. See Sasson, *Jonah,* 23, 282–83; Thomas B. Dozeman, "Inner-Biblical Interpretation of Yahweh's Gracious and Compassionate Character," *Journal of Biblical Literature* 108 (1989): 207–23.

18. John A. Miles Jr., "Laughing at the Bible: Jonah as Parody," *Jewish Quarterly Review* 65 (1975): 168–81; Arnold J. Band, "Swallowing Jonah: The Eclipse of Parody," *Prooftexts* 10 (1990); 177–95 and the review of scholarship (195n5); Sharp, *Irony and Meaning,* 176–86; Scholem and Schwab, "On Jonah," 356; Good, *Irony in the Old Testament,* 39–55.

19. On narrative links between Jonah and the prophets, including the refusal to serve and the desire to die, see Phyllis Trible, "Studies in the Book of Jonah" (PhD diss., Columbia University, 1963), 266–68.

20. For an excellent form-critical discussion of Jonah and genre, see ibid., 122–259.

21. Compare Trible's suggestion that action "reveals the inward feelings of people," that emotions "are not explicitly expressed" ("Studies in Jonah," 183).

22. On the translation and various suggestions, see Sasson, *Jonah,* 103–4.

23. See Trible's excellent discussion of aspects of personal and material religion in Jonah ("Studies in Jonah," 246).

24. On the relationship of this lament to biblical psalms of lament, on their relative chronology, on the authorship of the poem in Jonah, and on the role of this piece in the tale as parody, see Athalya Brenner, "Jonah's Poem out of and within Its Context," in *Among the Prophets: Language, Image and Structure in the*

Prophetic Writings, ed. Philip R. Davies and David J. A. Clines (Sheffield, UK: Sheffield Academic Press, 1993), 183–92.

25. The formulaic language concerning divine mercy found in many biblical passages and employed by numerous biblical authors in longer and shorter variations (Exodus 34:6–7; Numbers 14:18; Deuteronomy 7:8; Nehemiah 9:17; Joel 2:13; Psalms 86:5, 86:15, 103:8, 111:4, 145:8) has been the topic of scholarly inquiries into biblical intertextuality, questions concerning varying views of theodicy in ancient Israel, and, more specifically for our study, debates concerning worldview in Jonah and implications for the characterization of the prophetic protagonist; see Trible, "Studies in Jonah," 165.

26. See the discussion of translation of this difficult phrase and an overview of opinions in Sasson, *Jonah,* 286–87.

Bibliography

Abusch, Tzvi. "The Demonic Image of the Witch in Standard Babylonian Literature: The Reworking of Popular Conceptions by Learned Exorcists." In *Religion, Science, and Magic in Concert and in Conflict*, edited by Jacob Neusner, Ernest S. Frerichs, and Paul Virgil McCracken Flesher, 27–58. New York: Oxford University Press, 1989.

———. "Prayers, Hymns, Incantations, and Curses: Mesopotamia." In *Religion of the Ancient World: A Guide*, edited by Sarah Iles Johnston, 353–55. Harvard University Press Reference Library. Cambridge, Mass.: Belknap Press of Harvard University Press, 2004.

Ackerman, Susan. "'And the Women Knead Dough': The Worship of the Queen of Heaven in Sixth-Century Judah." In *Gender and Difference in Ancient Israel*, edited by Peggy L. Day, 109–24. Minneapolis: Fortress, 1989.

———. "Household Religion, Family Religion, and Women's Religion in Ancient Israel." In Bodel and Olyan, *Household and Family Religion in Antiquity*, 127–58.

———. "The Queen Mother and the Cult in Ancient Israel." *Journal of Biblical Literature* 112 (1993): 385–401.

———. *Under Every Green Tree: Popular Religion in Sixth-Century Judah*. Harvard Semitic Monographs 46. Atlanta: Scholars Press, 1992.

———. *Women and the Religion of Ancient Israel*. Anchor Yale Bible Reference Library. New Haven, Conn.: Yale University Press, forthcoming.

Albertz, Rainer. "Family Religion in Ancient Israel and Its Surrounds." In Bodel and Olyan, *Household and Family Religion in Antiquity*, 89–112.

———. "Personal Piety." In Stavrakopoulou and Barton, *Religious Diversity in Ancient Israel and Judah*, 135–46.

Albertz, Rainer, and Bob Becking, eds. *Yahwism after the Exile: Perspectives on Israelite Religion in the Persian Era*. Papers Read at the First Meeting of the European Association for Biblical Studies, Utrecht, 6–9 August 2000. Studies in Theology and Religion 5. Assen, Netherlands: Royal Van Gorcum, 2003.

Albertz, Rainer, and Rüdiger Schmitt. *Family and Household Religion in Ancient Israel and the Levant*. Winona Lake, Ind.: Eisenbrauns, 2012.

Amit, Yaira. "'There was a man . . . and his name was': Editorial variations and their tendenz." [In Hebrew.] *Beth Mikra* 30 (1984/85): 388–99.

Avigad, Nahman. "The Contribution of Hebrew Seals to an Understanding of Israelite Religion and Society." In *Ancient Israelite Religion*, edited by Patrick D. Miller, Paul D. Hanson, and S. Dean McBride, 195–208. Philadelphia: Fortress, 1987.

Avioz, Michael. "The Call for Revenge in Jeremiah's Complaints (Jer XI–XX)." *Vetus Testamentum* 55 (2005): 429–38.

Balentine, Samuel E. *Prayer in the Hebrew Bible: The Drama of Divine-Human Dialogue*. Minneapolis: Fortress, 1993.

Band, Arnold J. "Swallowing Jonah: The Eclipse of Parody." *Prooftexts* 10 (1990): 177–95.

Barag, Dan. "The Tomb of Jason Reconsidered." In *"Follow the Wise": Studies in Jewish History and Culture in Honor of Lee I. Levine*, edited by Zeev Weiss, Oded Irshai, Jodi Magness, and Seth Schwartz, 145–61. Winona Lake, Ind.: Eisenbrauns, 2010.

Barkay, Gabriel. "The Iron Age II–III." In *The Archaeology of Ancient Israel*, edited by Amnon Ben-Tor, 302–73. New Haven, Conn.: Yale University Press, 1992.

Barstad, Hans M. "After the 'Myth of the Empty Land': Major Challenges in the Study of Neo-Babylonian Judah." In *Judah and the Judeans in the Neo-Babylonian Period*, edited by Oded Lipschits and Joseph Blenkinsopp, 3–20. Winona Lake, Ind.: Eisenbrauns, 2003.

Baumgartner, Walter. *Jeremiah's Poems of Lament*. Translated by David E. Orten. Sheffield, UK: Almond Press, 1988.

Beck, Pirhiya. "The Drawings from Horvat Teman (Kuntillet 'Ajrud)," *Tel Aviv* 9 (1982): 3–68.

Becking, Bob. "Sour Fruit and Blunt Teeth: The Metaphorical Meaning of the *Mašal* in Jeremiah 31, 29." *Scandinavian Journal of the Old Testament* 17 (2003): 7–21.

Ben Zvi, Ehud. "The Urban Center of Jerusalem and the Development of the Literature of the Hebrew Bible." In *Urbanism in Antiquity: From Mesopotamia to Crete*, edited by Walter E. Aufrecht, Neil A. Mirau, and Steven W. Gauley, 194–209. Journal for the Study of the Old Testament: Supplement Series 244. Sheffield, UK: Sheffield Academic Press, 1997.

Berlinerblau, Jacques. *The Vow and "Popular Religious Groups" in Ancient Israel*. Sheffield, UK: Sheffield Academic Press, 1996.

Berquist, Jon L., ed. *Approaching Yehud: New Approaches to the Study of the Persian Period*. Semeia Studies 50. Atlanta: Society of Biblical Literature, 2007.

———. *Judaism in Persia's Shadow: A Social and Historical Approach.* Minneapolis: Fortress, 1995.

———. "Psalms, Postcolonialism, and the Construction of the Self." In Berquist, *Approaching Yehud,* 195–202.

Blenkinsopp, Joseph. "The Family in First Temple Israel." In Perdue, Blenkinsopp, Collins, and Meyers, *Families in Ancient Israel,* 48–103.

———. *Judaism: The First Phase; The Place of Ezra and Nehemiah in the Origins of Judaism.* Grand Rapids, Mich.: Eerdmans, 2009.

———. "The Nehemiah Autobiographical Memoir." In *Language, Theology, and the Bible: Essays in Honour of James Barr,* edited by Samuel E. Balentine and John Barton, 199–212. Oxford: Clarendon, 1994.

Bloch-Smith, Elizabeth. *Judahite Burial Practices and Beliefs about the Dead.* Journal for the Study of the Old Testament: Supplement Series 123. Sheffield, UK: Sheffield Academic Press, 1992.

Blum, Erhard. "Issues and Problems in the Contemporary Debate regarding the Priestly Writings." In *The Strata of the Priestly Writings: Contemporary Debate and Future Directions,* edited by Sarah Shectman and Joel S. Baden, 31–44. Zürich: TZV, 2009.

Bodel, John, and Saul M. Olyan, eds. *Household and Family Religion in Antiquity.* Oxford: Blackwell, 2008.

Brakke, David, Michael L. Satlow, and Steven Weitzman, eds. *Religion and the Self in Antiquity.* Bloomington: Indiana University Press, 2005.

Brenner, Athalya. "Jonah's Poem out of and within Its Context." In *Among the Prophets: Language, Image and Structure in the Prophetic Writings,* edited by Philip R. Davies and David J. A. Clines, 183–92. Journal for the Study of the Old Testament: Supplement Series 144. Sheffield, UK: Sheffield Academic Press, 1993.

Brettler, Marc Zvi. "Women and Psalms: Towards an Understanding of the Role of Women's Prayer in the Israelite Cult." In *Gender and Law in the Hebrew Bible and the Ancient Near East,* edited by Victor H. Matthews, Bernard M. Levinson, and Tikva Frymer-Kensky, 25–56. Journal for the Study of the Old Testament: Supplement Series 262. Sheffield, UK: Sheffield Academic Press, 1998.

Brown, Francis, S. R. Driver, and Charles A. Briggs. *A Hebrew and English Lexicon of the Old Testament.* Oxford: Clarendon Press, 1968. Reprint, with corrections, of the 1907 edition.

Brown, Peter. *The Cult of the Saints: Its Rise and Function in Latin Christianity.* Haskell Lectures on History of Religions, New Series 2. Chicago: University of Chicago Press, 1981.

Burkes, Shannon. *God, Self, and Death: The Shape of Religious Transformation in the Second Temple Period.* Leiden: Brill, 2003.

Campbell, Edward F., Jr. *Ruth: A New Translation with Introduction, Notes, and Commentary*. Anchor Bible. Garden City, N.Y.: Doubleday, 1975.

Carter, Charles E. *The Emergence of Yehud in the Persian Period: A Social and Demographic Study*. Journal for the Study of the Old Testament: Supplement Series 294. Sheffield, UK: Sheffield Academic Press, 1999.

Cartledge, Tony W. "Conditional Vows in the Psalms of Lament." In *The Listening Heart: Essays in Wisdom and the Psalms in Honor of Roland E. Murphy, O. Carm.*, edited by Kenneth G. Hoglund, E. Huwiler, J. Glass, and R. Lee, 77–94. Journal for the Study of the Old Testament: Supplement Series 147. Sheffield, UK: JSOT Press, 1987.

———. *Vows in the Hebrew Bible and the Ancient Near East*. Journal for the Study of the Old Testament: Supplement Series 147. Sheffield, UK: Sheffield Academic Press, 1992.

———. "Were Nazirite Vows Unconditional?" *Catholic Biblical Quarterly* 51 (1989): 409–22.

Carroll, Robert P. *Jeremiah: A Commentary*. Old Testament Library. Philadelphia: Westminster, 1986.

Cataldo, Jeremiah W. *A Theocratic Yehud? Issues of Government in a Persian Province*. London: T&T Clark, 2009.

Christianson, Eric S. *A Time to Tell: Narrative Strategies in Ecclesiastes*. Journal for the Study of the Old Testament: Supplement Series 280. Sheffield, UK: Sheffield Academic Press, 1998.

Clines, David J. A., and David M. Gunn. "Form, Occasion and Redaction in Jeremiah 20." *Zeitschrift für die alttestamentliche Wissenschaft* 88 (1976): 390–401.

Cooper, Alan. "In Praise of Divine Caprice: The Significance of the Book of Jonah." In *Among the Prophets: Language, Image, and Structure in the Prophetic Writings*, edited by Philip R. Davies and David J. A. Clines, 144–63. Journal for the Study of the Old Testament: Supplement Series 144. Sheffield, UK: Sheffield Academic Press, 1993.

Cross, Frank Moore. "The Cave Inscriptions from Khirbet Lei." In *Near Eastern Archaeology in the Twentieth Century: Essays in Honor of Nelson Glueck*, edited by James A. Sanders, 299–306. Garden City, N.Y.: Doubleday, 1970.

Culley, Robert C. "The Confessions of Jeremiah and Traditional Discourse." In *"A Wise and Discerning Mind": Essays in Honor of Burke O. Long*, edited by Saul M. Olyan and Robert C. Culley, 69–81. Brown Judaic Studies 325. Providence, R.I.: Brown Judaic Studies, 2000.

Daube, David. *Collaboration with Tyranny in Rabbinic Law*. Riddell Memorial Lectures 1965. London: Oxford University Press, 1965.

Davis, Ellen F. *Swallowing the Scroll: Textuality and the Dynamics of Discourses in Ezekiel's Prophecy*. Sheffield, UK: Sheffield Academic Press, 1989.

Day, John. *Molech: A God of Human Sacrifice in the Old Testament.* Cambridge: Cambridge University Press, 1989.

Day, Peggy L., "From the Child Is Born the Woman." In *Gender and Difference in Ancient Israel,* edited by Peggy L. Day, 58–74. Minneapolis: Fortress, 1989.

Dewrell, Heath. "Child Sacrifice in Ancient Israel and Its Opponents." PhD diss., Johns Hopkins University, 2012.

Diamond, A. R. *The Confessions of Jeremiah in Context: Scenes of Prophetic Drama.* Journal for the Study of the Old Testament: Supplement Series 45. Sheffield, UK: JSOT Press, 1987.

Doran, Robert. *The Stewards of the Poor: The Man of God, Rabbula, and Hiba in Fifth-Century Edessa.* Cistercian Studies Series. Kalamazoo, Mich.: Cistercian Publications, 2006.

Dozeman, Thomas B. "Inner-Biblical Interpretation of Yahweh's Gracious and Compassionate Character." *Journal of Biblical Literature* 108 (1989): 207–23.

Dundes, Alan. "On the Structure of the Proverb." *Proverbium* 25:961–73. Reprinted in Mieder and Dundes, *The Wisdom of Many,* 43–64.

———. "Proverbs and the Ethnography of Speaking Folklore." In *Analytic Essays in Folklore,* 35–49. Studies in Folklore 2. The Hague: Mouton, 1979.

———. "Who Are the Folk?" In *Interpreting Folklore,* 1–19. Bloomington: Indiana University Press, 1980.

Ebersole, Gary L. "The Poetics and Politics of Ritualized Weeping in Early and Medieval Japan." In *Holy Tears: Weeping in the Religious Imagination,* edited by Kimberley Patton and John Stratton Hawley, 25–51. Princeton, N.J.: Princeton University Press, 2005.

Erikson, Amy. "'Without My Flesh I Will See God': Job's Rhetoric of the Body." *Journal of Biblical Literature* 132 (2013): 295–313.

Eskenazi, Tamara Cohn, and Tikva Frymer-Kensky. *Ruth.* JPS Bible Commentary. Philadelphia: Jewish Publication Society, 2011.

Faust, Avraham. "Settlement Dynamics and Demographic Fluctuations in Judah from the Late Iron Age to the Hellenistic Period and the Archaeology of Persian-Period *Yehud.*" In *A Time of Change: Judah and Its Neighbors in the Persian and Early Hellenistic Periods,* edited by Yigal Levin, 23–51. Library of Second Temple Studies 65. London: T&T Clark, 2007.

———. "Doorway Orientation, Settlement Planning and Cosmology in Ancient Israel During Iron Age II." *Oxford Journal of Archaeology* 20 (2001): 129–55.

Feeley-Harnik, Gillian. "Naomi and Ruth: Building Up the House of David." In *Text and Tradition,* ed. Susan Niditch, 163–84. Semeia Studies. Atlanta: Scholars Press, 1990.

Fishbane, Michael. "Sin and Judgment in the Prophecies of Ezekiel." *Interpretation* 38 (1984): 131–50.

Foley, John Miles. *Immanent Art: From Structure to Meaning in Traditional Oral Epic.* Bloomington: Indiana University Press, 1991.

Fontaine, Carole R. *Traditional Sayings in the Old Testament.* Sheffield, UK: Almond Press, 1982.

———. "Wounded Hero on a Shaman's Quest: Job in the Context of Folk Literature." In *The Voice from the Whirlwind: Interpreting the Book of Job,* edited by Leo G. Perdue and W. Clark Gilpin, 70–85. Nashville, Tenn.: Abingdon, 1992.

Fox, Michael V. *Qoheleth and His Contradictions.* Journal for the Study of the Old Testament: Supplement Series 71. Sheffield, UK: Almond Press, 1989.

Fried, Lisbeth S. "The Political Struggle of Fifth Century Judah." *Transeuphratène* 24 (2002): 9–21.

Geertz, Clifford. "Religion as a Cultural System." In *The Interpretation of Cultures,* 87–125. New York: Basic Books, 1973.

Gerstenberger, Erhard S. *Israel in the Persian Period: The Fifth and Fourth Centuries B.C.E.* Biblical Encyclopedia 8. Atlanta: Society of Biblical Literature, 2011. Originally published in German in 2005.

———. "Jeremiah's Complaints: Observations of Jer 15:10–21." *Journal of Biblical Literature* 82 (1963): 393–408.

Ginsberg, H. L. "Job the Patient and Job the Impatient." In *Congress Volume: Rome, 1968,* 88–111. Vetus Testamentum Supplement 17. Leiden: Brill, 1969.

Goffman, Erving. *The Presentation of Self in Everyday Life.* Garden City, N.Y.: Doubleday, 1959.

Good, Edwin M. *Irony in the Old Testament.* Sheffield, UK: Almond Press, 1981.

Gordis, Robert. *The Book of God and Man: A Study of Job.* Chicago: University of Chicago Press, 1965.

———. *Koheleth: The Man and His World; A Study of Ecclesiastes.* New York: Jewish Theological Seminary of America, 1951.

Gottwald, Norman. *All the Kingdoms of the Earth.* New York: Harper & Row, 1964.

Grabbe, Lester L. *A History of the Jews and Judaism in the Second Temple Period,* vol. 1, *Yehud: A History of the Persian Province of Judah.* London: T&T Clark, 2004.

Gray, John. *The Book of Job.* Sheffield, UK: Sheffield Phoenix Press, 2010.

Green, Deborah. "Sweet Spices in the Tomb: An Initial Study of the Use of Perfume in Jewish Burials." In *Commemorating the Dead: Texts and Artifacts in Context,* edited by Laurie Brink and Deborah Green, 145–73. Berlin: de Gruyter, 2008.

Greenberg, Moshe. *Biblical Prose Prayer as a Window in the Popular Religion of Israel.* Taubman Lectures in Jewish Studies. Berkeley: University of California Press, 1983.

Greenstein, Edward L. "Jeremiah as an Inspiration to the Poet of Job." In *Inspired Speech: Prophecy in the Ancient Near East; Essays in Honor of Herbert B. Huffmon*, edited by John Kalter and Louis Stulman, 98–110. Journal for the Study of the Old Testament: Supplement Series 378. London: T&T Clark International, 2004.

———. "The Problem of Evil in the Book of Job." In *Mishneh Todah: Studies in Deuteronomy and Its Cultural Environment in Honor of Jeffrey H. Tigay*, edited by Nili Sacher Fox, David A. Glatt-Gilad, and Michael J. Williams, 333–62. Winona Lake, Ind.: Eisenbrauns, 2009.

Greenwood, Kyle R. "Debating Wisdom: The Role of Voice in Ecclesiastes." *Catholic Biblical Quarterly* 74 (2012): 476–91.

Gunkel, Hermann. *Introduction to Psalms: The Genres of the Religious Lyric of Israel.* Completed by Joachim Begrich and translated by James D. Nogalski. Macon, Ga.: Mercer University Press, 1998.

———. *The Legends of Genesis: The Biblical Saga and History.* New York: Schocken, 1964.

———. *The Psalms: A Form-Critical Introduction.* Translated by Thomas M. Horner. Philadelphia: Fortress, 1967.

———. *Reden und Aufsätze.* Göttingen: Vandenhoeck & Ruprecht, 1913.

Gyatso, Janet. *Apparitions of the Self: The Secret Autobiographies of a Tibetan Visionary.* Princeton, N.J.: Princeton University Press, 1998.

Haas, N. "Human Skeletal Remains in Two Burial Caves." *Israel Exploration Journal* 13 (1963): 93–96.

Habel, Norman C. *The Book of Job: A Commentary.* Old Testament Library. Philadelphia: Westminster, 1985.

Hachlili, Rachel. *Jewish Funerary Customs, Practices, and Rites in the Second Temple Period.* Supplements to the Journal for the Study of Judaism 94. Leiden: Brill, 2005.

Hanson, P. D. *The Dawn of Apocalyptic.* Philadelphia: Fortress, 1975.

Hass, Kristin Ann. *Carried to the Wall: American Memory and the Vietnam Veterans Memorial.* Berkeley: University of California Press, 1998.

Heider, George Charles. "The Cult of Molek: A New Examination of the Biblical and Extra-Biblical Evidence." PhD diss., Yale University, 1984.

———. *The Cult of Molek: A Reassessment.* Sheffield, UK: JSOT Press, 1985.

Hezser, Catherine. *Jewish Literacy in Roman Palestine.* Texts and Studies in Ancient Judaism 81. Tübingen: Mohr Siebeck, 2001.

Hoglund, Kenneth G. *Achaemenid Imperial Administration in Syria-Palestine and the Missions of Ezra and Nehemiah.* Society of Biblical Literature Dissertation Series 125. Atlanta: Scholars Press, 1992.

———. "The Material Culture of the Persian Period and the Sociology of the Second Temple Period." In *Second Temple Studies III: Studies in Politics, Class, and Material Culture,* edited by Philip R. Davies and John M. Halligan, 14–18. Journal for the Study of the Old Testament: Supplement Series 340. Sheffield, UK: Sheffield University Press, 2002.

Holtz, Barry W. "Midrash." In *Back to the Sources: Reading the Classic Jewish Texts,* edited by Barry W. Holtz, 177–211. New York: Summit, 1984.

Hurvitz, Avi. "The Date of the Prose Tale of Job Linguistically Reconsidered." *Harvard Theological Review* 67 (1974): 17–34.

———. "On the Term נעל שלף in Ruth 4:7." In *Shnaton I: An Annual for Biblical and Ancient Near Eastern Studies,* edited by Jonas C. Greenfield and Moshe Weinfeld, 45–49. Jerusalem: Israel Bible Company / Tel Aviv: M. Newman, 1975. [In Hebrew; English abstract, xiii–xiv.]

Hutton, Rodney R. "Are the Parents Still Eating Sour Grapes? Jeremiah's Use of the *Māšāl* in Contrast to Ezekiel." *Catholic Biblical Quarterly* 71 (2009): 275–85.

Isbell, Charles D. *Corpus of the Aramaic Incantation Bowls.* Society of Biblical Literature Dissertation Series 17. Missoula, Mont.: SBL, 1975.

Jackson, Kent P. "The Language of the Mesha Inscription." In *Studies in the Mesha Inscription and Moab,* edited by Andrew Dearman, 96–130. Atlanta: Scholars Press, 1989.

Janzen, J. Gerald. "Prayer and/as Self-Address: The Case of Hannah." In *A God So Near: Essays on Old Testament Theology in Honor of Patrick D. Miller,* edited by Brent A. Strawn and Nancy R. Bowen, 113–27. Winona Lake, Ind.: Eisenbrauns, 2003.

Jastrow, Morris, Jr. "The 'Nazir' Legislation." *Journal of Biblical Literature* 44 (1914): 266–85.

Joyce, Paul M. *Divine Initiative and Human Response in Ezekiel.* Journal for the Study of the Old Testament: Supplement Series 51. Sheffield, UK: JSOT Press, 1989.

Kaminsky, Joel S. *Corporate Responsibility in the Hebrew Bible.* Journal for the Study of the Old Testament: Supplement Series 196. Sheffield, UK: JSOT Press, 1995.

Katz, Steven T. "The 'Conservative' Character of Mystical Experience." In *Mysticism and Religious Traditions,* edited by Steven T. Katz, 3–60. Oxford: Oxford University Press, 1983.

Kellermann, Ulrich. *Nehemiah: Quellen, Überlieferung und Geschichte.* Beihefte zur Zeitschrift für die alttestamentliche Wissenschaft 102. Berlin: Töpelmann, 1967.

King, Philip J., and Lawrence E. Stager. *Life in Biblical Israel.* Louisville, Ky.: Westminster John Knox, 2001.

King, Thomas J. *The Realignment of the Priestly Literature: The Priestly Narrative in Genesis and Its Relation to Priestly Legislation and the Holiness School.* Princeton Theological Monograph Series. Eugene, Ore.: Pickwick, 2009.

Kirshenblatt-Gimblett, Barbara. "Toward a Theory of Proverb Meaning." In Mieder and Dundes, *The Wisdom of Many*, 111–20.

Knoppers, Gary N. "Revisiting the Samarian Question in the Persian Period." In *Judah and the Judeans in the Persian Period*, edited by Oded Lipschits and Manfred Oeming, 265–89. Winona Lake, Ind.: Eisenbrauns, 2006.

Knoppers, Gary N., and Lester L. Grabbe, with Deirdre N. Fulton, eds. *Exile and Restoration Revisited: Essays on the Babylonian and Persian Periods in Memory of Peter R. Ackroyd*. Library of Second Temple Studies 73. London: T&T Clark, 2009.

Knowles, Melody D. *Centrality Practiced: Jerusalem in the Religious Practice of Yehud and the Diaspora in the Persian Period*. Atlanta: SBL, 2006.

Kottsieper, Ingo. "'And They Did Not Care to Speak Yehudit': On Linguistic Change in Judah during the Late Persian Period." In *Judah and the Judeans in the Fourth Century BCE*, edited by Oded Lipschits, Gary N. Knoppers, and Rainer Albertz, 95–124. Winona Lake, Ind.: Eisenbrauns, 2007.

Kraemer, David. *The Meanings of Death in Rabbinic Judaism*. London: Routledge, 2000.

Krüger, Thomas. *Qoheleth: A Commentary*. Hermeneia. Minneapolis: Fortress, 2004.

La Cocque, André. *Ruth: A Continental Commentary*. Minneapolis: Fortress, 2004.

Lapsley, Jacqueline E. *"Can These Bones Live?": The Problem of the Moral Self in the Book of Ezekiel*. Berlin: de Gruyter, 2000.

Lenzi, Alan. "Invoking the God: Interpreting Invocations in Mesopotamian Prayer and Biblical Laments of the Individual." *Journal of Biblical Literature* 129 (2010): 303–15.

———, ed. *Reading Akkadian Prayers and Hymns: An Introduction*. Atlanta: SBL, 2011.

Leveen, Adrianne B. "Variations on a Theme: Differing Conceptions of Memory in the Book of Numbers." *Journal for the Study of the Old Testament* 27 (2002): 201–21.

Levin, Yigal, ed. *A Time of Change: Judah and Its Neighbors in the Persian and Early Hellenistic Periods*. Library of Second Temple Studies 65. London: T&T Clark, 2007.

Levinson, Bernard M. "'You Must Not Add Anything to What I Command You': Paradoxes of Canon and Authorship in Ancient Israel." *Numen* 50 (2003): 1–51.

Lewis, Theodore J. "Athartu's Incantations and the Use of the Divine Names as Weapons." *Journal of Near Eastern Studies* 70 (2011): 207–27.

———. "Family, Household, and Local Religion at Late Bronze Age Ugarit." In Bodel and Olyan, *Household and Family Religion in Antiquity*, 60–88.

————. "Job 19 in the Light of the Ketef Hinnom Inscriptions and Amulets." In *Puzzling Out the Past: Studies in Northwest Semitic Languages and Literatures in Honor of Bruce Zuckerman,* edited by Marilyn J. Lundberg, Steven Fine, and Wayne T. Pitard, 99–113. Leiden: Brill, 2012.

Lichtheim, Miriam. *Ancient Egyptian Autobiographies Chiefly of the Middle Kingdom: A Study and an Anthology.* Orbis Biblicus et Orientalis 84. Göttingen: Vandenhoeck & Ruprecht, 1988.

Lindars, Barnabas. "Ezekiel and Individual Responsibility." *Vetus Testamentum* 15 (1965): 452–67.

Lipschits, Oded. *The Fall and Rise of Jerusalem: Judah under Babylonian Rule.* Winona Lake, Ind.: Eisenbrauns, 2005.

Lipschits, Oded, and Manfred Oeming, eds. *Judah and Judeans in the Persian Period.* Winona Lake, Ind.: Eisenbrauns, 2006.

Malinowski, Bronislaw. *Magic, Science, and Religion, and Other Essays.* Garden City, N.Y.: Doubleday, 1954.

Mandolfo, Carleen. "A Generic Renegade: A Dialogic Reading of Job and Lament Psalms." In *Diachronic and Synchronic: Reading the Psalms in Real Time; Proceedings of the Baylor Symposium on the Book of Psalms,* edited by Joel S. Burnett, W. H. Bellinger Jr., and W. Dennis Tucker Jr., 45–63. London: T&T Clark, 2007.

Marsman, Hennie J. *Women in Ugarit and Israel: Their Social and Religious Position in the Context of the Ancient Near East.* Oudtestamentische Studiën 49. Leiden: Brill (for the Society of Biblical Literature), 2003.

Matties, Gordon H. *Ezekiel 18 and the Rhetoric of Moral Discourse.* Society of Biblical Literature Dissertation Series 126. Atlanta: Scholars Press, 1990.

Mazar, Amichai. *Archaeology of the Land of Israel.* New York: Doubleday, 1992.

McDannell, Colleen. *Material Christianity: Religion and Popular Culture in America.* New Haven, Conn.: Yale University Press, 1995.

McGuire, Meredith B. *Lived Religion: Faith and Practice in Everyday Life.* Oxford: Oxford University Press, 2008.

Menn, Esther. "No Ordinary Lament: Relecture and the Identity of the Distressed in Psalm 22." *Harvard Theological Review* 93 (2000): 301–41.

Meshel, Ze'ev. *Kuntillet ʿAjrud (Horvat Teman): An Iron Age II Religious Site on the Judah-Sinai Border.* Jerusalem: Israel Exploration Society, 2012.

Meyers, Carol. "The Family in Early Israel." In Perdue, Blenkinsopp, Collins, and Meyers, *Families in Ancient Israel,* 1–47.

————. "The Hannah Narrative in Feminist Perspective." In *"Go to the Land I Will Show You": Studies in Honor of Dwight W. Young,* edited by Joseph E. Coleson and Victor H. Matthews, 117–66. Winona Lake, Ind.: Eisenbrauns, 1996).

————. "Household Religion." In Stavrakopoulou and Barton, *Religious Diversity in Ancient Israel and Judah,* 118–34.

———. "Procreation, Production, and Protection: Male-Female Balance in Early Israel." *Journal of the American Academy of Religion* 51 (1983): 569–93.

Meyers, Carol L., and Eric M. Meyers. *Haggai, Zechariah 1–8.* Anchor Bible 25B. Garden City, N.Y.: Doubleday, 1987.

Middlemas, Jill. *The Troubles of Templeless Judah.* Oxford: Oxford University Press, 2005.

Mieder, Wolfgang. *"Proverbs Speak Louder than Words": Folk Wisdom in Art, Culture, Folklore, History, Literature, and Mass Media.* New York: Lang, 2008.

Mieder, Wolfgang, and Alan Dundes, eds. *The Wisdom of Many: Essays on the Proverb.* New York: Garland, 1981.

Miles, John A., Jr., "Laughing at the Bible: Jonah as Parody." *Jewish Quarterly Review* 65 (1975): 168–81.

Miller, Patricia Cox. "Shifting Selves in Late Antiquity." In *Religion and the Self in Antiquity,* edited by David Brakke, Michael L. Satlow, and Steven Weitzman, 15–39. Bloomington: Indiana University Press, 2005.

Miller, Patrick D. "Trouble and Woe: Interpreting Biblical Laments." *Interpretation* 37 (1983): 32–45.

Mol, Jurrien. *Collective and Individual Responsibility: A Description of Corporate Personality in Ezekiel 18 and 20.* Studia Semitica Neerlandica 53. Leiden: Brill, 2009.

Momigliano, Arnaldo D. *The Development of Greek Biography.* Cambridge, Mass.: Harvard University Press, 1993.

———. "Popular Religious Beliefs and Late Roman Historians." *Studies in Church History* 8 (1971): 1–18. Reprinted in *Essays in Ancient and Modern Historiography* (Oxford: Blackwell, 1977), 141–60.

Montgomery, James A. *Aramaic Incantation Texts from Nippur.* Philadelphia: University Museum, 1913.

Mowinckel, Sigmund. *Psalmenstudien: 'Awan und die individuellen Klagepsalmen.* Vol. 1. Kristiana, Norway: SNVAO, 1921.

Nakhai, Beth Alpert. "Varieties of Religious Expression in the Domestic Setting." In *Household Archaeology in Ancient Israel and Beyond,* edited by Assaf Yasur-Landau, Jennie R. Ebeling, and Laura B. Mazow, 347–60. Culture and History of the Ancient Near East 50. Leiden: Brill, 2011.

Naveh, Joseph. "Old Hebrew Inscriptions in a Burial Cave." *Israel Exploration Journal* 13 (1963): 74–92.

Naveh, Joseph, and Shaul Shaked. *Amulets and Magic Bowls: Aramaic Incantations of Late Antiquity.* Jerusalem: Magnes, 1985.

———. *Magic Spells and Formulae: Aramaic Incantations of Late Antiquity.* Jerusalem: Magnes, 1993.

Neusner, Jacob, Ernest S. Frerichs, and Paul V. McCracken, eds. *Religion, Science, and Magic in Concert and in Conflict.* New York: Oxford University Press, 1989.

Newsom, Carol A. *The Book of Job: A Contest of Moral Imagination.* Oxford: Oxford University Press, 2003.

———. *The Self as Symbolic Space: Constructing Identity and Community at Qumran.* Leiden: Brill, 2004.

Niditch, Susan. "The Challenge of Israelite Epic." In *A Companion to Ancient Epic,* edited by John Miles Foley, 277–87. Oxford: Blackwell, 2005.

———. "Experiencing the Divine: Heavenly Visits, Earthly Encounters, and the Land of the Dead." In Stavrakopoùlou and Barton, *Religious Diversity in Ancient Israel and Judah,* 11–22.

———. *Folklore and the Hebrew Bible.* Minneapolis: Fortress, 1993.

———. *Judges: A Commentary.* Louisville, Ky.: Westminster John Knox, 2008.

———. "Legends of Wise Heroes and Heroines." In *The Hebrew Bible and Its Modern Interpreters,* edited by Douglas A. Knight and Gene M. Tucker, 445–63. Philadelphia: Fortress; Chico, Calif.: Scholars Press, 1985.

———. *"My Brother Esau Is a Hairy Man": Hair and Identity in Ancient Israel.* Oxford: Oxford University Press, 2008.

———. *The Symbolic Vision in Biblical Tradition.* Harvard Semitic Monographs 30. Chico, Calif.: Scholars Press, 1980.

———. "Twisting Proverbs: Oral Traditional Performance and Written Context." In *Discourse, Dialogue, and Debate in the Bible: Essays in Honour of Frank H. Polak,* edited by Athalya Brenner-Idan, 125–28. Sheffield, UK: Phoenix, 2014.

———. *War in the Hebrew Bible: A Study in the Ethics of Violence.* Oxford: Oxford University Press, 1993.

———. "The Wronged Woman Righted: An Analysis of Genesis 38." *Harvard Theological Review* 72 (1979): 143–49.

Noth, Martin. *Numbers: A Commentary.* Translated by James D. Martin. London: SCM Press, 1968.

Obeyesekere, Gananath. *Medusa's Hair: An Essay on Personal Symbols and Religious Experience.* Chicago: University of Chicago Press, 1981.

O'Connor, Kathleen M. *The Confessions of Jeremiah: Their Interpretation and Role in Chapters 1–25.* Society of Biblical Literature Dissertation Series 94. Atlanta: Scholars Press, 1988.

Oden, Robert A. *The Bible without Theology: The Theological Tradition and Alternatives to It.* Cambridge, Mass.: Harper and Row, 1987.

Olyan, Saul M. "Family Religion in Israel and the Wider Levant of the First Millennium BCE." In Bodel and Olyan, *Household and Family Religion in Antiquity,* 113–26.

———. "The Search for the Elusive Self in Texts of the Hebrew Bible." In *Religion and the Self in Antiquity,* 40–50. Bloomington: Indiana University Press, 2005.

Orsi, Robert. "Is the Study of Lived Religion Irrelevant to the World We Live In?" *Journal for the Scientific Study of Religion* 42 (2003): 169–74.

Patton, Kimberley Christine, and John Stratton Hawley, eds. *Holy Tears: Weeping in the Religious Imagination.* Princeton, N.J.: Princeton University Press, 2005.

Penchansky, David. *The Betrayal of God: Ideological Conflict in Job.* Louisville, Ky.: Westminster John Knox, 1990.

Perdue, Leo G. "The Household, Old Testament Theology, and Contemporary Hermeneutics." In Perdue, Blenkinsopp, Collins, and Meyers, *Families in Ancient Israel,* 223–57.

Perdue, Leo G., Joseph Blenkinsopp, John J. Collins, and Carol Meyers, eds. *Families in Ancient Israel.* Louisville, Ky.: Westminster John Knox, 1997.

Person, Raymond L. *The Deuteronomic School: History, Social Setting, and Literature.* Atlanta: Society of Biblical Literature, 2002.

Polak, Frank. "Sociolinguistics and the Judean Speech Community in the Achaemenid Empire." In *Judah and the Judeans in the Persian Period,* edited by Oded Lipschits and Manfred Oeming, 589–628. Winona Lake, Ind.: Eisenbrauns, 2006.

Polk, Timothy. *The Prophetic Persona: Jeremiah and the Language of the Self.* Journal for the Study of the Old Testament: Supplement Series 32. Sheffield, UK: JSOT Press, 1984.

Pope, Marvin H. *Job: Introduction, Translation, and Commentary.* Anchor Bible. Garden City, N.Y.: Doubleday, 1965.

Propp, Vladimir. *Morphology of the Folktale.* Translated by Laurence Scott. Austin: University of Texas Press, 1968.

Römer, Thomas, ed. *The Books of Leviticus and Numbers.* Bibliotheca Ephemeridum Theologicarum Lovaniensium 215. Leuven, Belgium: Peeters, 2008.

Ruiz, Jean-Pierre. "An Exile's Baggage: Toward a Postcolonial Reading of Ezekiel." In Berquist, *Approaching Yehud,* 117–35.

Sasson, Jack M. *Jonah: A New Translation with Introduction, Commentary, and Interpretations.* Anchor Yale Bible 24B. New Haven, Conn.: Yale University Press, 1990.

———. *Ruth: A New Translation with a Philological Commentary and a Formalist-Folklorist Interpretation.* Baltimore: Johns Hopkins University Press, 1979.

Satlow, Michael L. "Giving for a Return: Jewish Votive Offerings in Late Antiquity." In *Religion and the Self in Antiquity,* edited by David Brakke, Michael L. Satlow, and Steven Weitzman, 91–108. Bloomington: Indiana University Press, 2005.

Schlesinger, Herbert J. *Promises, Oaths, and Vows: On the Psychology of Promising.* New York: Analytic Press, 2008.

Schniedewind, William M. "Aramaic, the Death of Written Hebrew, and Language Shift in the Persian Period." In *Margins of Writings, Origins of Cultures,* edited by Seth L. Sanders, 141–51. Chicago: Oriental Institute, 2004.

———. *How the Bible Became a Book: The Textualization of Ancient Israel.* Cambridge: Cambridge University Press, 2004.

Scholem, Gershom, and Eric T. Schwab. "On Jonah and the Concept of Justice." *Critical Inquiry* 25 (1999): 353–61.

Seow, Choon-Leong. *Ecclesiastes: A New Translation with Introduction and Commentary.* Anchor Bible 18c. New York: Doubleday, 1997.

———. "The Social World of Ecclesiastes." In *Scribes, Sages, and Seers: The Sage in the Eastern Mediterranean World,* edited by Leo Perdue, 189–217. Göttingen: Vandenhoeck & Ruprecht, 2007.

Sharp, Carolyn J. *Irony and Meaning in the Hebrew Bible.* Bloomington: Indiana University Press, 2009.

Sloane, David Charles. *The Last Great Necessity: Cemeteries in American History.* Baltimore: Johns Hopkins University Press, 1984.

Smart, Ninian. *Worldviews: Crosscultural Explorations of Human Beliefs.* New York: Scribner's Sons, 1983.

Smith, Daniel L. "The Politics of Ezra: Sociological Indicators of Postexilic Judean Society." In *Second Temple Studies I: Persian Period,* edited by Philip R. Davies, 73–97. Journal for the Study of the Old Testament: Supplement Series 117. Sheffield, UK: Sheffield Academic Press, 1991.

———. *The Religion of the Landless: The Social Context of the Babylonian Exile.* Bloomington, Ind.: Meyer-Stone, 1989.

Smith, Mark S. *The Laments of Jeremiah and Their Contexts: A Literary and Redactional Study of Jeremiah 11–20.* Society of Biblical Literature Monograph Series 42. Atlanta: Scholars, 1990.

Smith, Morton. *Palestinian Parties and Politics That Shaped the Old Testament.* London: SCM, 1987.

Stavrakopoulou, Francesca. "'Popular Religion' and 'Official' Religion: Practice, Perception, Portrayal." In Stavrakopoulou and Barton, *Religious Diversity in Ancient Israel and Judah,* 37–58.

Stavrakopoulou, Francesca, and John Barton, eds. *Religious Diversity in Ancient Israel and Judah.* London: T&T Clark International, 2010.

Stern, Ephraim. *Material Culture of the Land of the Bible in the Persian Period, 538–332 B.C.* Warminster, UK: Aris and Philips, 1982. Originally published in 1973 by the Israel Exploration Society (Jerusalem).

———. "The Religious Revolution in Persian-Period Judah." In *Judah and Judeans in the Persian Period,* edited by Oded Lipschits and Manfred Oeming, 199–205. Winona Lake, Ind.: Eisenbrauns, 2006.

Strawn, Brent A. "'A World under Control': Isaiah 60 and the Adapana Reliefs." In Berquist, *Approaching Yehud*, 85–116.

Talmon, Shemaryahu. "The Old Testament Text." In *Cambridge History of the Bible*, edited by P. R. Ackroyd and C. F. Evans, 1:159–99. Cambridge: Cambridge University Press, 1970.

Thompson, Stith, ed. and trans. *The Types of the Folktale: A Classification and Bibliography*. Folklore Fellows Communications 184. Helsinki: Suomalainen Tiedeakatemia, 1973. Expanded edition of Antii Aarne's *Verzeichnis*.

Trible, Phyllis. "Studies in the Book of Jonah." PhD diss., Columbia University, 1963. Ann Arbor, Mich.: Ann Arbor Microfilms.

Van Buren, E. Douglas. "Concerning the Horned Cap of the Mesopotamian Gods." *Orientalia* 12 (1943): 318–27.

Van Der Toorn, Karel. "Female Prostitution in Payment of Vows in Ancient Israel." *Journal of Biblical Literature* 108 (1989): 193–205.

Van Dijk, Jan, Albrecht Goetze, and Mary I. Hussey. *Early Mesopotamian Incantations and Rituals*. Yale Oriental Series: Babylonian Texts 11. New Haven, Conn.: Yale University Press, 1985.

Vanderhooft, David S. "The Israelite *MIŠPĀHÂ*, the Priestly Writings, and Changing Valences in Israel's Kinship Terminology." In *Exploring the "Longue Durée": Essays in Honor of Lawrence E. Stager*, edited by J. David Schloen, 485–96. Winona Lake, Ind.: Eisenbrauns, 2009.

———. "New Evidence Pertaining to the Transition from Neo-Babylonian to Achaemenid Administration in Palestine." In *Yahwism after the Exile: Perspectives on Israelite Religion in the Persian Era*, edited by Rainer Albertz and Bob Becking, 219–35. Studies in Theology and Religion 5. Assen, Netherlands: Royal Van Gorcum, 2003.

Watts, James, ed. *Persia and Torah: The Theory of Imperial Authorization of the Pentateuch*. Society of Biblical Literature Symposium Series 17. Atlanta: SBL, 2001.

Wendel, A. *Die israelitische-jüdische Gelübde*. Berlin: Philo Verlag, 1931.

Werline, Rodney. *Penitential Prayer in Second Temple Judaism: The Development of a Religious Institution*. Early Judaism and Its Literature 13. Atlanta: Scholars Press, 1998.

Westermann, Claus. *Praise and Lament in the Psalms*. Translated by Keith R. Crim and Richard N. Soulen. Atlanta: John Knox, 1981.

Whybray, R. N. *Ecclesiastes*. New Century Bible Commentary. London: Marshall, Morgan and Scott, 1989.

———. "The Identification and Use of Quotations in Ecclesiastes." In *Congress Volume: Vienna, 1980*, edited by J. A. Emerton et al., 435–51. Vetus Tetamentum Supplement 31. Leiden: Brill, 1981.

Williamson, H. G. M. *Studies in Persian Period History and Historiography.* Forschungen zum Alten Testament 38. Tübingen: Mohr Siebeck, 2004.

Wilson, Robert R. *Prophecy and Society in Ancient Israel.* Philadelphia: Fortress, 1980.

———. "Prophecy in Crisis: The Call of Ezekiel." *Interpretation* 38 (1984): 117–30.

Wright, Jacob L. "Commensal Politics in Ancient Asia." Pts. 1 and 2. *Zeitschrift für die alttestamentliche Wissenschaft* 122 (2010): 333–52.

Yasur-Landau, Assaf, Jennie R. Ebeling, and Laura B. Mazow, eds. *Household Archaeology in Ancient Israel and Beyond.* Culture and History of the Ancient Near East 50. Leiden: Brill, 2011.

Yoder, Christine Roy. "The Woman of Substance (אשת-חיל): A Socioeconomic Reading of Proverbs 31:10–31." *Journal of Biblical Literature* 122 (2003): 427–47.

Zevit, Ziony. *The Religions of Ancient Israel: A Synthesis of Parallactic Approaches.* New York: Continuum, 2001.

Zorn, Jeffrey R. "Tell en-Nasbeh and the Problem of the Material Culture of the Sixth Century." In *Judah and the Judeans in the Neo-Babylonian Period,* edited by Oded Lipschits and Joseph Blenkinsopp, 413–47. Winona Lake, Ind.: Eisenbrauns, 2003.

General Index

Amos, 115, 116, 117, 118
amulets, 91, 97, 100
angels, 55, 87; in visions, 99, 100, 108, 113–114, 116–117
apocalypticism, 14, 46–47, 118
autobiography, 8–9, 41, 44–45, 66–67; incantation and, 55, 73, 131; lament and, 68, 70

Babylonian conquest, 3, 10, 26, 36, 57, 61, 134, 136; blame for, 23; immediate effects of, 22, 37, 65, 99, 105; long-range effects of, 12, 56, 66
Babylonians, 10, 11, 55, 64
Buddha, 45
burial, 3, 15, 47, 90, 93, 97, 99, 105. *See also* Khirbet Beit Lei

chaos, 50, 74, 91, 105, 111; Geertz's definition of, 26–27, 39, 40, 52
community, 15–16, 24, 31, 38, 56–57, 118; and the individual, 22, 30, 38, 75, 134, 135, 138; leaders of, 69–70, 85, 115, 136; and ritual, 69, 75, 77, 82, 101
council, divine, 110–111, 112–113, 116–117
covenant, 24, 25, 28–29, 67
creation, 47, 87, 130
culture, U.S., 19, 72
curses, 21, 25, 28, 65, 68, 101; individual, 6, 25, 56, 59, 64, 66, 98; rituals of, 58, 69, 91–92, 98, 104, 105. *See also* theology, blessings-and-curses

Daniel, 29, 115, 117–118, 136
David, 13, 44, 62, 98, 104, 132; genealogy of, 4, 120
death, 35, 62, 76, 103, 111, 122, 125, 136; in Jonah, 61, 131–132; in Qohelet and Job, 37–40, 45–46, 49, 51, 52; and sin, 30–31, 121, 123; and suffering, 25–26; in war, 22, 74, 75. *See also* burial; Khirbet Beit Lei
demons, 54–55, 91, 100
divination, 115, 118–119
dreams, 2, 72, 105, 114, 117, 119, 124; efficacy of, 108–110, 112

Ecclesiastes, book of, 14–15, 32, 46, 105. *See also* Qohelet
Eden, 31, 51
Elijah, 16, 81, 86, 129, 132
embodiment, 15, 59, 93, 100, 102, 103, 115, 135; in Qohelet and Job, 51, 52, 57, 90, 136
emotion, 1, 9, 58, 67, 79, 106, 135, 136; in narrative, 90, 120, 124, 125; in prophecy, 66, 108, 114–115, 117–118; in Qohelet and Job, 41, 42, 43, 57; at tombs, 93, 95, 96
Enuma Elish, 111, 117

179

Scripture Index

Printed in the USA
CPSIA information can be obtained
at www.ICGtesting.com
JSHW081911110824
67835JS00002B/8